MORE PRAISE FOR
THE
PERFECTI
TRAP

"Thomas Curran is the world's leading expert on perfectionism, and he's written the definitive book on why it's rising."

—Adam Grant, #1 *New York Times* bestselling author of *Think Again*

"A clear-eyed look at how perfectionism and its capitalistic 'obsession with boundless growth' has contributed to mass discontent and insecurity . . . Smart, thorough, and reassuring."

—*Publishers Weekly*

"Curran delivers many useful lessons and valuable insights. . . . This book offers an alternative path to a fulfilling, productive life."

—*Kirkus Reviews*

"Beautiful, reflective, and rigorous . . . A fascinating and panoramic analysis of perfectionism in modern capitalist societies."

—Grace Blakeley, staff writer at *Tribune* magazine, host of the *A World to Win* podcast, and author of *Stolen* and *The Corona Crash*

"Packed with vivid and thought-provoking case studies, this book will transform how you think about success."

—Jake Humphrey and Damian Hughes,
coauthors of *High Performance*

"Makes a stirring and delightful case for getting over our culture's 'favorite flaw.' Curran's knack for empathetic storytelling is on display."

—Jonathan Malesic, author of *The End of Burnout: Why Work Drains Us and How to Build Better Lives*

THE
PERFECTION
TRAP

Embracing the Power of Good Enough

THOMAS CURRAN

SCRIBNER
NEW YORK   LONDON   TORONTO   SYDNEY   NEW DELHI

Scribner
An Imprint of Simon & Schuster, LLC
1230 Avenue of the Americas
New York, NY 10020

First Scribner trade paperback edition May 2024

SCRIBNER and design are trademarks of Simon & Schuster, LLC

Simon & Schuster: Celebrating 100 Years of Publishing in 2024

For information about special discounts for bulk purchases,
please contact Simon & Schuster Special Sales at 1-866-506-1949 or
business@simonandschuster.com.

The Simon & Schuster Speakers Bureau can bring authors to your live
event. For more information or to book an event, contact the Simon &
Schuster Speakers Bureau at 1-866-248-3049 or visit our website
www.simonspeakers.com.

Interior design by Erika R. Genova

Manufactured in the United States of America

1   3   5   7   9   10   8   6   4   2

Library of Congress Cataloging-in-Publication Data is available.

ISBN 978-1-9821-4953-6
ISBN 978-1-9821-4954-3 (pbk)
ISBN 978-1-9821-4955-0 (ebook)

For June

CONTENTS

PROLOGUE

Every last one of us in the West lives inside a culture knitted by perfectionistic fantasies. Like a holographic simulation of exaggerated reality, it's a place where images and moving pictures of perfect lives and lifestyles beam from billboards, movie screens, television sets, commercials, and social media feeds. Within the hologram, particles of unreality fire indiscriminately. Each one teaching us that we'd lead a happy and successful life if only we were perfect, and that everything will come crashing down if we stray too far from that ideal. This understanding is real, and alive, and all-consuming, and it's penetrated us so deeply that perfectionism lives in our interiors via a lingering and unshakable insecurity. Insecurity about what we don't have, how we don't look, and what we haven't achieved.

And yet, despite those immobilizing thoughts of deficit, we're seemingly gluttons for punishment. Interviewees call perfectionism their greatest weakness. Leaders in business, politics, sports, and the arts credit their success to it. Celebrities and life coaches educate us in the many ways we can maximize it for personal gain. In fact, so much of what we understand to be virtuous about work, money, status, and "the good life" in modern society constitutes perfectionism's most powerful driving force: an obsession with boundless growth and unrelenting moreness at any cost.

That cost has mounted exponentially. Epidemics of burnout and mental distress mark our hectic times. We seem to be drowning in discontentment, submerged in the thicket of never enough, preoccupied with perfection because everyone else seems so effortlessly perfect. Deep down, we know this isn't a normal or natural way to exist. We understand, by virtue of being human, that no one is perfect or could ever be made perfect. And we recognize, in our hearts if not our heads, that perfectionism's heavy armor is weighing us down.

But we wear it anyway. Because taking off the armor, and accepting the beautiful but imperfect person we are, is so unfathomably hard if it also means confronting our most basic assumptions about what's "great" and "good" in modern society and undergoing a complete apostasy of understanding about how we *should* exist in the world. When was the last time you caught a person, never mind an entire country, doing that level of introspection?

Yet that level of introspection is exactly what we must do if together we're going to escape the perfection trap. This so-titled book, *The Perfection Trap*, traces my journey to that conclusion. It started as a kind of meditation, a scratching of a persistent itch, but soon developed a dramatic narrative arc with one single thread coursing through it: perfectionism is the defining psychology of an economic system that needs each and every one of us to live in constant fear of being swallowed up by the quicksand of scarcity. The thrust of this argument is woven into thirteen chapters explaining what perfectionism really is, what it does to us, how fast it's currently rising, why it's rising, and the things we can do to escape it.

To make my case, I've used a mix of formal and informal data sources—for example, the results of psychological studies, clinical case notes, economic data, and psychoanalytic and sociological theories. I've also relied on anecdotal evidence from life going on around me in rather more heavy measure than one might expect from a social psychologist. For that, I make no apology. I'm unambiguously a numbers guy. I love statistics. I spend a great deal of my waking existence drilling them into students. But an idea cannot simply bear the weight of data to find validity in the real world. It must also bear the weight of lived experience or else it becomes a mere abstraction—a number, a trend line, an estimate around a band of many other possible estimates.

So from the get-go, let me point out a couple of things about this book. First, the reader will find many psychological, economic, and sociological ideas not so much spelled out but interspersed with, applied to, and tested by concrete experiences in my own life and the lives of others. Second, and perhaps more important, the reader should know that I've disguised identities and circumstances to tell the stories of those experiences. This has meant changing names and sometimes genders, altering places and times, making up locations, and occasionally combining several different voices into one, or one voice into many. I realize that these hidden identities and various disguises put tremendous demand on your trust, but not more demand, I hope, than a screenwriter would seek to earn through a well-crafted plotline. My intention is to portray the sense and meaning of what I've seen, heard, and experienced, if not precisely the circumstances in which those experiences occurred.

Because yes, I, too, am a perfectionist. And if there's one thing I want this book to be, it's a souvenir of solace from one perfectionist to another. The more time I've spent learning about my own perfectionism, the perfectionism of those around me, and the results of research studies looking into perfectionism's effects on health and happiness, the more I've come to realize that our stories are born of essentially the same root. Sure, we suffer perfectionism in our own special ways. But our journeys begin with the same core belief that we're not enough to matter to other people, or be loved by them, which is the same thing. You can learn that belief in many places, but most generally and most globally it's learned right here, in the flawless hologram that consumes and surrounds us.

I hope reading this book gives you comfort. I hope it helps you to gain perspective over what perfectionism does to you, and where it really comes from. I hope it gives you peace of mind knowing that none of this is your fault—that you are enough no matter how much your culture tries to convince you otherwise. I hope it gives you the tools to move toward self-acceptance. I hope it injects you with a resolve to pursue social and political causes that will establish a more psychologically attuned way of living, one that accepts human limits.

In other words, I hope this book helps you to learn a little more about yourself and the world you live in. And with that knowledge, I hope it helps you to experience more and more of the unparalleled joy that comes from accepting all of yourself and all of your imperfections for the astonishing little explosions of humanity that they are.

September 2022
London, England

PART ONE

WHAT IS PERFECTIONISM?

CHAPTER ONE

Our Favorite Flaw
Or Modern Society's Obsession with Perfection

I'm a perfectionist, so I can drive myself mad—and other people,
too. At the same time, I think that's one of the reasons I'm successful.
Because I really care about what I do.
Michelle Pfeiffer

In Nathaniel Hawthorne's 1843 tale "The Birthmark," an eminent scientist named Aylmer marries Georgiana, an impeccable young woman whose perfection is marred only by a small birthmark on her left cheek. The contrast of Georgiana's pristine face with this discolored mark of birth bothers the perfectionist Aylmer, and he can see nothing but his wife's one and only imperfection. "A crimson stain upon the snow."

For Aylmer, Georgiana's birthmark is her "fatal flaw." Soon, his revulsion rubs off on her, causing Georgiana to hate the distorted self-image that he's created. She pleads with him to use his scientific talent to fix her imperfection, "at whatever risk."

They devise a plan. Aylmer, a talented chemist, will experiment with a cocktail of compounds until a cure is discovered. He toils day and night, but the perfect concoction eludes him. One day, while he's distracted by his test tubes, Georgiana glimpses Aylmer's diary and discovers a catalogue of failures. "Much as he had accomplished," she observes, "his most splendid successes were almost invariably failures, if compared with the ideal at which he aimed."

Then suddenly, "Eureka!" Aylmer concocts an alchemic miracle: "Water from a heavenly fountain," which Georgiana hurriedly drinks before collapsing in a heap of exhaustion, waking the next day to find no trace of her birthmark. Aylmer delights in his success: "You are perfect!" he tells his now flawless wife.

But there's a sting in Hawthorne's tale. Although Aylmer's potion corrected Georgiana's blemish, it did so at the expense of her life. The birthmark vanishes—and soon after, so does Georgiana.

Not long after Hawthorne penned "The Birthmark," another Gothic writer, Edgar Allan Poe, wrote an equally chilling study of perfectionism's tragic psychology. In Poe's short story, "The Oval Portrait," a wounded man seeks shelter in a derelict mansion on the Italian peninsula. His servant tries to stem his wounds, but eventually has to give up. The wounded man assesses his situation as too grave, so holes himself up in one of the mansion's many bedrooms to die.

Lying there on the bed, shivering and delirious, he becomes enchanted by the many paintings hanging on the bedroom walls. Next to him, a small book is perched on the pillow, which claims to explain them. As he adjusts the candelabrum to illuminate the pages, his eye catches a portrait of a young woman in an oval frame tucked away in a nook behind the bedpost. The man is mesmerized. He thumbs open the book and finds the entry describing the painting's story.

The woman in the oval portrait was the young bride of a gifted but troubled painter. She was "a maiden of rarest beauty," but her husband was so obsessed with his artistry that he paid her little attention. One day, the painter asked his wife if he could paint her portrait. She accepted, thinking this was, at last, her chance to spend some precious time with her husband. She entered his studio and there she patiently sat, in a dark, high-turreted chamber, as the painter immortalized her earthly beauty.

But rather like Aylmer, the painter was a perfectionist. He "took glory in his work, which went on from hour to hour and from day to day." Many weeks passed. The painter became so lost in his art that he didn't notice his wife was ailing. "He would not see that the light which fell so ghastly in that lone turret withered the health and the spirits of his bride, who pined visibly to all but him."

Even still, she submitted uncomplainingly to her husband's perfectionism. And the painter became so fixated on capturing his wife's likeness that he eventually gazed only at the portrait. "He would not see that the tints which he spread upon the canvas were drawn from the cheeks of her who sat beside him." More weeks passed. The painter's wife grew weaker. Then, just like that, he applied the final brushstroke to his masterpiece and bellowed, "This is indeed life itself!"

He turned to his wife to find that she'd died.

★   ★   ★

It's not easy to read Hawthorne and Poe through the lens of 2023. Their tales cut eerily close to home. Hawthorne's Georgiana could quite easily be one of the many men and women who've died or been maimed by plastic surgery in the quest for bodily perfection. Poe's painter, likewise, bears haunting hallmarks of stressed-out bankers or lawyers, working all hours of the day and night to close a deal or write a contract at the expense of precious time with their family and friends.

The parallels are indeed striking. Yet, what's arguably more illuminating about these stories is the contrasts. Back in Jacksonian America, perfectionism was the stuff of popular Gothic horror, something to be ridiculed and most certainly avoided. These days, the focus of perfectionism's psychology is rather different. It's much more of a lionized quality now, something we might look for or admire, a trait that says we're working hard, that we're giving it everything we've possibly got.

Of course, unlike Hawthorne's Aylmer or Poe's painter, we're not entirely naive. We're aware of perfectionism's collateral damage, counted in hours of relentless striving, untold personal sacrifices, and heaps of self-imposed pressure. But that's sort of the point, isn't it? Perfectionism is the insignia of self-sacrificial success in modern culture, the badge of honor that conceals an altogether more fragile reality.

Which is why job interviews tend to be especially revealing of our willingness to embrace perfection. Inside the jeopardy of these ordeals, we learn a great deal about how we want to be judged, and the masks we wear to convince our interviewers that we really are worth the investment.

The most revealing part of the cross-examination is always the answer to that killer question: "What's your biggest weakness?" How we respond invariably reveals what we think are socially acceptable weaknesses—weaknesses that prove we're right for the job, weaknesses that we're so much better for having. "My biggest weakness?" we respond, trying to give the impression we're searching the depths of our character to find it.

"I'd have to say that's my perfectionism."

This answer is well-worn. Indeed, according to surveys, recruiters commonly cite the phrase "I tend to be a bit of a perfectionist" as the most overused cliché in job interviews.[1] But get past the cliché, ask ourselves why we do this, and it makes perfect sense to signal our suitability in this way. After all, in a hypercompetitive, winner-takes-all economy, *average* is a decidedly dirty word. Admitting you're happy to do just enough is an admission that you lack the ambition and personal resolve to better yourself. And we don't think employers are looking for anything less than perfection.

We don't think society looks for anything less than perfection, either. Unlike in Hawthorne and Poe's day, perfectionism in the modern world is a necessary evil, an honorable weakness, our favorite flaw. Living inside this culture, we're so invested in its absurdities that we scarcely recognize them as absurdities at all. But look closer. Hawthorne's Aylmer and Poe's painter are chilling warnings of the true cost to lives spent scaling the dizzying heights of perfection. In this book, we'll uncover what perfectionism really is, whether it actually helps us, why there might be more of it than ever, and what to do about all these things.

✷   ✷   ✷

Let's start, shall we, by getting rational. Because when we do, we see that lionizing perfectionism is a completely irrational thing to do. By definition, perfection is an impossible goal. You can't measure it, it's often subjective, and it's destined to be forever out of reach for mere mortals like us. "True perfection," joked correctional psychologist Asher Pacht, "exists only in obituaries and eulogies."[2] It's a red herring; a fool's errand. And since perfection is always beyond the possible, since chasing it is such an utterly hopeless quest, the cost for those who try must be very high indeed.

So why does it feel like striving for perfection is the only way to succeed? And are we right to feel that?

To begin answering these questions, I want to turn back to January 17, 2013. A shell-shocked Lance Armstrong sits in a leather wingback chair, looking outward into a grand, old-fashioned reading room. His legs are crossed, his breathing labored, his hands moving skittishly back and forth from his lap to his face. It's almost as if he knows in his bones that this will turn out to be one of the most-watched interviews in American broadcasting history.

His interviewer, Oprah Winfrey, is a master of her craft. She doesn't face him straight on like most interviewers. Instead, she sits at a careful angle so that Armstrong must turn his head, deliberately, to face her. After several straightforward questions, Winfrey goes all-in for her headline confession. And as she does so, she pauses for a dramatic second, lifts her head from her notes, fixes her gaze on Armstrong, and coolly invites him to admit that his seven Tour de France titles were won with the help of performance-enhancing drugs.

"Yes," Armstrong confirms. He'd been a prolific doper.

Winfrey then invites Armstrong to explain himself. And that's when something remarkable happens. His demeanor completely changes. His torso straightens, his chin lifts. He'd been waiting for this moment. Staring Winfrey right in the eye, he tells her firmly that he "didn't do it to gain an advantage." Doping, in his mind, was simply leveling the playing field. "The culture was what it was," he tells her defiantly. "It was a competitive time; we were all grown men, we all made our choices."

Armstrong chose to dope because everybody else was doping.

How we behave is influenced by how others behave. We like to think we're as free as birds, that we're completely unique individuals, and certainly very different from most people around us. But in actual fact, we're not unique in the slightest. Just like Armstrong described to Winfrey, our basic instinct is to act more like sheep. The very last thing we want to be is shunned, ostracized, or excommunicated from the herd. So every day, knowingly or otherwise, we carefully measure our behavior to stay within the bandwidth of what's socially acceptable or "normal."

Rather than some divine individuality, the social wind is what really moves the weather vane of how we tend to think, feel, and behave. When we're working, parenting, studying, or posting to social media, especially if we're filled with fear or doubt—and we're filled with those feelings a lot these days—we tend to go with the herd. And we do this even when herd behavior is decidedly unhealthy, like in Armstrong's case. So when everyone else seems to be perfect, our own sense that perfection is the only way to succeed starts to seem decidedly rational.

It's hard to escape this kind of culture. Recent research shows that we all have a certain intolerance for imperfection, whether that be in our work, school grades, appearance, parenting, sports, or lifestyle. The difference, to quote psychoanalyst Karen Horney, "is merely quantitative."[3]

Some of us have slightly more intolerance, some slightly less; most are in the middle. And that middle bit of the perfectionism spectrum—the average—is fast increasing over time. We'll look at how fast later. But for now, let's talk about what's underneath this collective scramble for perfection and whether we should be at all concerned.

*   *   *

I'm a university professor and one of the few people worldwide who studies perfectionism. Over the years, I've been working on all sorts of problems, such as identifying perfectionism's distinguishing features, looking at what correlates with perfectionism, and figuring out why it seems to be the defining characteristic of our time. In the process, I've listened to many clinicians, teachers, managers, parents, and young people coming of age in the modern world. The view from the frontline is that perfectionism is very much the new zeitgeist.

This fact was confirmed to me in 2018 when an invitation arrived in my inbox from a woman named Sheryl. She'd contacted me on behalf of TED and wanted to know whether I'd like to speak at their upcoming conference in Palm Springs, California. Perfectionism, Sheryl told me, was a topic of enormous interest to TED's membership. "Our people," she said, "see perfectionism in their own lives, their children's lives, and the lives of those they work alongside." She wanted me to tell the conference what perfectionism was, what it does to us, and why it seems so widespread. "I'd love to," I told her. So that month I sat down with TED's speechwriters to pen a twelve-minute talk titled "Our Dangerous Obsession with Perfection."

I'm proud of myself for making it through that talk, but I've grown to dislike the title. It's far too personal. It places the onus on us, on *our* obsession with perfection. Writing this book—buried in that tricky art of collecting thoughts in neat little sentences, then tweaking and distilling them into something plain for others to read—has been clarifying. Through it, I've found gaps in my thinking that I didn't know existed.

And I've started to see things in the data and all around me, things I'd somehow missed or simply couldn't see.

Perfectionism is not a personal obsession—it's a decidedly cultural one. As soon as we're old enough to interpret the world around us, we begin noticing its ubiquity on our televisions and movie screens, billboards, computers, and smartphones. It's right there in the language our parents use, the way our news is framed, the things our politicians say, how our economy works, and the makeup of our social and civic institutions. We radiate perfection because our world radiates perfection.

My flight to the TED conference in Palm Springs departed from the shiny new Terminal 2 at Heathrow Airport. Terminal 2 is the Queen's Terminal, named after Queen Elizabeth II. She opened the original Queen's Building at Heathrow in 1955, which was demolished in 2009 to make way for the new £3 billion global gateway.

The Queen's Terminal is a breathtaking piece of commercial architecture. According to *Guardian* journalist Rowan Moore, its central waiting area is the "size of the covered market at Covent Garden." And the vision for passenger experience is much the same. It's a "great social gathering space," says architect Luis Vidal, "like a piazza or a cathedral." Walking through the Queen's Terminal, one certainly gets a sense of this romanticism. From the top of the gallery that skirts the building's periphery lies a grand expanse, punctuated by sweeping curves, clean edges, brightly colored billboards, and floor-to-ceiling glass.

In this superstructure, the lines between what's real and what's not are blurred. Advertising is the principal culprit. Even by modern standards, Queen's Terminal ads are an especially curious form of corporate artistry. "Outthink infection" is IBM's call to an enlightened passenger, who'll presumably read it on their way to board a plane in the middle of a pandemic. Microsoft tells us how its cloud can turn "chaos into clockwork," while HSBC charitably reassures us that "climate change doesn't do borders."

But perhaps the most striking aspect of the marketing at the Queen's Terminal is the lifestyle branding. One billboard shows a besuited man, impeccably groomed, roaming courageously from one destination to another, aided by an especially benevolent car-sharing app. Another shows a grinning businesswoman, expensive suitcase in hand, being cheerily greeted by the concierge of an oh-so-helpful airline. These are not isolated examples. From the billboards to high-end fashion outlets to the almost too deliciously on-brand Perfectionists' Café, the terminal is a microcosm of what we celebrate: exaggerated, impossible ideals of perfect lives and lifestyles.

Yet sitting right there in the Perfectionists' Café, I couldn't help but dwell on the fanciful nature of the idealism being trumpeted. Because when viewed in the harsh light of what's happening in the real world, this building conjures a hyperfunctional, ambrosial land that's simply unrecognizable. The immaculately besuited man beaming down at me from the electronic billboard doesn't appear to have legged it to check-in because the car park is thirty minutes from the terminal. The grin on the businesswoman's face seems almost goading when you've had to slalom through security, only to find the flight's delayed.

Is coffee at the Perfectionists' Café perfect? It's not even hot. Your gate is finally called and of course it's the one at the other end of the terminal, down the escalator and a one-kilometer walk under the taxiway. You get there only to find no seats at the gate and a queue of disgruntled passengers snaking out of the waiting area and into the walkway. Tired and in need of a stiff drink, you find a space to sit and begin to ask yourself whether this meeting could just as well have been convened online.

Stop right there and really think about this. It's staggering, isn't it, how different this building's idealism is from reality? The aspirational taglines, the picture-perfect imagery, the sparkle of transatlantic travel— all of it points to a chasm not just here but in culture at large. Houses, vacations, cars, fitness regimes, beauty products, diets, parenting tips, life coaches, productivity hacks—you name it, we're living inside a hologram of unattainable perfection, with the imperative to constantly update our lives and lifestyles in search of a flawless nirvana that simply doesn't exist.

We're just human. And deep down we know, better than we'd like to admit, that all humans are fallible, flawed, and exhaustible creatures. The more this holographic culture scrambles all sense of reality, the more it insists we fight against our most humanizing fallibilities and the slow march of Mother Nature, the more our perfectionism will trap us in pursuit of a chimera—rendering us helpless as our health and happiness plummet. We'll talk about perfectionism's impact on these things later in the book. For now, though, let's return to the Queen's Terminal so I can tell you a little bit about my own struggle with our favorite flaw.

Back in the Perfectionists' Café, waiting patiently for my flight to be called, I tried to nurse threadbare nerves by flicking through the most popular TED Talks on my laptop. I must have watched hundreds in the run-up to mine. I studied each one, searching for the secret formula. The best speakers seemed to exude bulletproof confidence, as if storytelling were as second nature as eating or drinking. I'm far less sure of myself. What if I couldn't muster the courage to go onstage? What if I forgot my lines? What if I panicked in front of all those people?

Perfectionists like me tend to deal with anxiety by overthinking. We suppose that covering every possible base is the most fail-safe method of holding things together, forgetting that overthinking is itself a handicapping form of anxiety. Sure, I've never absolutely bombed a presentation using the overthinking method—but I've never truly aced one, either. At the age of just twenty-nine, and against all odds, here I was flying to California as one of TED's much-hyped "thought leaders." On that big red speaker's circle, I needed to look like I was worth the $5,000 entrance fee.

One of my great struggles is being unable to sit comfortably next to success. I'd rather pass it off as luck or happenstance than accept acclaim that, deep down, I don't believe I deserve. That deficit thinking—or insecurity—is perhaps the most pernicious aspect of perfectionism. Because when you're constantly striving for more success—not to mention petrified of failure—even a rather high level of achievement can feel decidedly empty. Worse than empty, in fact, since perfectionism exposes our dreams as nothing more than dead ends. For the perfectionist, success is a bottomless pit that depletes us in its pursuit, while the answer to that deeper question—"Am I enough?"—is always over the horizon.

And just like the horizon, it recedes as we approach.

Constantly feeling never enough is a punishing way to go through life. Despite my outward achievements, and despite what is on one level an earnest desire to lead an enlightened and compassionate life, feeling never enough means I'm never contented; I move away from people, avoid tricky situations, and end up presenting as awkward, unreliable, and generally commitment-phobic. I'm restless, panicked, oscillating between relative stability and medicated relapse, prone to self-doubt and self-criticism, torn about who I really am, caught inside a cycle of overachievement in pursuit of a credentialized success that, in my heart of hearts, I don't truly believe in.

As far as I can tell, to move toward perfection is to alienate ourselves from ourselves, or worse, to never find ourselves at all.

Nursing lukewarm coffee in the Perfectionists' Café, watching the hectic crisscrossing of Queen's Terminal passengers, I reflected for a moment on whether I might have been better off working with my father, a construction worker by trade, on his building sites. Drilling holes, sanding wood, laying bricks for a living, marrying a local girl, owning a modest house, perhaps even driving a decent car and raising a couple of kids. I *would* have missed out on the collection of fancy degrees, Russell

Group professorship, and this glittering book deal. But I wouldn't be working around the clock, and I wouldn't be restless with fear, either. And maybe, just maybe, I'd have glimpsed that elusive horizon.

Then again, maybe not. These days, is anyone truly spared the perfectionistic fantasies that plague our consumerist lives?

To one extent or another, I suspect I'm caught in a trap familiar to everyone living in the modern age—entangled in a thicket of never enough, unable to make sense of what all the relentless perfecting is for. Endless amounts of work, consumption, and self-improvement summoned in pursuit of no particular end point. Yes, there's some heritability to perfectionism. And yes, strict, harsh, and traumatic early life experiences also matter, and they matter rather a lot. But while genes and those experiences load the deck, our culture asks us to keep playing perfect aces hand after hand after hand.

Lance Armstrong faced a dilemma: stay clean at the back of the pack, or dope and compete with the leaders. "The culture was what it was . . . We all made our choices." At the time, Armstrong's choice worked out handsomely for him, but for other cyclists, doping was a risky decision. Some even lost their lives. And for what? If, as Armstrong insists, every cyclist was doping, then this arms race imperiled each cyclist's health without making any rider more likely to succeed.

The same destructive arms race is playing out in wider culture right now. Because if all we see around us is a scrambled reality of limitless perfection, then the hardest thing to accept is that we're just human. Life becomes an endless court of appeals for our flaws. We feel exhausted, empty, and anxious most of the time. And despite everything we throw at life—the relentless striving, wellness rituals, life hacks, retail therapy, filtering, concealing, and tinkering—the law of the herd means that none of it will ever make us any more likely to succeed, or, more pointedly, feel like we're ever enough.

This is the contemporary reading of Hawthorne and Poe, which basically says we're all doomed to be Aylmer and the painter now. But I'm not so sure that's quite right. In fact, I think we're more like the forgotten women in these tales. Like them, we could be quite content with our imperfect lives if only our chinks, flaws, and curved edges were allowed to simply exist—exactly as they are—rather than being magnified and blown out of all proportion by an overbearing influence bent on airbrushing the most imperceptible blemishes from view.

The deeper we fall into our culture's perfection trap, the more perfectionism will drain the life from our lives. It's high time we talked seriously about our favorite flaw, starting by looking at what it really is and how it really affects us.

CHAPTER TWO

Tell Me I'm Enough
Or Why Perfectionism Is So Much More Than High Standards

"What I am, at any given moment in the process of my becoming a person, will be determined by my relationships with those who love me or refuse to love me."
Harry Stack Sullivan[1]

Rafferty's bar and grill is a stone's throw from Toronto's downtown Union Station. It's a hip gastro joint frequented by white-shirted, dark-tied businesspeople who nurse mugs of coffee during the day, and at night, by elegant, well-dressed shoppers who sip trendy, ornate cocktails. The front patio offers a view of a busy intersection: people scuttling on the sidewalk, lights flashing green to red, streetcars clicking by and crisscrossing east and west.

It's a sunny summer evening in 2017, and I was out on Rafferty's patio with esteemed professors Gordon Flett and Paul Hewitt. We were enjoying a couple of cold beers and they were telling me about their work histories. Gord was dressed in typical academic attire: plaid shirt, tucked neatly into chinos, and walking shoes that are both comfortable and functional. This, combined with his playful, kindly face gave him the air of a local tour guide, and his excitable demeanor had much the same energy.

Paul's presence was altogether more meditative. He's a quiet, reflective, wide-eyed bundle of knotted complexity, sporting trendy circular glasses and wearing a pressed white shirt that shimmered in the evening sun. He talked only when necessary, and whenever he did, he glowed with a gentle intensity, as if momentarily enchanted by some solemn piece of fact. That intensity gave him the aura of a brooding psychologist, which is exactly what he is.

These starkly different men share a common goal. For well over three decades, they've made it their mission to examine the inner workings of perfectionism and discover why it seems to turn up so often in their therapy rooms and lecture halls. Listening to them, I sense that their work is far more than a job. It's intensely personal, as if the study of perfectionism has become an additional child to nurture. I was in Toronto to watch these titans speak about perfectionism. Their dedication to their cause had me intrigued, so I sat down with them to understand more.

Paul reflected on their journey matter-of-factly. He seems to know that their single-minded, sacred mission is somewhat unusual by modern academic standards. He explained: "I got fire in my belly for this thing and couldn't let it go." Back in the mid-1980s, as a budding clinical psychologist, Paul was working with patients whose stresses and strains—from school to work to parenting—seemed to be tied to their need to do things perfectly. His early case notes described perfectionism as a malignant force. Left unchecked, he told me, "perfectionism triggers a downward spiral, one that's extremely difficult to reverse."

He went on. "But few people saw perfectionism as a damaging characteristic, at least not in its own right."

"They still don't see it that way!" Gord shot back, his face splitting into a knowing grin.

"But they should."

In a roundabout way, these men were grumbling good-naturedly about the long-standing reluctance of psychological science to take perfectionism seriously, or at least seriously enough. The mainstream thinking is that perfectionism is something of a pop-psychology topic, the kind of thing that's drenched in armchair psychoanalysis. Sure, perfectionism *can* be problematic—in the same way conscientiousness gone too far can be problematic—but it's certainly nothing that merits serious, systematic inquiry.

We know this is true because the bible of psychiatry—the *Diagnostic and Statistical Manual of Mental Disorders*—doesn't consider perfectionism to be a character trait of much concern.[2] On the rare occasion that it's mentioned in diagnostic criteria, it tends to be one of many symptoms associated with obsessive-compulsive disorder (OCD).

Gord explained the problem: "The mainstream view of perfectionism is way too narrow. We know perfectionism has many faces, some of which are relevant to OCD, but some of which are not, and we also know that perfectionism is in all sorts of psychological ailments, not just the compulsive types."

Paul leaned over and looked in my direction. "There's that, and there's also the fact that perfectionism is way rifer than people realize. It's not a dichotomy or a classification so much as it's a spectrum. When we talk about perfectionism, we're not talking about some people, or even about whether one is or isn't a perfectionist; we're talking about *all* people, and the extent to which they're more or less perfectionistic."

He continued. "Our research shows an enormous breadth and depth to perfectionism. Even so, it's tough to make inroads when the consensus is the way it is."

If Paul's therapy room observations had taught him anything, it's that to grasp perfectionism fully we're going to need to consider that breadth and depth. Which is why expanding and distinguishing between different types of perfectionism, and then measuring and testing them, became the cornerstone of Paul and Gord's ground-breaking work. And that's also why I was in Toronto; to find out all about them.

*　　　*　　　*

What is this breadth and depth Paul talks about? And why does it matter? To answer those questions, we need to go back to when Paul first started looking into this curious personality trait. "Most people think perfectionism is really high standards," he explained, "but it was clear early on in my clinical work that this simply wasn't the case." Paul's notes revealed a web of symptoms, which went far beyond personal standards and self-imposed pressures.

"I was seeing in case after case people who felt compelled to be perfect not just to ape their own impossible standards, although they did this in great measure, but also to ape the impossible standards they felt were being imposed on them by others, and that they themselves imposed on those around them."

These different faces—self-directed, socially imposed, and other-directed—had Paul thinking. What if perfectionism was more than just a set of high goals or standards? "It quickly became clear that perfectionism is not really about striving at all, certainly not in the way you'd strive to ace a test or pitch the perfect fastball. It's an entire worldview—a way of existing that defines how we perceive ourselves and interpret the things other people do and say."

That statement was eye-opening, and it got me thinking about my own perfectionism. I used to believe it was all about hard work, dedication, and meticulousness. I assumed that I simply had excessive standards for myself, standards that defined me as a perfectionist. But actually, when you look closer, high standards turn out to be only half the story. What also matters is why people like me need to set those excessive standards in the first place. Paul thinks we're putting ourselves through the wringer for validation from other people that we're worth something in the world. "Until we recognize the simple fact that perfectionism is about how we relate to each other," he told me, "we'll continue to misunderstand it."

And with that statement, I thought about my late grandfather. He was, in many ways, a perfect example of the distinction Paul's trying to make—between high standards on the one hand and perfectionism on the other. As a child, I used to sit for hours in wide-eyed bewilderment as Pappy, a master carpenter, fashioned everyday things like bannisters, chairs, and window frames from the very first plank to the final ferrule.

I marveled at his craft. Every Sunday, I'd scuttle through the estate to his bungalow and watch intently as he showed me how to cut pieces of reclaimed timber into perfectly measured strips of wood. Then he'd delicately carve and contour each strip, carefully mark and saw the strips with military precision, before slotting them crisply together. He'd fix them tightly with screws and tenderly sand and polish the finished article. The contours of his wares were perfectly formed, the wood deliciously smooth, the end result a piece of immaculate, functional art.

These are unquestionably the traits of a person with extremely high standards. But they're not the traits of a perfectionist. When my grandfather was done in his workshop, he gathered up the wares he'd lovingly crafted and delivered them to their new homes, then simply left them there, without loitering for a   five-star review. He brought everyday things into the world for other people to use and appreciate. As far as he was concerned, his wares needed to exist way more than their maker needed to be recognized or praised.

That absence of a burning need for approval is what Paul's driving at when he says perfectionism is not about our own standards, but the standards we think are expected of us by other people. Of course, Pappy didn't always get things right. But he always got them done. The dreaded three-star review had no meaning in his world, and even if it did, someone else's dim opinion was simply part and parcel of life. Shit happens. So long as he tried his best, he felt no need to make amends or ask for approval, to continually reinvent himself, or fail better, as they say in corporate-speak. He took pride in his craft alone, and if he should miss a bit of varnish on a corner joint or leave a screw tip jutting imperceptibly out of the wood, he'd simply let those mistakes wash through him—as sure a sign of his fallibility as his wrinkles or sciatica.

That's the thing about high standards: they don't have to come with insecurity. Only perfectionism grafts the two together. As Paul understands it, perfectionism isn't about perfecting things or tasks, nor is it about striving for especially high standards in, say, your assignments, appearances, parenting, or relationships. It's far, far deeper than that. It's about perfecting *ourselves*, or to be more exact, perfecting our *imperfect selves*; going through life in defensive mode, concealing every last blemish, flaw, and shortcoming from those around us.

That way of thinking about perfectionism was a breakthrough for me. Because when you view perfectionism from the angle of deficit thinking so extreme that you spend your entire life hiding from the world, it's absolutely not the gold-plated emblem of self-sacrificial success that we mistake it for. Although there's something of my grandfather's exactitude in my blood, his conscientiousness and my perfectionism mean we're very, very different people. And our lives, as a consequence, are lived with completely different outlooks and inner dialogues.

Perhaps the biggest misconception about perfectionistic people is that our primary concern is to pull off some act of brilliance. Unlike narcissists, with whom we're often confused, we simply don't believe the bulletproof narrative we're trying to write for ourselves. Although we set our gaze on perfect standards, we aim to attain them not so much because of what they leave in the world, or even how brilliant they make us look, but because getting something exactly right relieves shame-based fears of not being good enough to matter, or be loved by other people, which is the same thing.

These shame-based fears should be emphasized, since a distinction between the external things we do and the internal things we feel is easily missed in conversations about perfectionism. Shame is the self-conscious emotion telling us we're unworthy of love and approval. It's what happens when we think we've been rejected or, worse, ignored, because we couldn't be more. Shame stings. It reaches into every sphere of our existence, infecting the way we view ourselves in relation to other people. And shame's why the perfectionists' great preoccupation with perfection is many orders of magnitude greater than the pride felt by conscientious types like my grandfather. It's a preoccupation that reaches into the very essence of *who we are* and how inadequate we think we must surely appear to other people.

My life so far has been one long quest for well-above-average achievements and, with them, other people's recognition as props for self-esteem that's more brittle than bone china. My grandfather had no such hang-up. Sure, he was driven to prove to himself and other people that he was a skilled craftsman, but he did so with a humble, patient determination that refused to be cracked by fickle opinion. Keep in mind how differently those high and low in perfectionism interact with other people because those interactions are critical to understanding why, as Paul says, perfectionism is so much more than the high standards we set ourselves.

Because perfectionism is—can only ever be—a relational trait; a self-esteem issue, arising not in a vacuum within individuals, but in our social world and through the interactions we have with those around us. It starts with an inner dialogue that says, "I'm not attractive enough, cool enough, rich enough, skinny enough, healthy enough, intelligent enough, productive enough," and finishes with a brute realization: "So whenever my shortcomings are revealed, other people will notice, and I'll be a less acceptable person in their eyes." Every ounce of energy from that realization onward is used to hide our real selves from the world and do everything we possibly can to strengthen what we think are threadbare, perfection-contingent ties binding us to other people.

⋆　　⋆　　⋆

It was the late-1980s when Paul met Gord at York University. Both had recently earned their PhDs, and both were appointed to lecture on psychology. As a young scholar of depression measurement, Gord was enchanted by Paul's early work on perfectionism. Over time, the two men began to forge a close collaboration and friendship. "I'd always been fascinated by perfectionism," Gord said, "so I jumped at the chance to work with Paul . . . If we could pinpoint a set of characteristics and a tool to measure perfectionism, we knew we could start to build an evidence base."

They began with a pool of self-descriptive statements that Paul had written a few years earlier. These statements included descriptions of perfectionistic thoughts, feelings, and behaviors that people could agree or disagree with—for example, "I strive to be perfect" or "I must be flawless"—and were based on what his patients had taught him about the things perfectionists typically think, feel, and do. "My patients showed me what perfectionism is," Paul said. "I simply listened very carefully and created a pool of items that reflected its core features."

And that's where Gord came in. With his expertise in measurement and personality psychology, and his energy and enthusiasm, they combined forces and melded extremely well. Over the following years, they began pooling perfectionism items, dishing them out to diverse samples, before distilling the items down, rewriting them, deleting them, and dishing them out again. Finally, after doing all of that heavy lifting, they arrived at an optimal solution that seemed to best describe perfectionism's structure. "When we'd done the validation work," Gord told me, "we had the bones of a theory that summarized perfectionism's core traits."

To properly convey their theory, it helps to create a graphic of what Paul and Gord discovered. As you can see in the figure on page 30, their theory is multifaceted. Perfectionism is not just one thought, feeling, or behavior, like high goals or standards. It's much more than that. It's a problematic relationship with ourselves, in which we demand too much or are overly self-critical, and it's also a problematic relationship with other people, in which we believe that those around us demand perfection and that we demand perfection from other people, too.

Recognizing that perfectionism contains these multiple faces— private and public, personal and relational—Paul and Gord called their theory the Multidimensional Model of Perfectionism and introduced it to the world in a 1991 paper published by the *Journal of Personality and Social Psychology*.[3] What does this model show? It shows perfectionism is a living, breathing worldview starting with the core deficit belief that we're not perfect enough and that our imperfections should be concealed from those around us. Within that core belief are various faces that perfectionism takes and, within those faces, characteristics that distinguish one face from another.

These multiple faces, when Paul and Gord first described them, offered a new way to study perfectionism. Rather than a solitary protagonist—exceptionally high standards—here we have an array of personal and relational characters to call forth. What follows is a biography of each, alongside illuminating case examples.

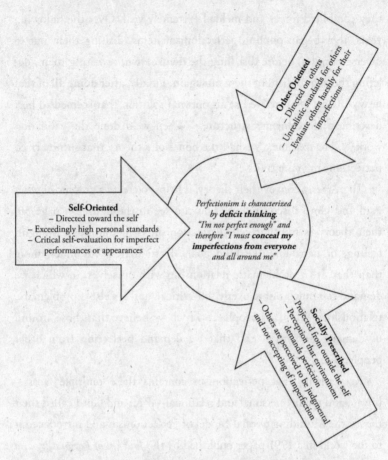

Other-Oriented
– Directed on others
– Unrealistic standards for others
– Evaluate others harshly for their imperfections

Self-Oriented
– Directed toward the self
– Exceedingly high personal standards
– Critical self-evaluation for imperfect performances or appearances

*Perfectionism is characterized by **deficit thinking**. "I'm not perfect enough" and therefore "I must **conceal my imperfections from everyone** and all around me"*

Socially Prescribed
– Projected from outside the self
– Perception that environment demands perfection
– Others are perceived to be judgmental and not accepting of imperfection

Paul Hewitt and Gordon Flett's Multidimensional Model of Perfectionism.

> *SELF-ORIENTED PERFECTIONISM is directed from within. It involves a way of existing in the world that says, "I must be perfect and nothing but perfect."*

Self-oriented perfectionism is perhaps the first thing we'd think about if conjuring the image of perfectionism in our mind's eye. For example, the workaholic colleague or overzealous student. An "internal compulsion and sense of internal pressure to be perfect" is how Paul and Gord define the traits of self-oriented perfectionism. It can be very motivating, but, ultimately, the motivation spills over into the exhausting obligation to be perfect and nothing but perfect.

Track cyclist Victoria Pendleton describes a particularly vivid case of such self-imposed pressure. Pendleton is a once-in-a-generation athlete, one of Britain's most decorated Olympians. But she's also renowned for her inability to recognize her achievements. In a 2008 interview given to *Guardian* journalist Donald McRae, Pendleton recalled that cycling was "a constant struggle."[4] She found it difficult to take any lasting satisfaction from accomplishment. "People say, wow, you've achieved it all this year, two world championship wins and an Olympic gold medal," she told McRae. "And I think, yeah, but how come I feel so unsatisfied and under pressure all over again?"

Perhaps the most visible feature of self-oriented perfectionism is this hypercompetitive streak fused to a sense of never being good enough. Yet hypercompetitiveness reflects a paradox of sorts, because, oddly enough, people high in self-oriented perfectionism can recoil from competition due to fear of failure and fear of losing other people's approval. "Being caught between a need for success and a fear of failure is the basic tension of the self-oriented perfectionist," Paul told me. "On the one hand, there's a need to strive relentlessly in the hope of being respected by and acceptable to those around us, and on the other, there's a need to do everything one possibly can to prevent the shame of falling short."

This conflicted existence sees self-oriented perfectionists flipping between perfecting and scolding themselves, and prone to self-sabotaging behaviors like overthinking and procrastination.

And yet, self-oriented perfectionists often do things that others would consider to be exceptional. You just wouldn't know it, since they tend to diminish evidence of success and cruelly belittle themselves at the first sign of struggle. Their compulsive tinkering, iterating, and general perfecting of themselves are evidence that they take their imagined shortcomings at face value, and insist on their being completely real.

Pendleton is a good example of this. She seems to place irrational importance on excessive standards for her self-worth. Not being quite good enough to satisfy these standards is a recurring theme running through her self-analysis. Through cycling, she "just wanted to prove that [she was] really good at something." She explained to McRae, "I haven't quite done that yet, at least not to myself. I know I could ride so much better, with more ease, with more finesse . . . I'm nowhere near as good as I should be."

Pendleton accepted later in her interview with McRae that she's "an insecure person," "emotional," and "a self-critical perfectionist." Her account illustrates the absence of self-compassion that's found among people high in self-oriented perfectionism. And it reminds me of one of Paul's most frequent clinical observations, namely that shame and rumination are omnipresent within the suffering perfectionist. His case notes compiled from hundreds of therapeutic interactions reveal how self-oriented perfectionists develop a distorted image of themselves, one that "goes beyond self-dislike to a form of self-loathing."

As a mentor to many high-achieving young people, I sadly see a lot of that self-loathing. One student, Anne, really sticks out. Like Pendleton, she was ambitious, hardworking, and exceptionally talented. Yet no matter how well she did, whenever we chatted, she always recast her successes as abject failures. In meetings, Anne routinely talked about how first-class grades weren't enough, how she hadn't worked sufficiently hard, and how she'd let herself and other people down.

Anne's perfectionism is far from unique among students these days, but it did strike me as particularly extreme. If I could hear her inner dialogue, it would sound something like this: "I can't possibly be bright or talented if I'm trying so much harder than other people but not doing so much better." To self-oriented perfectionists like Anne, the very fact they put in so much effort is evidence that they're not bright or talented at all. Their need to be perfect serves only to magnify the imperfections that they loathe in themselves.

The truth is that people high in self-oriented perfectionism feel compelled to play an unwinnable game, which involves shooting for perfection simply to exonerate themselves from the shame and embarrassment of not being perfect. "It's an exhausting way of going through life, needing to be perfect, correcting or concealing what's imperfect," Paul told me. "And that leaves absolutely no room for respite or compassionate self-reflection."

> SOCIALLY PRESCRIBED PERFECTIONISM is directed from the environment. It involves the belief that others expect me to be perfect.

Perfectionism is more than just having excessive personal standards; it also has a particularly pernicious social root. Paul and Gord call this *socially prescribed perfectionism*, and it entails an all-encompassing belief that everybody, at all times, expects us to be perfect. When we fall short of that impossible benchmark, the belief is that other people are scathing in their judgment.

According to Paul and Gord, socially prescribed perfectionism expresses itself in illusions of constant judgment, which leave you always trying to live up to everyone else's standards. People prone to these illusions hear snide comments about their shortcomings everywhere they go. Even benign statements can be interpreted as jabs at their imagined imperfections. There's an inner dialogue that says you should act, appear, and perform how everyone else expects you to. And everyone else expects you to be perfect.

Socially prescribed perfectionism can resemble self-oriented perfectionism. But in this case, the need to be perfect comes from pressures in the outside world. Socially prescribed perfectionists believe they'll be judged harshly if they're imperfect, so they shoot for perfection to secure the validation and approval of other people, often people they don't even know. In a world that radiates perfection, the belief that we're being judged is very much rooted in actual, lived experience. Yet it doesn't have to be. Socially prescribed perfectionism is simply a lens through which we interpret the demands of other people, real or imagined.

One of my university friends, Nathan, is a socially prescribed perfectionist. He's a quiet lad, unassumingly meticulous and extremely high achieving, but prone to low moods and mild outbursts of anxiety. That constellation of characteristics was decidedly peculiar in the teaching college we attended, and it was a peculiarity for which he received a tremendous amount of "banter." He shrugged most of it off good-naturedly, but I could tell it affected him.

I reconnected with Nathan recently and learned he hadn't lost his quiet fire for doing things perfectly. He works high up in finance nowadays, which didn't surprise me. But even so, he still sees himself as something of a failure. Not relative to where he comes from—on that count he's an overachiever. But relative to the people around him, whom he believes are far more capable. "They're super talented, they set the bar ridiculously high," he told me. "It's impossible to 'keep up'; they know I'm not doing the numbers they are."

I told him, "You must be doing something right, otherwise they wouldn't keep promoting you." He didn't seem to see the relevance of that fact, or if he did, he quickly dismissed it. "There's never a time when I'm not expected to do more," he said. "Even when I beat my targets, it's not enough—the better you do, the better you're expected to do."

Nathan's insecurities clearly haven't left him. He still feels under constant surveillance, wondering whether people will think he's excelling in sufficient measure. Only now, the intensity of corporate culture has left him more fearful about exposing his inner frailties than he's ever been before.

Somewhere else you see a lot of this fear is show business. Celebrities are, after all, constantly under the microscope, subject to inescapable pressures that stem from unrelenting performance and appearance ideals. That's why so many public figures are self-confessed perfectionists. And if you read their testimonies, you'll find their stories almost always feature socially prescribed pressures.

Demi Lovato's story is particularly illustrative. Lovato, an exceptionally talented performer, has enjoyed an incredibly successful career—but this success has come at tremendous personal cost. The roots of her struggles are vividly described in the 2017 documentary *Simply Complicated*. From a young age, "I was a perfectionist," Lovato says, "and I really wanted to be the best of the best of the best." Being propelled into the limelight as a teenager on Disney's *Camp Rock* took its toll, she says. "The fame started to creep into my life, I started feeling pressure to look a certain way, to sing music that I felt people would like, rather than sing music that I would like."

Lovato describes the pressures of being a high-profile entertainer. "There was pressure to succeed, you know, numbers on charts." Pressure is a theme echoed in her 2011 interview with MTV's James Dinh. "There's a ton of pressure out there to meet impossible standards," Lovato told Dinh. "To look right, be smart, be thin, talented, and popular, and many of us feel like we have to be everything to everyone."[5]

Like self-oriented perfectionists, socially prescribed perfectionists live their lives trying to repair their imagined imperfections. However, in the latter's case, the primary motive is to meet the expectations of other people with the express aim of gaining their acceptance, love, and approval. "These unmet relational needs are what truly derail perfectionistic people and what makes it so damaging," Paul told me. "Socially prescribed perfectionists suffer just as much in this respect because they're forever concealing imperfections from people around them."

In Lovato's self-analysis, we see corroboration for this. Socially prescribed perfectionism makes for a hugely pressured life, spent at the whim of everyone else's opinions, trying desperately to be somebody else, somebody perfect. "It's pressure," Gord added, "but pressure combined with a profound sense of helplessness."

> *OTHER-ORIENTED PERFECTIONISM is directed outward. It involves the belief that other people must be perfect.*

The final face of perfectionism that Paul and Gord identified was *other-oriented perfectionism*. This is perfectionism turned on other people, like friends, family, or coworkers. Although I should stress that while "other people" often means those close to the other-oriented perfectionist, it doesn't have to. Targets of their ire can just as well be people in general. "The more the other-oriented perfectionist feels themselves to be a measure of all things," Gord explained, "the more they insist upon their standards being measured up to."

Other-oriented perfectionists are easy to spot, since they're the ones who tend to fly off the handle when you haven't met their standards. There are obvious problems with this kind of behavior, not least for relationships. If you require others to be perfect and you're critical of them, there's invariably going to be a clash. Think, for example, about the quarrels you've had with a demanding boss, critical coach, or judgmental friend. It's seldom pretty.

Other-oriented perfectionists set impossible standards for other people because they're compensating for their own imagined imperfections—what Freud called "projection." "These people are by nature self-conscious," Paul said, "and their other-oriented perfectionism is an unconscious means of diverting attention away from the self."

It all reminds me of my first boss. Middle-aged and well presented, not posh but certainly giving it a good go, Tammy ran an exclusive health club on the outskirts of town. I was eighteen when she took me on as a trainee gym supervisor—my dream job. It soon unraveled. Tammy had difficulties with her perfectionism, difficulties she regularly turned on her subordinates. She was irritable, anxious, and overbearing. If she got it in her head that you weren't performing, which was often, she'd get hostile and generally suspicious of everything you did. She'd pace up and down the gym floor, picking out every speck of dirt or sweat that hadn't been cleaned, letting you know, bluntly, that it wasn't good enough. I used to seethe at Tammy's brash management, but her behaviors are now clearer to me as a reflection on herself. My errors were a reminder of her errors—she couldn't tolerate me missing something, just as she herself couldn't tolerate missing something.

And when something truly bad happened, she lost it. One day, the gym pool malfunctioned, spilling too much chlorine into the water. Since I was responsible for checking the pool, Tammy went straight to me for an explanation. She was visibly stressed, yelled expletives, and right there in front of puffed-out gym-goers, threatened to sue me for any damages. When the pool maintenance person arrived and informed her that the problem was nothing of my doing, she paused for a moment, as if contemplating an apology, before briskly ushering me back to work. I walked out the door instead.

We've all experienced an other-oriented perfectionist like Tammy. But perhaps the most infamous was Steve Jobs. Jobs is widely credited with transforming Apple's fortunes from a failing company in 1996 to the $1 trillion multinational business it is today. Upon Jobs's death in 2011, Apple's new CEO, Tim Cook, wrote that "Apple has lost . . . a creative genius." "The world has lost a visionary," added President Obama.

Visionary genius, Jobs surely was, but as Walter Isaacson's biography details, the man was complicated. "There are parts of his life and personality that are extremely messy, and that's the truth," Jobs's wife, Laurene Powell, told Isaacson.[6] *Atlantic* journalist Rebecca Greenfield's attempt to get to the bottom of Jobs's complexity implicates his perfectionism.[7] "Perfectionism is the disease that plagued Jobs," writes Greenfield, citing Malcolm Gladwell's *New Yorker* anecdote about Jobs's exacting standards for the decoration of a New York hotel.

He arrives at his hotel suite in New York for press interviews and decides, at 10 p.m., that the piano needs to be repositioned, the strawberries are inadequate, and the flowers are all wrong: he wanted calla lilies.[8]

Typical of the other-oriented perfectionist, Jobs used his perfectionism as an instrument of power. "[He] had the uncanny capacity to know exactly what your weak point is, know what will make you feel small, to make you cringe," a friend told Isaacson. When *Gawker*'s Ryan Tate interviewed some of Jobs's ex-colleagues, they told him much the same. He was "rude, dismissive, hostile, spiteful," they recalled, the type of boss who would manipulate employees as a way to inspire them.[9]

These accounts show the extent to which Jobs went well beyond the brash manager who might get irate every now and then. "He screams at subordinates," writes Gladwell in the same *New Yorker* piece, and he's documented in Isaacson's biography as telling his public relations assistant that her suit is "disgusting." Ultimately, "he couldn't handle anything less than perfection," Greenfield writes, and when he fell short of that impossible benchmark, he "took it out on others."

There's a lot in that description of Jobs. Despite his outward achievements, his perfectionism gave him fragile self-esteem, which was easily threatened, and this threat caused him to lash out frequently. Other-oriented perfectionists like him have a win-at-all-costs attitude, which is fine. But when your dominance is threatened, it can evoke a lot of rage, and in some cases quite aggressive behavior. "This is not something conducive," Paul said, "to warm, harmonious relations."

Anne, Pendleton, Nathan, Lovato, Tammy, Jobs—these people are far from alone. I could have written an anthology filled with profiles of perfectionists and tales of their tensions. But I've chosen to spotlight these characters because their different experiences are especially instructive if we're to grasp the breadth and depth of perfectionism and the many faces it has. Each of these people needs to be perfect. Yet this need is visited on them differently, depending on the type of perfectionism most at play.

The three perfectionism dimensions are often described as independent entities. This helps provide clarity, but it's an oversimplification. Self-oriented, socially prescribed, and other-oriented perfectionism are far from independent of each other. On the contrary, much like the watercolors on a painter's palette, Paul and Gord's dimensions bleed into each other, such that people can possess high levels of one, two, or even all three.

Take Steve Jobs. We've seen how he adopted demanding and, at times, hostile attitudes toward his coworkers in a manner reminiscent of other-oriented perfectionism. Yet he also, according to Rebecca Greenfield, "approached even the most mundane tasks . . . with thoughts of perfection." She illustrates this tendency with a quote lifted from Isaacson's biography in which Jobs is weighing up the purchase of a washing machine.

> We spent some time in our family talking about what's the trade-off we want to make. We ended up talking a lot about design, but also about the values of our family. Did we care most about getting our wash done in an hour versus an hour and a half? Or did we care most about our clothes feeling really soft and lasting longer? Did we care about using a quarter of the water? We spent about two weeks talking about this every night at the dinner table.

"All for a washing machine," Greenfield wryly observes. Jobs is an excellent example of a person for whom boundaries between perfectionism's personal and relational elements are blurred. In his mind, there was no separation. If he was going to haul himself over coals for every minor imperfection, then why should others escape the same torment?

Not everyone's perfectionism expresses like Jobs's. Mine is mostly directed inward, impostor-like, and has me worrying about public displays of imperfection. Lovato's seems mostly directed from outside, and has her trapped by unrelenting pressures. In other words, we're gloriously complex creatures, our circumstances are many and varied, and as such, there are infinite kinds of perfectionistic people. "We normally see one dimension stand out," Paul told me, "but that doesn't mean people can't have thoughts, feelings, and behaviors associated with the others. In fact, it's quite typical for perfectionists to have high levels of all dimensions."

The one constant, the thing that binds all perfectionistic people together, is the place it all begins—a lingering and unshakable insecurity that no matter what we do, we're not perfect enough.

The intricate interplay of self-oriented, socially prescribed, and other-oriented perfectionism is why Paul and Gord treat perfectionism as a spectrum. "Our dimensions are like the threads of a spider's web," Gord explained. "All threads are part of the same web, but every web has its own distinctive structure."

How far each thread stretches depends on where each person is on each perfectionism spectrum. Some are higher on, say, self-oriented perfectionism, while others are lower on socially prescribed and other-oriented perfectionism. If we plot these webs, they might look something like the following chart.

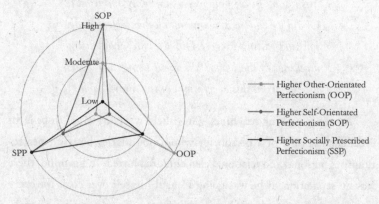

Hypothetical perfectionism profiles based on where people score on the spectrums of self-oriented, socially prescribed, and other-oriented perfectionism.

Of course, knowing how far our threads of perfectionism fan out requires a tool to measure them. That's why, back when Paul and Gord embarked on their journey, the very first thing they did was develop a perfectionism scale using those self-descriptive statements Paul had written. Their Multidimensional Perfectionism Scale is a paper and pencil questionnaire with forty-five statements about self-oriented, socially prescribed, and other-oriented perfectionism. People must agree or disagree with each, according to a seven-point scale.

You can assess where you fall on each spectrum with this adapted version of Paul and Gord's Multidimensional Perfectionism Scale. Answer each question with "strongly disagree," "disagree," "only slightly disagree," "unsure," "only slightly agree," "agree," or "strongly agree."[10]

Self-oriented perfectionism

_____ I must be perfect at the things that matter to me.

_____ If I screw up or fall short, I'm hard on myself.

_____ I hold myself to an exceptionally high standard.

_____ If I do not appear or perform perfectly, I feel a lot of guilt and shame.

_____ I strive to be perfect.

Socially prescribed perfectionism

_____ When I slip up or fall short, people are right there waiting to criticize me.

_____ Everyone else is perfect and they're judging me if I'm not perfect, too.

_____ Those close to me will accept nothing less than perfection.

_____ People tend to get upset with me if I don't do things perfectly.

_____ Everybody expects me to be perfect.

Other-oriented perfectionism

_____ I find it difficult to tolerate substandard performances from those around me.

_____ If people aren't trying their absolute hardest, I let them know.

_____ Everyone should totally excel at things that are important to them.

_____ When someone close to me screws up or falls short, it's important to call them out.

_____ I dislike being surrounded by people who've got low standards.

If you mainly answered "agree" or "strongly agree" for one, two, or all three sets of questions, then you're probably quite high on each perfectionism dimension. If you wavered between "only slightly agree" and "only slightly disagree," you're probably somewhere in the middle. And if most of your answers were "disagree" or "strongly disagree," then good news: you're unlikely to be especially perfectionistic.

These individual differences in the makeup of perfectionism mean that not everything you'll read in this book will apply to you, even if you scored yourself high on one or more dimensions. Paul and Gord developed the Multidimensional Perfectionism Scale to capture the full array of perfectionistic thoughts, feelings, and behaviors, some of which will apply a great deal, others not so much. That's the most interesting thing about perfectionism: there's no one-size-fits-all.

Paul and Gord also developed the Multidimensional Perfectionism Scale as a research tool, one that can pinpoint precisely where people fall on the various spectrums of perfectionism. Alongside this simple tool, their labs, and labs across the world, could assess other areas of people's lives—their mental health, the quality of their relationships, or how well they're performing in school or work, for example. Using these measures, a vast volume of scientific work has amassed over the years—abstracts, papers, and meta-analyses—that together reveal some astonishing answers to pressing questions such as: What's the effect of perfectionism on mental health? Is it essential for success? And where does it come from? So let's look at the fruits of that research.

PART TWO

WHAT DOES PERFECTIONISM
DO TO US?

CHAPTER THREE

What Doesn't Kill You
Or Why Perfectionism Does So Much Damage to Our Mental Health

"I wrote all the morning, with infinite pleasure, which is queer, because I know all the time that there is no reason to be pleased with what I write, and that in six weeks or even days, I shall hate it."

Virginia Woolf[1]

Two beers into my chat with Paul and Gord and I was wrapped in my own thoughts. Their words had me wondering exactly what perfectionism does to us, in part because one of the many people caught in its trap was me. I wanted to know why these men had such a glib view of perfectionism, why their illuminating reflections seemed to portend a decidedly gloomy turn in our conversation.

I asked them, "What exactly is the problem with perfectionism?" They premised their concerns on the fact that, to their minds, perfectionism lurks beneath the surface of mental distress. "If you want to know why so many young people are struggling these days," Paul remarked, "you've got to look at perfectionism."

As I would come to realize, it's an entirely valid point. No sooner had Paul and Gord developed their perfectionism scale than researchers were looking at whether perfectionism contributes to all manner of afflictions, such as depression, anxiety, bulimia, self-harm, and suicide. "Our scale unlocked the potential for a systematic program of research," Gord told me. "Sadly, what we found was a depressing picture."

Much of the research Gord's referring to is correlational. Correlational studies involve researchers giving people the Multidimensional Perfectionism Scale and outcome measures such as anxiety or depression in a one-shot survey. Suppose Paul and Gord's thinking about perfectionism is correct. In that case, people with a lot of anxiety will have high levels of perfectionism, people with a little anxiety will have moderate levels, and people with almost no anxiety will have low levels. This is a positive correlation; someone who scores high on perfectionism also scores high on anxiety.

Correlation, of course, does not equal causation. But when enough correlations tend in the same direction, you know something's up. "Time and time again our labs, and labs around the world, find perfectionism to have sizable correlations with markers of mental and emotional distress, problematic thought patterns, and body image concerns—sometimes very sizable indeed," Paul told me.

Of Paul and Gord's perfectionism dimensions, self-oriented perfectionism is the most complex. On the surface, research can seem to indicate that it's benign or that it somehow promotes self-esteem and positive emotions. But these outcomes belie vulnerability to psychological difficulties that come from tying self-worth to achievement and being unable to derive a lasting sense of satisfaction from success. We saw a vivid example of this psychology with Victoria Pendleton's self-reflections in the last chapter.[2]

Across hundreds of studies, self-oriented perfectionism correlates with goodies like self-esteem and happiness, but it also correlates with a lot of very bad things, like depression, anxiety, hopelessness, body image worries, and anorexia.[3] There's even concerning evidence that self-oriented perfectionism contributes to thoughts of suicide, albeit with only a very small effect size, which means the effect is detectable, but other factors are more important.[4] The ill effects of self-oriented perfectionism are substantiated in recent comprehensive reviews, which found that it positively correlates with anxiety and predicts increases in depression over time—an effect that can sometimes be concealed in one-shot studies.[5]

Other-oriented perfectionism is a curious case, since it's mostly studied in the context of relationships. But findings here, too, are troubling. Many studies have discovered links between other-oriented perfectionism and higher vindictiveness, a grandiose desire for admiration and hostility toward others, as well as lower altruism, compliance with social norms, and trust.[6,7,8,9] In intimate relations, other-oriented perfectionism is also problematic. It's closely linked with significant issues in the bedroom, greater partner conflict, and lower sexual satisfaction.[10,11]

These insights about self-oriented and other-oriented perfectionism paint a pretty bleak picture. But they're not Paul and Gord's biggest concern; that's socially prescribed perfectionism. People with high levels of socially prescribed perfectionism typically report elevated loneliness, worry about the future, need for approval, poor-quality relationships, rumination and brooding, fears of revealing imperfections to others, self-harm, worse physical health, lower life satisfaction, and chronically low self-esteem.[12] They're also highly vulnerable to severe mental distress. For example, in correlational studies, they'll often report higher hopelessness, anorexia, depression, and anxiety disorders, and like self-oriented perfectionism, socially prescribed perfectionism also correlates with thoughts of suicide—but to a far greater degree.[13]

Rory O'Connor, a British psychologist who studies suicide, has a theory on socially prescribed perfectionism's link. "It's not necessarily you setting standards for yourself that's potentially risky; it's what you think others expect of you," he told *The Psychologist* magazine. "If you think that you've failed to meet their expectations, you may internalize this as self-critical rumination, and for some [that initiates] a self-critical cycle of failure and despair."[14] Without intervention, O'Connor thinks, this cycle can end tragically.

And that's not all. There's a compounding effect of socially prescribed perfectionism when it's combined with self-oriented perfectionism. Gord explained: "Whether it be depression, anxiety, self-esteem, rumination, or body image concerns, it doesn't matter the outcome, high socially prescribed perfectionism laced with high self-oriented perfectionism is a hazardous mix, one that can amplify problems by many orders of magnitude." That compounding effect is evident across hundreds of studies showing that the effects of socially prescribed perfectionism on mental distress are magnified by self-oriented perfectionism.[15]

Far from just an inner compulsion or something that leads only to obsessive tendencies, perfectionism looks like it's an underlying risk factor for mental and emotional distress more generally. In other words, there's an aggressive, aggravated vulnerability built into perfectionism. This vulnerability is real and alive and becomes the lens through which perfectionists view what's happening to them in ways that make them extremely susceptible to a whole plethora of mental health problems. And that's the reason Paul and Gord are so concerned: they're convinced perfectionism lurks hidden beneath more visible markers of mental and emotional distress—anxiety disorders, body image concerns, depressed mood—which appear to be ominously on the rise.

Perhaps that's not a shocking revelation. After all, perfectionism wouldn't be our favorite *flaw* if there wasn't some sting in the tail. But I wonder, do we fully appreciate the extent of the pain that perfectionism can inflict? And exactly why is it that perfectionism stings so much in the first place? We've seen that it correlates with a whole host of mental health problems, but we're yet to take a deep dive into why that is. To do so, we're going to need to bust a few myths—starting with one of modern culture's most dubious maxims.

★   ★   ★

What doesn't kill you makes you stronger. In recent years, Friedrich Nietzsche's words have coagulated into something of a cliché. You'll find them written on the walls of school corridors, gymnasium locker rooms, university libraries, and embossed on mugs, T-shirts, and bumper stickers. Pop star Kelly Clarkson used them as the chorus for her number one smash hit "Stronger," which explores themes of empowerment and bouncing back from heartache. As Freud reminded us, suffering is an inevitable part of life. But these days, Nietzsche's words have been invoked to bestow upon suffering a kind of magical, transformative power.

Society desperately wants to believe this magical power, too. We're bombarded with self-made, can-do fantasies in which we're told we should endure—even embrace—struggle and strife if we're going to succeed. Visit any bookstore and browse the self-help section; you'll find hundreds of titles promising to give you the power of "positive thinking" or make you more "resilient." Life coaches fill social media platforms with the same messaging: "Wake up, it's time to grind," "Push through the pain," "Nothing worth having comes easy."

All of which means modern-day conventional wisdom basically says that you must always grow, remain unblinkingly positive, and roll with the punches every time you're knocked down. When bad things happen, no problem: dust yourself off, get back up, and keep striving for a better outcome next time. Ordinary forms of suffering, like feeling unhappy, confused, a bit tired, or simply dwelling in a state of grief, animosity, or sadness after a stressful event—these are traits of the weak, the idle, the unambitious. People need to be tough, uncompromising, and fearless. Superheroes versus the wimps.

This curious relationship with suffering is why I think we're kind of relaxed about those correlations between perfectionism and mental distress. We've taken it for granted that perfectionism hurts because we think that hurt, far from being destructive, is the secret to a life well lived. What doesn't kill you makes you stronger.

Paul and Gord don't think that's right, and I'm inclined to agree with them. Perfectionism isn't the caped crusader we've mistaken it for. It's not self-sacrificing tenacity, it's self-sabotaging tumult. It's the inevitable end point of Nietzsche's famous maxim, the one we don't often talk about, but the one the reclusive, tormented, and insomniac man himself was ultimately met with all the same.

So let's take a look at the true extent to which perfectionism takes over our lives. Let's appreciate the sheer enormity of what really happens when things go wrong. Let's talk frankly about my own losing battle with perfectionism.

★   ★   ★

My ex-girlfriend was named Emily, but everyone always called her Em. Not me, I never called her by her name, except perhaps when we first dated back in high school. To me, for the several years we were together, she was simply "hun." If I were to suddenly call her Em or, worse, Emily, she'd surely know something was terribly wrong.

"Emily," I messaged her, panicked. "I need to know what's going on."

"I'm getting home at 6:30," she messaged back. "I'll tell you everything."

But six thirty came and Emily hadn't arrived. Since she was late, I walked out to the courtyard of our apartment block for some fresh air. I remember the sun's dusty hue, which left long shadows over the lawn. I remember the distinctive smells of a warm summer evening. The neighbors were making dinner and it was time to do the same, but I couldn't bring myself to think, never mind cook.

Suddenly, Emily's car roared into view, turned left through the gates, and disappeared down the ramp to the car park beneath our block. I walked back to the building, up the stairs, and into our apartment, where I sat and waited.

Emily stayed in her car for some time; much longer than usual. She knew something was up because one evening I'd seen messages from an unknown number flash up on her open phone. She said the messages were just flirtatious jokes with a colleague that'd got out of hand. And I believed her because I loved her. But then, not long after, another less subtle message suddenly appeared. At once, she realized I deserved an explanation.

Emily's key turned in the lock and the door burst open. She wheeled around in the hallway for a moment, grappling with her coat and keys. I could hear her heavy breathing as she walked along the corridor to join me in the living room. "Let's do this in the bedroom," she said, staring straight through me.

Emily knelt in front of me as I perched on the side of the bed. Her head bowed, she took a deep breath and I, in turn, immediately did the same, hoping this wouldn't hurt too much, that the confession wouldn't scar me. She began by explaining the messages, which were from a man she'd met on a night out.

"I was drunk, we got to chatting in the smoking area," she told me.

Without saying another word, the muffled choke in Emily's voice at the end of that sentence told me what was coming next. I looked away, swept the cold sweat from my palms, and noticed my skin had turned a reddish pale in anticipation.

"One thing led to another, and I was back at his house," she continued, barely able to get her words out.

There was a definite pause as Emily collected herself. I waited to see if she would turn back before making the final, painful confession. I could tell she wanted to, but I insisted she say what she had to say.

"We slept together, Thom, I'm so sorry."

The release seemed to embolden her. And to my surprise, she wasn't done. She described several people she'd made out with while we were long-distance dating at our separate universities. And then she explained a couple of occasions when she'd been unfaithful subsequent to that. Guilt had been eating away at her for months, and she was hurriedly listing everything she could possibly remember.

Emily knew that what she was doing was right and fair. I'd forgotten every good reason by this point and certainty wished I hadn't asked. Right there, in that most vulnerable of moments, we were experiencing perhaps the greatest emotional distress of our young adult lives—exposing ourselves to painful truth, to shame, to fear, to heartbreak.

Emily did something unexpected on her final confession. She stopped midway through, reached out, and offered me her trembling hand. This gesture felt outrageous, yet somehow profoundly caring. I didn't take it, but I wish I had.

We were young. We just made mistakes.

Placing her hand back on her thigh, Emily finished what she had to say, let out a soft screech of pent-up tension, and breathed deeply to bring her heart rate under some sort of control. What happened immediately after that is a blur. I remember only the sorrow and my motionless body, and Emily kneeling there, breathless, staring at me in hopeless sadness.

The aggravated vulnerability that lurks in perfectionism surfaces whenever things go wrong. And the more exposed we are in those situations, the more damage perfectionism will do. It's so encompassing, has us so utterly fixated on our frailties, weaknesses, and imperfections, that it'll violently amplify moments of vulnerability, leaving absolutely no band-width for the mobilization of the emotional resources required to cope with what comes next. Ordeals like the heartbreak I experienced in that tender period of young adulthood are very ordinary forms of human suffering—part and parcel of life's uneven camber. Even so, when they happen to visit you unannounced, as they invariably will from time to time, perfectionism makes it feel like everything and all around you is collapsing.

The morning after Emily confessed, I got in the shower and drenched myself in cold water. The splash of cool spray on my tired face momentarily roused me from my torpor. I hadn't slept. All night I'd tortured myself with horrible imagery, grief about losing Emily, criticism of myself and my failings. And yet, despite feeling as low as I'd ever felt, despite looking as shattered as I'd ever looked, I got out of the stall, patted myself dry, put on my clothes, and went to work.

I sat at my desk like I did every day. I went to meetings, responded to emails, chatted with colleagues as if nothing had happened. Inside, I was a mess of emotion, resentment, and grief. I'd opened myself fully to Emily and it felt like she was rejecting me in the most brutal of ways. Her confessions had left me confronting the full extent of my shortcomings—the shortcomings I now had ample reason to loathe. I chastised myself. I asked how it could happen. I questioned my appearance, my body, my masculinity. I felt weak and embarrassed, my self-esteem in ruins.

Perfectionism amplifies stresses like this. It makes us hypersensitive to chinks in our armor, trying desperately to rescue the perfect outward persona that we've worked so hard to create. When we experience stressful situations, we worry about how others will view us. We ruminate about their judgment. We feel intensely self-conscious for not being the person we think we should've been. Every time researchers put people in the lab and expose them to a stressful situation like public speaking or competitive failure, it's always the people who score higher on perfectionism that report the most trepidation, the most guilt, and the most shame.[16]

Although plagued by these emotions, perfectionists can stay remarkably agile. They can fake the perfect life for a very, very long time, even when faced with quite significant stress, and even when preoccupied with really quite scathing self-criticism. Research shows that people high in perfectionism continue to persevere well beyond comfort when confronted with setbacks, and tend to display quite compulsive behaviors, especially in the workplace.[17] Their fear is that they'll be rejected or disapproved of if they don't carry on striving, or at least appear like they're striving.

I suffered after what happened with Emily, but somehow I held it together. I did so because the anticipated social judgment of doing the opposite—baring my vulnerability and allowing myself space to heal—was unthinkable. I didn't tell anyone what happened. I repressed the sorrow and concealed the shame from view. I confided in no one, sought help from no one. Studies show those high in perfectionism rarely reveal their stress or anguish, rarely seek help to manage mental health problems or go to therapy.[18] They'll bury their problems as deep as they possibly can, treat them as if they never existed, and lean further into their perfectionism as a way of holding things together.

That's a disastrous way to cope. Forcing yourself to carry on through adversity sets off a cruel cycle that prolongs stress and squeezes it into every other sphere of life. This coping strategy aims to salvage the perfect image of ourselves that we want others to see. But it's a salvation that carries a heavy price. For the perfect person we're trying to imitate is now even farther from view, carrying emotional baggage on top of all that impression management.

We become even more exhausted and burned out. Life becomes an almost heroic battle just to maintain the perfect facade, which by now is as brittle as porcelain, made up of nothing stronger or more lasting than a put-on smile, fake exuberance, and the fumes of pent-up fear. Stress, setbacks, failure visit us again and again, the judgment keeps piling up, and we turn on ourselves for being unable to snap out of it. Until one day, the tension becomes too much to bear and something pops. The dam breaks, the anxiety pours out.

I'll never forget my first panic attack. It was about three, perhaps four months after I broke up with Emily. I hadn't told anyone why we split; only that it was mutual. I was at the office. I remember sitting at my computer one afternoon, like I did every day, tired, on my third coffee, working on something I'd been up with the night before.

From nowhere, a white flash appeared in my vision. It fizzed away in the periphery as an annoyance at first, then slowly moved into sight, obscuring my view, making it impossible to focus. I didn't know why. I still don't really know why. But apparently flashes like this are a common symptom of acute stress—one of the many helpful ways our bodies manage anxiety by churning out even more of it.

I'd never experienced anything like it. I panicked. I couldn't catch my breath. My hands began to shake; my heart started to throb. I leapt from my desk, rushed to the kitchen, and poured myself some water. But it was no use. I moved to the common room and lay on the sofa. I closed my eyes for several seconds, fingered my pulse, and took several deep breaths in the bewildered company of concerned colleagues.

I knew I needed to get out of there, but I didn't want to draw attention to myself.

My heart carried on racing. I breathed deeper and harder, trying desperately to slow it. The reverse happened: my heart began to pound as if it were thumping out of my chest. All my senses now seemed to tremble together. The stuffy air got thicker, tightening my throat, tingling my skin. I started to gasp, gently at first, and then uncontrollably as my body turned into a vehicle for something dreadful.

That's the odd thing about panic: the things you do to suppress it just

57

make it worse. Panic feeds panic. Worry gives way to fear and you begin to wonder whether you're in the middle of a fate altogether darker. Disoriented and frightened, you ask yourself: How can my heart possibly beat this hard? Why won't it stop? Am I dying? I thought and thought, but couldn't find the answers.

Then I melted.

I was sure this was it. I scurried down the stairs and hurried out into the street, closely followed by concerned colleagues. Out in the open air, I crouched to the oily concrete, put my head between my legs, and sucked the air. The outside world seemed to slip away momentarily. Just me and my roaring panic.

The instant I felt like I was going to finally pass out, I pulled out my phone and dialed the emergency services. My thumb trembled as it hovered over the call button for what seemed like an eternity. And then, by some happenstance I can't fully account for, my body just seemed to come back to me. My heart stopped pounding. I was able to speak.

"Don't worry," I told onlookers. "I'm fine."

I wasn't fine. I was shaken and vulnerable. In that terrifying moment, perfectionism had blown out of all proportion what was a painful but not life-altering ordeal. My despair—and shame—at what happened with Emily was amplified to the point of crisis. And my emotional plunge had elongated the stress, snowballing anxiety into every other sphere of my life.

After that panic attack, I experienced many more. I still do, now and then. I developed all kinds of weird and wonderful complaints, like a tightness in my throat, dizziness, palpitations, and a ringing in my ears that remains to this day as a lingering reminder. I slipped into a depression that oscillated between brief interludes of doing okay and long stretches of listlessness, tension, and intense tiredness. At worst, the fatigue was so immobilizing that I became incapable of peeling myself out of bed or concentrating on simple tasks, like proofreading or responding to emails.

I saw all these symptoms as the enemy within. I believed that a real man should be able to pull himself together and overcome his inner tensions. But that wasn't true. When I simply couldn't keep on pushing through the symptoms, when the anxiety was too much to cope with and things felt completely hopeless—as if I'd never feel "normal" again—I sought the help of a psychologist. She was able to show me that I was suffering from profound amounts of self-loathing, shame, and grief, which were being expertly covered up and aggravated by my perfectionism.

That realization didn't just shift the way I thought about our favorite flaw. It's the very reason I'm still here, doing the research, writing this book, and bringing the perils of perfectionism out into the open.

As far as I can tell, were it not for reality, I'd be quite okay. But that's the problem, isn't it? Life comes at us hard, sometimes really hard. The world isn't the Elysian utopia projected on television screens, depicted on airport billboards, or smattered across social media feeds. It's messy, disorientating, chaotic. The financial system is unstable by design, cost of living is spiraling; recessions, natural disasters, wars, and pandemics emerge out of nowhere; we lose our jobs, we break people's hearts, people break ours, those close to us pass away, and the arrow of time ceaselessly, and indifferently, accelerates ever forward.

Setbacks, hassles, failures, mistakes, layoffs, heartbreaks, fallouts— these are part and parcel of life. Almost everything we set out to do, somewhere along the line, will meet us with implacable resistance. "Not this time," we tell ourselves. "Maybe next time!" We can no more control that fact than we can alter the direction of the wind or the rhythm of the tides. Often, for no good reason, we get caught in the cross fire of an unpredictable world—that's just fate, and fate's nothing personal.

Even so, perfectionism makes shame stick to fate's cross fire like hot tar on cold concrete. If only we perfectionists could accept that so much of what occurs in this world is far beyond our control. How much healthier we'd be if we could view the trajectory of our lives with calm equanimity. Instead, we feel culpable for every bad thing that happens to us, taking each setback personally as further evidence that we're irredeemably flawed.

When bad things happen to us, we don't, as a rule, console ourselves. We find no solace in the fact that, for example, we live in a tilted society that predisposes many to disadvantage, or that we tried at something but just happened to fail, or that we got distracted, or had a bad night's sleep, or simply screwed up, as we do from time to time. There's no self-compassion to be found when we're lied to, ignored, or cheated on. We conceal our vulnerabilities and do all we possibly can to maintain the perfect, cheerful, unblinkingly positive pretense. What doesn't kill you, we think, makes you stronger.

Viewed from this angle, perfectionism is rather like running on a treadmill at maximum velocity. You're breathless, but since everyone's watching, you somehow find it within yourself to keep putting one foot in front of the other. Until suddenly, from nowhere, someone throws a rag on the belt, it trips you up, and you lose your balance. You stumble around trying to collect yourself, but there's no action you can take— the centrifugal force has already gathered you up and it's about to spit you out. Anyone who's been tossed off the back of a treadmill will know it's painful. And they'll also know that trying to get back on without first stopping the belt is enormously foolhardy.

Yet, engulfed by the fear of what accepting such defeat must look like to those around them, that's exactly what perfectionists do, and that's exactly why perfectionism is a risk factor for all manner of mental health struggles—not just the compulsive types.

Contrary to Nietzsche's maxim, perfectionists aren't strengthened in the trying times. They're weakened. Left untreated, repeated knockdowns so injure perfectionists' self-esteem that they begin to feel helpless, and in extreme cases, like mine, hopeless. No wonder perfectionism is so enormously damaging. "There's this assumption that perfectionism means we're more resilient," Paul told me. "But actually, perfectionism is the opposite of resilience—anti-resilience, if you will. It makes people extremely insecure, self-conscious, and vulnerable to even the smallest hassles. If you don't seek help, it's easy to see how that vulnerability creates substantial distress."

Perfectionism, then, is incredibly painful. If we let it, it'll spread self-criticism, fear, insecurity, anxiety, and depression into every part of our waking existence. And it'll aggressively magnify and elongate those thoughts and feelings when things go wrong. But what about the upside? What about the favorite part of our favorite flaw? What about performance?

CHAPTER FOUR

I Started Something I Couldn't Finish
Or the Curious Relationship between Perfectionism and Performance

"Perfection is man's ultimate illusion. It simply doesn't exist in the universe . . . If you are a perfectionist, you are guaranteed to be a loser in whatever you do."
David Burns[1]

As the night progressed, nondescript techno music was thudding through the patio speakers, the beers were starting to kick in, and we were in high spirits. Before the trendy nighttime crowd descended on Rafferty's bar and grill, I needed to unpack a thorny subject with Paul and Gord. I wanted their take on the favorite part of our favorite flaw, the supposedly good part, the part that says you're giving it everything you've possibly got and then some. Perfectionistic people might feel miserable, but can they channel their need to be perfect into doing great things?

Success, meanly measured in units of pay and credentials, is by far the most controversial subject in perfectionism circles. It's hard to succeed nowadays; you've got to sacrifice yourself, keep pushing through the pain, and even then most won't make it to the very top—that's just the nature of the zero-sum battle in the modern economy. "To get ahead in this world," I asked Paul, "aren't we going to need a little bit of perfectionism?"

He looked understandably confused at the question, as though I hadn't quite grasped the severity of what he'd been saying. I pressed him. "Let me put it another way: The crystalline experiences of perfectionists, the data your lab and other labs have amassed, are these merely cautionary tales about something we simply cannot succeed without?"

Although this is a debated subject, Paul wasn't inclined to give an equivocal answer. He's spent far too many years working with suffering perfectionists to sit on the fence. Practicing on the front line, he can't possibly fathom why anyone would give a positive, adaptive, or healthy slant to this trait. He told me, "I often hear people say that perfectionism is necessary for success in this or that field—they'll say things like 'If you shoot for perfection, you'll land on excellence,' or some variation of that theme.

"But it's quite foolish," he continued, "since to leave the matter here would be to let whoever's making that statement off with perhaps the most pernicious myth of them all—that perfectionism is essential for success."

Paul and Gord hold one man primarily responsible for propagating that myth: American psychologist Don Hamachek. In 1978, writing for the journal *Psychology*, Hamachek did something controversial, something that *still* rankles researchers like Paul and Gord. His sin? He was the first high-profile thinker to draw a distinction between unhealthy and healthy perfectionism.

Unhealthy perfectionism, Hamachek argued, is the kind of perfectionism we've just discussed—a rigid and compulsive need to be perfect and nothing but perfect. Healthy perfectionism, on the other hand, is rather different. It's part of perfectionism that supposedly involves "hard work and doing one's level best." Skilled artists, careful workers, and craftspeople like my grandfather are healthy perfectionists, according to Hamachek, and they can set high goals for themselves without descending into a pit of self-loathing. They can even find satisfaction, he believed, in the striving itself.[2]

Many perfectionism scholars besides Paul and Gord have also questioned Hamachek's distinction. Fellow American psychologist Thomas Greenspon, for example, took special umbrage. In a paper titled "Healthy Perfectionism Is an Oxymoron!," Greenspon wrote that Hamachek's healthy perfectionists are far from perfect. "Correct, proper, better than average, and surely, the best one can be," he said, "but not perfect."[3]

Correctional psychologist Asher Pacht went further. In a 1984 *American Psychologist* article, Pacht remarked that he preferred not to use the "healthy" label when describing perfectionism. He believed perfectionism was a malignant feature of a neurotic, much like Paul and Gord do. It's a term Pacht used carefully, and "only when describing a kind of psychopathology."[4]

"Variations of this disagreement still rage on in the perfectionism literature," Gord told me. "Certain labs maintain that something in the drive and naked ambition of perfectionistic people can be considered positive, and other labs, like ours, think that's not the case." He went on. "If you ask me, Greenspon was right, healthy perfectionism is indeed an oxymoron. Striving for something that can't possibly be attained is the very opposite of healthy, and it stores up only misery for those who try."

As far as I can tell, the crux of this debate can be drawn out to a seemingly logical set of hypotheses that have remained open for many decades in our field. The first hypothesis is that perfectionism pushes us to work harder in the pursuit of great things. And if that's true, the second hypothesis is that perfectionism must, therefore, make us more likely to succeed. Researchers have wrestled for decades trying to reconcile these two matters. What they found is a complicated picture, one that may very well surprise you.

★　　★　　★

Whether there's anything positive about perfectionism is an age-old debate. But before we get into it, let's be clear about one thing. When we talk about "positive," "healthy," or even "normal" perfectionism, what we're really talking about is self-oriented perfectionism—the type that seems to contain those go-getting qualities of hard work, grit, and time on task. This is not the case for socially prescribed and other-oriented perfectionism. No one's arguing that these traits are in any way adaptive.

Many papers report links between self-oriented perfectionism and motivational outcomes. In diverse domains such as school, sports, and work, self-oriented perfectionism reveals itself to be a highly potent motivating force, correlating with a powerful work ethic and contributing to dogged persistence in even the most mundane of tasks.[5,6] There's even compelling evidence that it can contribute to pathological forms of striving—most notably workaholism.[7] These findings are perhaps not surprising given what we know about self-oriented perfectionism and the unrelenting standards it contains. The critical question is whether all that breathless striving translates into better performance.

To answer that, let's start with studies looking at performance in school. When I first started researching perfectionism, I was extremely interested in its effects on high schoolers. But back then, papers reporting links between perfectionism and high school performance were a relatively novel thing. So I was pleased to discover recently that a couple of labs have begun to do some serious research on whether perfectionism predicts academic achievement. And even more recently, a couple of groups have published meta-analyses on the topic.

One of those meta-analyses aggregated studies in which students were split into two achievement groups: high for those at the top of the class and low for those at the bottom.[8] The reasoning here is that if students in the high-achieving classes report higher levels of self-oriented perfectionism than those in the low-achieving classes, then self-oriented perfectionism probably gives an achievement boost. Pooled together, fourteen studies testing these differences found no such achievement boost. The variance shared between self-oriented perfectionism and performance was about 1 percent. In practical terms, that's tiny, and it means that knowing what a student scores on self-oriented perfectionism tells you next to nothing about whether they're likely to end up in high-achieving classes.

So let's take a different approach. Instead of aggregating studies that split students arbitrarily based on academic achievement, another researcher aggregated studies reporting correlations between students' perfectionism and achievement metrics like exam scores and grade point averages (GPAs).[9] Eleven studies reported such correlations, and across them, self-oriented perfectionism shared roughly 4 percent of the variance in academic achievement.

Now, 4 percent sounds like something. And I suppose, on the margins, it's somewhat meaningful. Indeed, for rote forms of learning requiring a lot of time on task, say reciting times tables or committing important passages to memory, you could argue that there's some benefit to being high in self-oriented perfectionism. But we need to set those marginal gains against what's lost: a proclivity to really quite serious mental health struggles.

Okay, so the evidence for school performance is mixed, but what about work? Surely perfectionism has performance benefits in the high-octane, high-pressure, modern-day workplace. A recent meta-analysis looked at the correlation between perfectionism and various measures of job performance, such as productivity and number of outputs.[10] Effects are a little difficult to decipher, since self-oriented and socially prescribed perfectionism were added together with other perfectionism measures. But the results are instructive, nonetheless. Across ten studies, the variance the perfectionism measure that contained self-oriented perfectionism shared with job performance was zero, nada, zilch. Seemingly, self-oriented perfectionism has absolutely no link to success at work.

Which is perplexing. Because given the hours self-oriented perfectionists put in, the all-nighters they pull, the sheer effort they expend on even trivial tasks, you'd think they'd be far more successful. But that's not the case. Instead, results of these meta-analyses point to something of a success paradox, where the things perfectionists do to succeed end up thwarting their chances of success. In other words, perfectionists appear to suffer considerable pain for no apparent gain. And to better understand this puzzling fact, we need to take another trip to Canada and meet Patrick Gaudreau.

★   ★   ★

It was early 2018 and I was in Ottawa to talk at Patrick Gaudreau's lab. Patrick's a French-Canadian psychologist studying perfectionism at the University of Ottawa. He's young, far younger than most professors. And I would describe him as quite hip. His slender frame and tanned face are always impeccably paired with stylish glasses, trendy shirts, sneakers, and blazers. He speaks assertively and in an unmistakable French-Canadian accent.

In the corridor of his office, Patrick greeted me with a smile. We chatted for a while before he walked me to the auditorium, where I was due to speak. And when I was done, Patrick put up his hand. He asked me whether I had a theory about why perfectionists can't turn striving into prolonged success. There are many reasons, I said, but the main one is probably mental health: low mood, depression, anxiety, and so forth, have a habit of getting in the way of high performance.

Patrick sat back and chewed on that answer. He looked unconvinced, but nodded and moved the discussion on to a different topic.

After the talk, he took me for dinner downtown at Le Cordon Bleu's training restaurant. As we sat down, he circled back to our earlier exchange. "I've been chatting to economists," he told me, and it had got him thinking: Is there something in the theory of diminishing marginal productivity? What he was envisioning was an inverted-U relationship between striving and performance, which is depicted in the figure on the opposite page.

In Patrick's mind, perfectionists are rather like overfertilized crops. When fertilizer is first applied, the crops will readily absorb the chemicals and use them to hasten their growth. However, after growing a certain amount, the crops will become less and less responsive. Amounts of fertilizer that would've grown the crops by inches when they were seedlings will scarcely grow them by a hair's breadth when they're ready for harvest. If more fertilizer is applied to eke out more growth, the crops will become poisoned and wither. Far from hastening growth, fertilizer now has exactly the opposite effect.

What Patrick's essentially saying is that human striving, like the growth of crops, is not infinite. You can't forever move forward without, at some point, reaching a threshold beyond which you end up wrecking yourself. Eventually, the performance boost to additional striving dissipates to zero. And if you don't stop there, if you don't recognize that more striving will equal no more performance, then you'll enter a zone of declining returns, in which more striving backfires. That's the zone perfectionists regularly find themselves in.

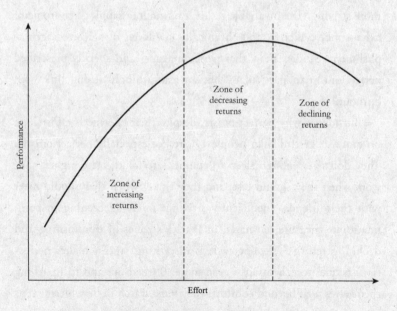

Visual representation of Patrick's theory of diminishing returns.
Adapted from Gaudreau (2019).[11]

It's a catch-22. Perfectionists are hopeless overstrivers—they just can't help themselves. They tinker and iterate to the minute detail. They reshape and rework things well beyond what's needed. As if to reinforce that explanation, Patrick glanced at the open kitchen, where trainee chefs were preparing food in hurried harmony. Here we were in one of the best culinary schools in the world. Perfection was supposedly the standard the chefs were expected to meet.

He looked back at me and smiled. Sure, perfection is the benchmark. "But even a cook in search of the perfect whipped cream can still over-work it into butter."

Canadian psychologist Fuschia Sirois agrees with Patrick. She thinks perfectionism hinders performance not only because of the overstriving, but also because of what she calls drained self-regulation. Self-regulation is a bit like mental energy. And it's drained when re-plenishing behaviors—like exercise, quality time with friends, and getting enough sleep to feel sufficiently rested—are sacrificed for yet more striving. The invariable result is burnout, a sapping syndrome of exhaustion, cynicism, and chronically low levels of perceived accom-plishment. Studies show that perfectionism—and socially prescribed perfectionism in particular—has an astonishingly strong link with burnout.[12]

Burnout is why perfectionists, despite their enormous efforts, are no more successful than people who're not especially perfectionistic. They don't get enough sleep to compensate for the late nights, they work when they should rest, and they tinker when they should meet with their friends. Inefficiently striving, rarely succeeding in com-mensurate measure, ensnared in Patrick's zones of diminishing and declining returns. The spectacle is dispiriting, and it makes perfec-tionists question themselves even more. Burned-out and still pushing themselves well beyond comfort, they must watch in bewilderment as other people achieve the very same things with far less work and far more rest.

As the night ended, my discussion with Patrick turned to other, healthier ways to strive. Rather than shooting for perfection, he believes we could be shooting for excellence. That "involves the pursuit of excellence only," Patrick says. "After reaching [excellence], excellence strivers will have successfully completed their goals."[13] Unlike perfectionists, people who focus on excellence know when high standards have been met and they can let things go without the fear of doing them imperfectly.

I like Patrick's take. It sounds very much like the healthy, conscientious striving that people like my grandfather seemed to possess in abundance. In fact, a focus on excellence sounds very much like what Don Hamachek mislabeled as "healthy perfectionism" all those years ago.

And yet, as I listened to Patrick speak about excellence, something didn't feel quite right to me. I didn't know what it was. I still didn't know as I reflected on our time together the next day. Only when I got back to London and had a coffee with my friend Amy, a clinical psychologist, did it make sense.

"Patrick Gaudreau's research seems to be showing some really nice findings for the benefits of pursuing excellence over perfection," I told her. "What do you think about that?"

"It feels right," she replied, idly browsing the sandwiches. "But I wonder whether there's a danger down the line of excellence turning itself right back into perfectionism?"

Her brusque intonation told me she had a strong view on that.

"I'm listening," I said.

"Being able to let things go when they're excellent is fine, and much healthier than the unrelenting rigidity of perfectionism. But I'm not sure it's a long-term solution. Excellence is still a really high bar. All those inner directives and pressures to excel are still there, and they'll whip up anxiety the minute we do something that's not quite excellent, or even just average.

"Put it this way," she said. "If I were to tell a perfectionist to strive for excellence instead of perfection, I'm not sure I'd be earning my money. It's a good distinction to play around with. I'm just not so sure it's the antidote."

Amy's reflections put my own muddled thoughts into perspective. Patrick's research indicates clearly that when you recalibrate your goals a little, shoot for excellence rather than perfection, you'll get all the performance goodies without the mental health problems.[14] And that's fine. The theory is sound. The data is robust.

But what happens over the course of time is still an open question. And in this "never enough" age, where there're always more things to buy, credentials to accrue, new targets to aim for, more money to make, striving for excellence will still compel you to always keep moving forward. And avoid, at all costs, the indignity of being seen to regress, or stand still, which these days might as well be the same things.

Certainly, the ability of excellence strivers to let things go when they're excellent enough is a decidedly healthy trait. But excellence remains a nebulous and lofty goal, and like all nebulous and lofty goals, it'll get more and more difficult to reach as each success sets a new floor. What striving for excellence can't solve, in other words, is the dilemma of failure. And this brings me to an arguably more important reason why perfectionists find lasting success so elusive: at some point the going will get tough, and when it does, perfectionists will do everything they possibly can to avoid the sting of defeat.

So let's take a look at that fear of failure, which, as we'll see, is an all-lane roadblock in the way of high performance for perfectionistic people.

★　　★　　★

Failure is essential to life. Without it, our existence would be defined by one long victory lap, which none of us would find especially stimulating. Sports fans know this in their bones. Remove the possibility that their side could lose, and few would turn up to watch the procession.

Cycling provides perhaps the most enjoyable failure theater. Think of the Tour de France. At the end of mountain stages, a captivating monodrama usually unfolds. Cameras set the viewer's gaze squarely on the diehards, who've shed the Peloton, and are farthest up the incline. All of them have tiredness and tension in their legs. Rather than a smooth revolution of the pedals, they appear jaded, their shoulders chop from side to side, their legs wade through the revolutions as if they're riding through molasses.

Yet amid the collective anguish there's always one cyclist, smuggled away in the bunch, who's measured his effort slightly better than everyone else. His breathing looks controlled, his shoulders rock-solid, his legs spinning in fluid synchrony. With perhaps a kilometer to the summit, suddenly, just like that, he'll flick the gears on his bicycle and arise from the saddle, stamping the pedals as hard as he possibly can.

Seeing this unfold is agonizing for the exhausted competitors. They grimace with raw hurt. They gallantly try to stay on the coattails of the now runaway leader, knowing, in their heart if not their legs, that the race is already over. One hundred meters to go, hands littered with blisters, calves cramping with excess lactate, they must sit down on their saddles and watch in resignation as the elated victor crosses the finish line to raucous applause.

The brave losers roll in one by one behind him, their heads bowed, their exhaustion compounded by bitter disappointment.

Success is sweet. But failure is so intimately revealing of what it means to be human. That's why, when we study perfectionism, we like to see what happens when perfectionists fail. We set them impossible goals, create competitions that they cannot possibly win, and when they fail, we take a good look at how they respond.[15]

British psychologist Andy Hill and I spearhead much of this research. And to get the maximum effect, we harness the anguish of sports. In one study, we set up a cycling sprint challenge and invited volunteer cyclists to race in fours against each other.[16] After they'd raced, no matter where they finished, we told them that they'd finished last.

Afterward, we asked the cyclists how they felt. All of them reported higher guilt and shame compared to when they'd first stepped foot in the lab—they'd just tasted bitter defeat, after all. But it was the cyclists with the highest levels of self-oriented and socially prescribed perfectionism who reported the steepest spikes in guilt and shame.

In the previous chapter, we saw why perfectionistic people are so sensitive to setbacks like this. Their self-worth hangs on the outcomes of their efforts, so naturally they feel intently self-conscious when they've failed. But there's something else perfectionists do when they fail, something of importance not just to their mental health, but to their performance, too: they withhold subsequent effort.

Because you can't fail at something you don't attempt.

In another study, Andy Hill teased out this curious form of self-sabotage.[17] Once again, he set up a cycling challenge, only this time the cyclists were racing against themselves. Following a sham fitness test, he set the cyclists a goal of covering a certain distance in a time that should have been comfortable. The cyclists worked flat-out to accomplish the goal, and when they were done, Andy delivered the bad news: you failed.

He then told them to have another go, and that's when something astonishing happened. The cyclists who scored low on self-oriented perfectionism said the effort they put in on the second trial did not change. If anything, they said they'd worked slightly harder. The cyclists who scored high on self-oriented perfectionism, however, did the opposite. They stopped trying. On the second attempt, after the first failure, their effort fell off a cliff. This difference-in-difference is called an interaction effect, and I've plotted the mean effort scores for the two trials in Andy's study in the figure below.

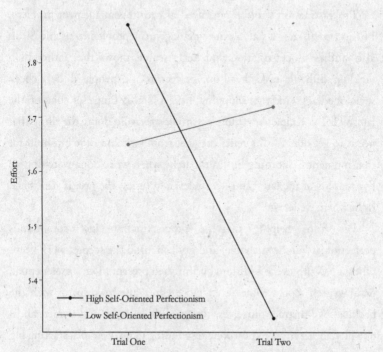

*Effort scores as a function of high and low
self-oriented perfectionism in Hill et al. (2010).*

Withholding effort in this way is what's called perfectionistic self-preservation. People high in perfectionism, as we've seen, strive extremely hard to meet their excessive standards. But that, in many ways, is only half the story. Because when things get tough, the trepidation is so fierce that it makes perfectionists reluctant to put forward any subsequent effort that might further expose them to failure. So, to make other people's discovery of their shortcomings a little more difficult, they simply stop trying when faced with a challenge that's highly likely to end in defeat.

Unfortunately, real life isn't at all like Andy's experiment. You can't just withdraw from most tasks without consequences. There are deadlines to meet and bosses to please. That's why perfectionists, when they can't remove themselves from the picture, tend to do the next best thing: procrastinate.

Procrastination is often portrayed as a time-management problem. But in actual fact, it's an anxiety-management problem. Fuschia Sirois also studies procrastination and her research shows that rather than tackling difficult tasks head-on, perfectionistic people dither, check social media, go internet shopping, have a Netflix binge, or cook up the latest TikTok recipe. Anything, essentially, to avoid doing the thing that needs to get done.[18] The relief they get from switching the brain off for that moment is soothing but, ultimately, when we're done watching all five seasons of the latest must-see television series, the task is still there, right where we left it.

Far from helping matters, procrastination just compounds perfectionists' anxiety, shame, and guilt. Behind the scenes, work keeps piling up. With every additional unfinished presentation, unseen email, or unwritten report comes even more effort just to keep up with the backlog. We distract ourselves, tinker, dawdle, redo, and iterate, all in one Herculean effort to postpone responding to testy emails, starting big projects, or sending out substandard work. In other words, perfectionists use procrastination as a way of getting through struggle, challenge, and failure without cognitive and emotional damage. But eventually, they're just damaged by the passage of time.

Self-sabotage, whether in the form of complete withdrawal of their efforts or simply procrastination, is another reason why perfectionists struggle to perform. They're overstrivers who often push themselves to the point of burnout. But they're also inefficient allocators of where that overstriving is channeled, putting off and avoiding challenging tasks with a low probability of success, preferring instead to channel their efforts toward the completion of more straightforward tasks with a high probability of success.

In a knowledge economy that demands just-in-time innovation, that particular allocation of resources makes perfectionism hugely incompatible with the ways in which modern products and services are created.

And that's not all. Perfectionists don't simply anticipate failure and do everything they possibly can to offset incoming shame. They also anticipate other people's rejection with a similar zeal and avoid placing themselves in tricky social situations where they might be critically judged. The result is an almost total avoidance of non-mandatory meetings, talks, job interviews, and the like, where the calculation is made that they're going to be evaluated, very possibly unfavorably. This, again, is self-defeating, since it means perfectionists are far less likely to apply for higher-grade jobs or ask for things like a promotion or raise.[19]

Yet more reasons why perfectionism isn't the secret to success we so often think it is.

Back, then, to our original dilemma. Does perfectionism motivate us to work hard? And if it does, what's the evidence that all that work pays off? We've just acquired two pieces of information that help us to answer those questions. First, perfectionists indeed work hard, but it's far *too* hard, and they're extremely inefficient in where it's allocated, making them highly susceptible to exhaustion and burnout. And second, although hard work is indeed a signature of the perfectionist, that doesn't mean they're always working. When the going gets tough, they tend to avoid the things that need doing until the passage of time forces them into action. Together, these two behaviors—inefficient overwork and avoidance—conspire to create a success paradox that makes perfectionists no more likely to succeed.

So why, then, do we still believe the successful perfectionist myth? The answer is survivor bias.

Survivor bias is the mental error of learning only from life's winners. And there are plenty of those in the perfectionism camp. Demi Lovato, Steve Jobs, Andre Agassi, Michelle Pfeiffer, Virginia Woolf, Serena Williams—the list goes on and on. These are all high-profile figures who, in their triumphant climbs to the top, exhibited intelligence, daring, drive, and, yes, a high dose of perfectionism.

Then again, many others exhibit the exact same traits. They just exhibit them outside the spotlight, striving relentlessly and in significant discomfort without a Grammy, Booker prize, or Olympic medal to show for it. Since the experiences of these perfectionists are hidden and out of sight, the experience of perfectionists who did "make it" lead us to incorrectly conclude that perfectionism must be the secret to success.

Because when the only people television shows, podcasts, blue tick accounts, and YouTube channels care about—and learn from—are the winners (or to be more exact, the outliers), then we'll invariably see perfectionism in high performance when no such relationships exists. Survivor bias duped Don Hamachek. And it's also duped us—as a society—into putting perfectionism on a gilded pedestal and calling it our favorite flaw.

Which means that if we're going to bust the successful perfectionist myth once and for all, we're going to need to view it from a different angle. Rather than looking to the few perfectionists whose circumstances, physiology, smarts, or sheer good fortune propelled them to the very top, we must look to the great majority of perfectionists who didn't quite scale those dizzying heights. Because when we do that, as Andy Hill discovered in his experiments on failure, we see something rather different. Perfectionists overstrive to the point of burnout, and also, at the same time, will self-sabotage their chances of success if it means avoiding the unbearable guilt and shame of defeat.

That's not the ticket to success. On the contrary, despite all the breathless striving, perfectionism makes us no more likely to succeed—

genertating a great deal of distress and self-doubt in the process. The answer to perfectionism's success paradox lies not in simply dialing it back a bit. It lies in learning to embrace the inevitability of setbacks, failures, and things not going quite as we planned. And being able to sit comfortably next to those humanizing experiences, to let them be, not needing to rehabilitate them on the redemptive arc of excellence, not needing to strive them out of existence—themes we'll pick up again toward the end of this book.

For now, though, let's keep on looking at our obsession with perfection. If it isn't healthy or making us any more successful, why does it feel like perfectionism's more widespread than ever? And are we right to think that?

CHAPTER FIVE

The Hidden Epidemic
Or the Astonishing Rise of Perfectionism in Modern Society

"Perfectionism is highly prevalent, is linked with mental health problems, and has become a global problem, especially among young people."
Gordon Flett and Paul Hewitt[1]

As the night drew to a close out on the patio at Rafferty's bar and grill, I wanted to know what Paul and Gord made of today's culture. Things have changed quite a bit since they first started researching perfectionism. Competition at school and college is much fiercer than it used to be, we've got widescreen televisions, tablets, and smartphones projecting unrealistic ideals at us 24/7, and social media platforms, with their photoshopped images of perfection, have become ubiquitous, occupying almost a quarter of our waking existence.[2]

We've discussed perfectionism's harms and its puzzling relationship with performance. But I wondered: What about its prevalence? Did these men think perfectionism was getting worse? I asked Paul, "Are you seeing more cases in your clinic?"

He looked straight at me. "I've never been busier, nor have the therapists I work with; it's everywhere."

Gord went further. "There's so much anxiety, worry, and stress in young people. I think we're in the midst of a perfectionism epidemic." With that statement, he glanced over at Paul. "You can't look past impossible pressures as major culprits."

Anyone who spends time with young people would surely agree with Gord. This is pressure that the National Education Association calls an "epidemic,"[3] the Association of Child Psychotherapists calls a "silent catastrophe,"[4] and the Royal College of Psychiatrists calls a "crisis."[5] A 2017 survey asked about twenty-five thousand elementary and high school students in Toronto whether they felt the need to be perfect.[6] More than one in two said that they did, which is bad enough. But 34 percent of elementary school students and 48 percent of high schoolers went further and said they felt under specific pressures to appear physically perfect in every possible way.

A 2016 report commissioned by Girlguiding in the UK found similar trends.[7] In its data, 46 percent of girls age eleven to sixteen and 61 percent of girls age seventeen to twenty-one said they felt a need to be perfect. Five years earlier, in a 2011 report, those percentages were just 26 and 23, which reflects increases of 77 and 165 percent, respectively.[8] A narrative review recently conducted by Paul and Gord estimates that about one-third of children and adolescents are currently reporting high levels of perfectionism.[9] Sure enough, not every young person feels the need to be perfect, but there's certainly enough in the available data to make you wonder what on earth's going on.

"The avalanche has already happened," Paul told me. "We're going to be treating this for some time." And on that rather melancholy note, we called it a night. I'd learned enough, and besides, hip, young twentysomethings were circling our seats in the hope that these three weary-eyed professors might soon vacate them. We said our goodbyes, and I watched as Paul and Gord disappeared into the Toronto night to take their trains home.

I wouldn't see Paul and Gord again in person after that night, but our conversation stayed with me. Each day, the epidemic they warned about was confirmed by the evidence of my eyes and ears. It was right there in the corridors of university campuses, the everyday chitchat between colleagues, and the social media profiles of friends whose real lives couldn't be further from those they carefully curated online. So in the winter of 2017, I set myself a challenge. I wanted to find out if Paul and Gord were right; I wanted to know if perfectionism really was the rumbling avalanche that they believed it was.

It was a tricky task and I was only able to do it by using Paul and Gord's Multidimensional Perfectionism Scale in a slightly different way. Since its development in the late eighties, this tool has been used in thousands of research projects—most of which sample college students in the US, Canada, and the UK. Instead of using that treasure trove of data to study relationships like it was designed to do, I used it like a historical tracker to compare young people across generations, and figure out whether they're reporting higher or lower levels of perfectionism over time.

The hard part was retrieving that many responses. So I roped in my colleague Andy Hill, who we met in the last chapter, to help. We split the workload and began scouring databases, search engines, and repositories for every single study that reported scores for college students' self-oriented, socially prescribed, and other-oriented perfectionism. When we were done, we'd scraped information from well over forty thousand American, Canadian, and British students who'd completed Paul and Gord's scale somewhere between 1988 and 2016.[10] Then we set about stringing out the data in chronological order, running our preliminary checks, and crunching the numbers.

Which is when we saw something astonishing: perfectionism was rising, and it was rising really, really fast.

In 1988, the average young person was high to very high in self-oriented and other-oriented perfectionism (most people slightly agreed or agreed with statements), and moderate to low in socially prescribed perfectionism (most people neither agreed nor disagreed with statements). Not the healthiest profile in terms of personal expectations, admittedly, but good news regarding socially prescribed perfectionism—young people seemed to report that expectations and pressures on them weren't excessively demanding.

By 2016, however, that profile had drastically changed. Self-oriented and other-oriented perfectionism had edged even higher, which was bad enough. But it was the trend for socially prescribed perfectionism that really worried us. It surged from low to moderate in 1989 to moderate to high in 2016. Projecting those increases into the future shows us where we might be headed. By 2050, based on the models we tested, self-oriented perfectionism will move above the very high threshold (most people agree with statements), and socially prescribed perfectionism will move above the high threshold (most people slightly agree or agree with statements).

That spells trouble, not just now, but in the future. Unlike similar traits such as neuroticism or narcissism, perfectionism doesn't seem to resolve itself as we get older. In fact, there's evidence that it gets worse. In a big meta-study summarizing dozens of smaller studies that followed people over years and decades, researchers found that those who start off high in perfectionism become more prone to anxiety and irritability, and less prone to conscientiousness as they age.[11]

Perfectionism, then, is a self-fulfilling prophecy that only gets worse over time. When perfectionists fall short of their excessive standards, they form an opinion of themselves that basically says they're not good enough. They set even higher standards to compensate, thinking that overshooting their previous efforts will somehow neuter the failure. But since their standards were excessive in the first place, they just set themselves up to fail, and so begins a cycle of never-met, upwardly spiraling expectations, setting the stage for more and more perfectionism as they get older.

The question now is whether these trends are continuing. Is perfectionism still trending upward? Or is it coming down from its high watermark? To answer that, for this book, I added the most up-to-date perfectionism data to the models Andy and I tested And when I reran the numbers, the results were even more troubling.

> *SELF-ORIENTED AND OTHER-ORIENTED PERFECTIONISM continue to rise, but the pace remains steady—so keep an eye on them.*

In the figures on pages 86 and 87, I've plotted young people's perfectionism scores against the year the data was collected. Black circles are the US data points, light gray Canada, and dark gray the UK. The data points are proportional to the number of students giving their data in each study (more students equals bigger circles), and the best-fitting line for the relationship between perfectionism and time is plotted through them.

Looking at the best-fitting lines, you can see that increases in self-oriented and other-oriented perfectionism are gradual, but nonetheless noteworthy. By noteworthy I mean statistically significant, or, in other words, their increases are noticeable enough for the null finding—that there's no increase at all—to be highly unlikely. We know that no increase at all is unlikely because the margins of error in our models—the gray shaded areas on either side of the trend lines—do not go over the straight horizontal lines showing what would've happened if nothing had changed.

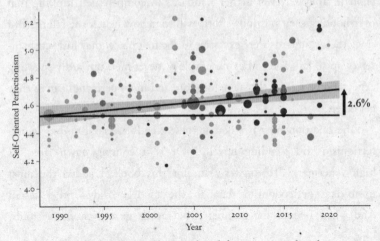

*College students' self-oriented perfectionism scores plotted
against the year of data collection.*

What is the extent of this increase? In crude terms, young people today score about 2.6 percentage points higher on the scale of self-oriented perfectionism and 1.5 percentage points higher on the scale of other-oriented perfectionism than young people in 1988. That seems quite small, but we must remember that we're dealing here with a spectrum that's concentrated within a narrow range (i.e., 1: strongly disagree, to 7: strongly agree). Even significant differences can look quite trivial.

Rather than use crude percentages, then, let's instead ask where today's average young person would score if they were filling out the surveys of self-oriented and other-oriented perfectionism in 1988. If we ask this question, we get a better sense of how different today's young people are, comparatively, to young people in the late 1980s. Today, the average young person reports self- and other-oriented perfectionism scores that would've been at the fifty-sixth and fifty-seventh percentile of scores in 1988—a 12 and 14 percent increase, respectively. Not enormous, but certainly not trivial, either.

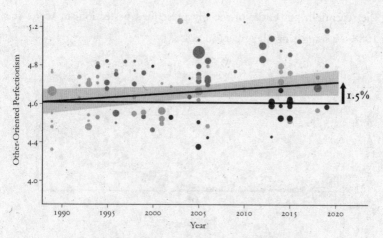

College students' other-oriented perfectionism scores plotted against the year of data collection.

SOCIALLY PRESCRIBED PERFECTIONISM *continues to rise, but now it's rapidly accelerating upward—so it's probably time to panic.*

What of socially prescribed perfectionism? Well, if I told you the trend was so peaked that I needed to relax the straight-line assumption in my reanalysis to capture it, then that should provide a clue. The straight-line assumption basically says that something is changing at a constant pace, which is the case for self-oriented and other-oriented perfectionism. But it's not the case for socially prescribed perfectionism. Right now, socially prescribed perfection is following an exponential trajectory, one that bends as the rate of increase accelerates over time.

As can be seen in the figure on page 88, levels of socially prescribed perfectionism were more or less flat until around 2005. Then something happened and they began to skyrocket. From the bottom of the trajectory to the top, socially prescribed perfectionism is about 7 percent higher today in crude terms. In comparative terms, that difference is even more dramatic. Today's typical young person would've scored at the seventieth percentile of socially prescribed perfectionism scores in 1988—a staggering 40 percent increase.

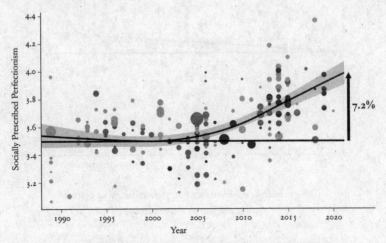

College students' socially prescribed perfectionism scores plotted against the year of data collection.

Worse, that rate of increase is still curving. And left unchecked, it will, by its own logic, continue to curve upward far more quickly than we might expect. That's how exponential growth works: slowly, then fast. Anyone paying attention to COVID-19 case data will know this, and they'll also know that once a trajectory starts to curve, it's time to panic. On these projections, socially prescribed perfectionism will break through the very high threshold by 2050, overtaking self-oriented perfectionism as the leading perfectionism indicator.

If there's one dimension of perfectionism you wouldn't want to rise like this, it's socially prescribed perfectionism. We saw in chapter 3 how this dimension stands out as by far the most extreme form of perfectionism—extreme since it contains a set of harmful beliefs that obligate us to appear perfect in publicly recognizable ways. Those who report high levels of socially prescribed perfectionism are confronted daily with their inability to live up to impossible expectations, and each time their imperfections are unveiled, which is often, they feel completely exposed and defeated—trapped in a life that's always on public display, thinking about the judgments other people are making.

We also saw in chapter 3 that socially prescribed perfectionism is the path to many and varied psychological problems. And the main signs of those problems—anxiety disorders, major depression, loneliness, self-harm, and thoughts of suicide—are rising in almost perfect lockstep.[12] We really are in the grip of a perfection trap—and that's not good news.

★　　★　　★

I've described my time with Paul and Gord because their work stands out as pioneering.[13] Rather like them, I'm convinced that perfectionism is best understood as a relational trait, rooted in deficit thinking, and keeping us always preoccupied with thoughts about how much less-than we must surely appear to others. And even if Paul and Gord's theory wasn't pioneering in this respect, no framework comes close to theirs in sheer depth, and none matches the extent to which theirs has withstood the test of observation, experience, and time.

Over the years, in one way or another, many of their insights have found their way into popular self-help, sometimes without credit. Not that they seem to care—their mission has never been for notoriety. On that red-hot night, out on the patio of Rafferty's, I had an education in two men's selfless dedication to understanding something that's fast becoming a major public health concern. If we want to really get a handle on what's going on, we need to listen to them.

Because when we do so, we learn several important facts. First, that perfectionism is a relational trait with many faces; second, that it contributes to a plethora of mental health problems; third, that it has no relationship with success; and fourth, that it's rising at an explosive pace. My own role in adding this last fact is bittersweet. Sweet because it's reassuring to confirm in data what we see and hear but bitter because the exponential shape of socially prescribed perfectionism's rise means that pressures to be perfect will cascade further and faster than even our very worst fears.

Certainly, a great frequency of socially prescribed perfectionism tells us that something is seriously wrong with the conditions under which we live. It tells us, in essence, that society's expectations are well beyond the capacity of most people to meet. And since those expectations are all-consuming, the problems they end up creating get buried under a weight of conventional wisdom that has essentially normalized our favorite flaw. Right there in open daylight, disguised in plain sight by its very ubiquity, perfectionism is today's hidden epidemic—the conspicuous vulnerability that's wreaking all sorts of havoc among those who're coming of age in modern society.

All of which poses the questions: Why is this happening? Where are these pressures to be perfect coming from? And how on earth did we let them become the mood music for our lives?

PART THREE

WHERE DOES PERFECTIONISM COME FROM?

CHAPTER SIX

Some Perfectionists Are Bigger Than Others
Or the Intricate Nature and Nurture of Perfectionism's Development

"Human character is built upon a biological base which is capable of enormous diversification in terms of social standards."
Margaret Mead[1]

I'll never forget the morning after Andy Hill and I published the paper showing that perfectionism was rising. There I was, a sport psychology lecturer at the University of Bath, a regional college in the southwest of England, astounded to learn that our research was being featured in hundreds of national and international outlets, written up by prominent bloggers and dissected by influential news anchors and podcasters. Within days, I was powdering up to appear on television, discussing the implications of a perfectionism epidemic in front of millions of viewers and listeners. When the furor finally settled, our paper was the most covered piece of research in the one-hundred-and-thirteen-year history of *Psychological Bulletin*, the academic journal that published it.

"I've never seen anything like this," my university's media officer told me. "It's the biggest news story we've had for ages, perhaps ever." The sheer amount of interest caught me unprepared. It's a period of my life that remains a bit of a blur. I can't remember what I said or whether any of it was even remotely intelligible. But what I do remember is that rising perfectionism seemed to strike a nerve among those I spoke to. Many told me that it was their aha moment, the data they could point to and say, "That's the problem; it's perfectionism!"

If our paper revealed a brewing epidemic, the public response confirmed it. People see perfection everywhere these days, they feel the pressure to be perfect, and they want to know why. That's the reason Sheryl from TED got in touch. She wanted me to answer that pressing question at their conference in Palm Springs.

The energy of the city is all I remember of Palm Springs. But what energy. It's an almost ethereal place—a fading of desert set back against the San Jacinto Mountains. The aura of nouveau riche is thick here. Freshly laid roads have been gouged from red-dirt tracks. Battalions of expensive resorts and lush golf courses are drilled into the arid sand.

The resort hosting the TED conference was nestled to the city's south, tucked away in an alcove called La Quinta. On my arrival, glamorous young twentysomethings and graying suburbanites clustered by the check-in desk, jangling their weekend luggage. They were bused in by private-hire SUVs, arriving every ten minutes.

Coming from a less glamorous place, one could easily have viewed what was going on as if it were happening in a totally different universe. Standing by the grand entrance, watching resort life, all the eye can see is a dreamland of manicured perfection and an army of groundskeepers assiduously tending to every nook and cranny. People dart by. The sound of affluence is shrill. The language of privilege carries in the gentle desert breeze.

One legacy of my upbringing is that I'm never quite comfortable in such surroundings. So I don't usually make a habit of hanging around resorts for the rich and famous. Even so, on the rare occasion my line of work thrusts me headlong into them, I get to taste the "good life." And every time I taste it, I just feel underwhelmed and out of place, as if the exhausting chase to get there wasn't really worth it, as if I never should've chased after that mythical ideal at all.

Sheryl greeted me at the resort entrance with a beaming smile and showed me the auditorium where I'd be speaking. The sheer scale of the operation did nothing to settle my nerves. Stagehands, camera operators, and sound engineers were working away in hurried harmony. As we watched them from the gallery, I asked her, "How many people are registered for the conference?"

"About four hundred—thousands more online," she replied.

"That's a lot!" I snapped back, feeling my face flush.

The next day, I left my villa and strolled to the opening ceremony. A man of about forty, short brown hair, slim, wearing an immaculately fitted navy jacket and freshly pressed trousers, was addressing the audience. I had no idea who he was—I still don't have any idea—but TED had paid him big bucks to open their conference. On that imposing stage, he carried himself with an air of invincibility, completely unfazed by the lights, cameras, and hundreds of onlookers hanging on his every word. His talk was clever, entertaining, and funny, but serious in just the right measure, and finished with a crescendo that had everyone—including me—on their feet in raucous applause.

I thought how awesome he was, and wondered how unimpressive my remarks were going to seem in contrast.

My talk was scheduled for the final session on the very last day, so I got to see the ebb and flow of things.

Things that are subtle, but nonetheless revealing. The audience, for example, preferred colorful anecdotes over hard data. Humanizing experiences provoked rapture. And curiously, while complex but enlightening talks about groundbreaking discoveries were appreciated, powerful personal testimony was what ultimately raised the roof.

Something else struck me about the audience. As far as I could tell, they had a subtle way to tell presenters what they *really* thought. Awe-inspiring talks that wowed them were greeted with a standing ovation. But the more run-of-the-mill stuff received polite, seated applause. In the greenroom before going onstage, audience reception was a fervent topic of debate. "Do you think you'll get a standing ovation?" speakers asked each other. I was too wrapped up in my own thoughts to get involved in that chitchat. But deep down, I'd been asking myself the very same question.

The speaker before me left the stage, and the audience in the packed auditorium hushed. My turn had arrived, and in an instant, Sheryl was urgently ushering me onstage in that typical American style of unadulterated enthusiasm, with sweet, if a little overzealous, words of encouragement.

"You've got this!" she said, smiling from ear to ear.

I did not think I had this.

I walked out gingerly, my eyes fixed on the blinding white light attached to the upper-gallery scaffolding straight ahead of me, before positioning myself smack in the middle of TED's famous red circle.

I'd practiced this talk countless times, pouring over other talks and fine-tuning the delivery. But now, as I looked out at the sea of faces staring back at me, all that preparation seemed to vanish from my mind. TED's production team has cut it from the recording, but if you look closely, you'll see my right leg wobbling like an untended hose. And if you listen carefully, you'll hear my voice cracking as I cleave my memory for the next line, and then the next, and then the next. Inside, I was shaking in terror. I still don't really know how, but somehow, I held it all together. I made it through.

As I uttered the final sentence, I looked straight at the audience. I longed for their standing validation. I needed it. Several seconds passed. Still seated, they applauded politely. Several more seconds passed and I willed them to stand. But they would not. So with a sinking feeling of defeat, I turned around and walked from the stage, to be chaperoned by Sheryl back to the greenroom.

"That was awesome!" she said, her face beaming.

"Thanks," I replied.

I'd pushed past my perfectionism just to show up in Palm Springs. I'd stubbornly refused to let my nerves get the better of me and recited fifteen minutes of word-for-word prose on probably the biggest stage I'll ever occupy. And yet, despite those remarkable feats, guess what part of my TED Talk experience I'd ruminate on in the hours, days, weeks, and months that followed?

★   ★   ★

Am I simply *destined* to feel like this? Or is my perfectionism nurtured by the environment I happen to inhabit? These are age-old questions, not just for perfectionism but for personality traits more generally. Are they the result of nature—the inherited equipment with which we begin life? Or are they the result of nurture—the circumstances we're met with?

The case for nature is pretty clear. Over the last three decades, behavioral geneticists have studied differences between identical twins, fraternal twins, and adopted siblings. Identical twins share the same DNA, fraternal twins share about half, and adopted children share none. If we compare the similarity of traits across these types of children, we can estimate how much is due to genetics. And results yield remarkably consistent conclusions. Identical twins are more alike than fraternal twins, who're more alike than adopted children. When the numbers are crunched, it turns out that genetic heritability is very high indeed. About half of the way we turn out is inherited, predetermined, out of our hands to do anything about.[2]

Not so long ago, researchers in Spain gave Paul and Gord's Multidimensional Perfectionism Scale to almost six hundred pairs of adolescent twins living in Valencia.[3] From this sample, they estimated that about 30 percent of self-oriented perfectionism is inherited. The figure for socially prescribed perfectionism is a little higher, at about 40 percent. Via the invisible hand of genetics, then, perfectionistic parents appear to pass on a certain amount of perfectionism to their offspring.

The Spanish research also found an extremely high genetic correlation between self-oriented and socially prescribed perfectionism. So if you start life disposed to self-oriented perfectionism, you're likely to struggle with socially prescribed perfectionism, too (and vice versa). Genes are the indiscriminate, enlivening lottery of life. Through absolutely no fault of our own, we're just destined to have some self-oriented and socially prescribed perfectionism.

It should be noted, however, that DNA is not a predefined script. It's an instruction manual, and a molecular process called epigenetics highlights which bits of the manual to read given the conditions we're faced with. Molecules called methyls are an especially important feature of epigenetics. They deactivate DNA sequences in response to things like starvation, acute stress, and trauma, which can lead to changes in cell structure and functioning.

This matters for the heritability of perfectionism. Epigenetic modifications are passed across generations, and therefore any conditions favorable to perfectionism that our ancestors may have experienced are likely, at least in part, to live on in our genes today. A lot of perfectionism is inherited, but we cannot know how much of that heritability is ancient DNA and how much is recent epigenetic modification.

And there's another consideration, one that also involves the environment. Although genetic estimates explain why people differ from one another, they say nothing about the average itself. Which means that although genes help explain why I might be more of a perfectionist than you, they don't explain why the average level of perfectionism is increasing for *everyone*. My research is extremely important in this respect because it doesn't just show how the average level of perfectionism is rising; it also shows that the circumstances we're met with after birth must matter to perfectionism's development—and they must matter rather a lot.

So, if circumstances matter, how exactly is perfectionism nurtured? The obvious answer—by the things our parents do—is not necessarily the correct one.

★   ★   ★

In 1960, a promising developmental psychologist named Judith Harris was kicked out of Harvard while working on her doctorate. The letter terminating her studies, signed by George A. Miller, the acting chair of psychology, said, "We are in considerable doubt that you will develop into our professional stereotype of what a psychologist should be."[4] Harris left Harvard to teach briefly at MIT before spending several years as a lab assistant in New Jersey. By the late 1970s, however, a cruel hereditary condition called systemic sclerosis caught up with her. As the disease progressed, she became increasingly housebound, unable to work.

Confined to her bed, Harris gave her life to doing the one thing she could do: write. In the decade between the early 1980s and early '90s, she wrote several college textbooks on the curious psychology of child development. But something rankled Harris about those texts. She began questioning the entire premise upon which they were written, and eventually she threw in the towel altogether. "I gave up writing textbooks," she said, "because one day it suddenly occurred to me that many of the things I had been telling those credulous college students were wrong."[5]

Harris had a radical theory of child development. She believed that the way parents raise their children doesn't matter much to the way children grow up. Children, she said, are influenced more by their genes and their culture than by their parents. It was a provocative take, one that flew in the face of conventional wisdom. Anxious parents, for example, are well known to raise anxious children, conscientious parents raise conscientious children, and, yes, there's evidence that perfectionistic parents raise perfectionistic children. Across the child development literature, correlations between parenting and child temperament are very strong indeed.

But look closer. These correlations aren't evidence for parental influence. Of course parents and children are alike; they have many of the same genes. And besides, even if genes were an irrelevance, correlation doesn't prove causation. Perhaps effects go from child to parent, and not vice versa. Harris's big idea was that we've overestimated the role of parents at the expense of other, more important factors, like genes, and forces well beyond the household.

Harris was heavily criticized for airing these ideas. But, unperturbed, she continued to carefully hone her arguments. She did so alone from her home in New Jersey, without ready access to university infrastructure, paywalled articles, and expensive textbooks. And yet, despite these obstacles, wisdom poured out of her. In 1994, thirty-four years after being kicked out of Harvard, Harris submitted her evidence to the prestigious *Psychological Review*. The paper was published the following year to extensive acclaim.[6]

It's hard to describe how big a feat this was. Many professors will go their entire careers without publishing in *Psychological Review*. For a woman of that era to do it on her first go, unaffiliated and with a chronic illness, is simply astonishing. The only way she could have done it was with writing that was clear, impeccably researched, and devastatingly persuasive. Her paper was deemed so outstanding that in 1998 it was given an award by the American Psychological Association for exceptional contribution. In the irony of ironies, that award was named after one George A. Miller—the Harvard bigwig who'd given her the boot.

We've just seen that Harris was correct about genes—the genetic heritability of traits is extraordinarily high. However, it was her thinking about the environment that proved most divisive. She believed that culture has far more power over the way we turn out than parents. By culture, Harris meant the world outside of the household; for example, our friendship groups, the fads of popular media, the values projected by advertising and influential people, and the way civic institutions like governments, schools, and colleges are organized and structured.

To support these ideas, Harris asked us to look again at those twin studies. Because when we do so, we see that parenting has almost no influence on the types of people children become. Adult twins who grew up in the same household are, astonishingly, no more alike in their traits than twins who grew up in different homes. The variability of traits attributed to the household, or in other words the parenting, is virtually zero. "If we left a group of children with the same schools, neighborhoods and peers, but switched parents around," Harris writes, "they would develop into the same sort of adults."[7]

Judith Harris was herself a mother. From this vantage point, she saw that child-rearing was often reduced to little more than helpless spectating. And as she delved into the evidence, the combined effects of genes and culture on child development was a reality that became more and more difficult to refute. Her writing tells us something essential about human nature: our traits are neither the innate total of biology nor a helpless reflection of the conditions we're met with. They're an intricate blend of both.

We're quite different, but we're also more or less the same. Certain evolutionary constants are necessary for survival, as in the need to eat, reproduce, and fit in, and then there are genes, which are concrete and unchangeable. Beyond these fixed entities is a plasticity of personality that—save the most terrible examples, such as abuse, abandonment, and neglect—is molded not by our parents, nor by our personal agency, but by our common culture.[8]

And when it comes to the influence of culture on human development, few people have been more influential than German psychoanalyst Karen Horney. Her clinical observations are lucid and provide a blueprint for the shared symphony of human personality types in developed societies. Perfectionism, she argued, is the price we all pay for our place in the orchestra.

Born in Blankenese, Germany, in 1885, Karen Horney was the youngest of several children. Her father, a ship's captain in the merchant marine, was an overbearing conservative. And his meanness surrounded Horney from an early age. He was a "cruel disciplinary figure," she writes in her diary, a "man who makes us all unhappy with his dreadful hypocrisy, selfishness, crudeness and ill-breeding."

Horney found refuge in her mother. She had greater ambitions for Karen, whose father wanted her to stay at home and take over as the housemaid. When Horney was fifteen, her mother got her a place at a high school in Hamburg where she could study medicine. Her father protested, claiming he couldn't afford the tuition. "He who has flung out thousands for my stepbrothers, who are both stupid and bad," Horney writes in her diary, "first turns every additional penny he has to spend for me ten times in his fingers."[9]

Her mother stood her ground and sent her to Hamburg anyway.

But this early episode left a mark. According to biographer Bernard Paris, Horney "was so ambitious because she needed to compensate for feelings of rejection by her family."[10] At school, Paris writes, she harbored "a dream of glory through academic achievement . . . a need to feel herself an exceptional person with a special destiny." Her perfectionism led to a crushing fatigue that she blamed on her need to be "above average." Transcripts from her therapist suggest that this achievement anxiety was borne of the fear of being "judged ordinary." Her troubles made school "an ordeal," says Paris, "but she was gifted enough to do well."

And well she did. After graduating from Hamburg, Horney used her medical background to train as a psychologist. She quickly ascended through the ranks as a pioneering critic of Freudian theory via her impressive essays on feminine psychology. In fact, she became so well regarded for her thinking that in 1932 she emigrated to teach psychoanalysis first in Chicago, as associate director of Chicago's Institute for Psychoanalysis, and shortly thereafter in New York, as a dean of the New York Psychoanalytic Institute.

It was in New York that Horney began to extend her thinking on patriarchal culture to postwar American culture more broadly. Reflecting on her own background, and the testimony of her many patients, she saw a pattern. Although everyone's troubles were expressed slightly differently, there was a basic similarity of mental distress. "Neurotic persons have essential peculiarities in common," she writes, "and these basic similarities are essentially produced by the difficulties existing in our time and culture."[11]

According to Horney, such difficulties are borne of excessive competitiveness and a quasi-religious faith in personal fate over fortune. "From its economic center, competition radiates into all activities," Horney writes. "[It] permeates love, social relations and play . . . and is a problem for everyone in our culture."[12]

Competitive, individualistic cultures create very specific dilemmas for people. "Contradictory tendencies" that, Horney says, we're "unable to reconcile."[13] For example, living inside a culture where rivalry in consumption is so vigorous that it creates a desire for goods the average paycheck can't afford is decidedly frustrating for the average person. As is living in one where expectations of status and wealth soar so high that they're simply impossible for most of us to attain.

These contradictory tendencies, Horney believed, drive wedges within us. We develop an idealized image of ourselves—someone rich, cool, attractive—which we use to ward off the anxiety of not feeling like we're enough. By identifying with this image, we conform ourselves to culture's ideal, and this conformity helps us to feel less alone with our inadequacies. But conformity has a price: inner conflict between the perfect person our culture lionizes and the imperfect person we really are.

Furthermore, the wider the gap between our ideal and actual selves, the more inner conflict we experience, and the more uncomfortable we feel in our own skin. "Having placed [ourselves] on a pedestal," Horney writes, "[we] can tolerate [our] real self still less and start to rage against it, to despise [ourselves] and to chafe under the yoke of [our] unattainable expectations." We get defensive, fearful of others, and even more fearful of exposing our imperfections to the world. These fears weaken self-worth, and weakened self-worth opens the gate to an excessive craving for love and dependency on other people's approval.

So, to feel safe, connected, and of worth, we wear the mask of perfection. Our perfect self, Horney says, is a complete armory of should: "should be able to endure everything, to understand everything, to like everybody, to be always productive—to mention only a few inner dictates."[14] And since these dictates are inescapable, she calls them "the tyrannies of should."

Reading these words, I realized: this woman was a genius. Because that's it, isn't it? I *should* be cooler, fitter, stronger, happier, more productive, not eating too much, not eating too little, either, taking regular exercise, making time to rest, seeing friends, drinking in moderation, hustling and grinding and saying yes to every possible opportunity, practicing self-care, cooking up a storm, raising smart and respectful kids. These are urgent (and often contradictory) directives that we regularly fire at ourselves. And society fires them, too. They're scattered all over the gallery walls of Instagram, dripping from episodes of the Kardashians, and plastered across posters and billboards. There's no other action we can take to bring these pressures into some sort of unity than to chase perfection. For if not by perfection, then how else will we be someone who society recognizes and accepts?

Perfectionism is the chrysalis of that tyranny; the lens through which we view a world that just keeps tossing us more and more ideals of who we should be. In Horney's own life, the pressures were different, but no less weighty. Aggressive patriarchy made its own demands of women, and they taught her that "tyrannies of should" present dilemmas that only being someone else, someone perfect, can resolve. Later on, over thousands of clinical interactions, she saw remarkably consistent impacts of that tyrannical culture, right there, in the roots of other people's troubles. In the eloquent words of one of her patients: "My cast-iron should system. My complete armor of should: duty, ideals, prides, guilt. This ridged and compulsive perfectionism was all that held me up. Outside of it and all around lay chaos."[15]

"Many of [Karen Horney's] ideas about personality development," American psychologist Scott Barry Kaufman wrote in a 2020 article for *Scientific American*, "are backed by modern personality psychology, attachment theory, and findings on the effects of traumatic experiences on the brain."[16] All of that's categorically true. But Kaufman doesn't dwell enough, I think, on Horney's most profound contribution: the idea that it's our adaptation to *culture* that's causing our innermost tensions. Because that observation is almost prophetic in its anticipation of what we recognize today as a societal obsession with perfection.

Karen Horney died of cancer at the age of sixty-seven, having lived a tumultuous, courageous, and at times troubled life. Despite this, she never wavered from searching for the truth about the neuroses that afflicted her and her patients, and the cultural conditioning that gave rise to them. If you feel seen by Karen Horney, then you, like me, will find in her a close friend. Just like friends are supposed to do, she'll help you feel less confused about your perfectionism, less alone with your feelings of never enough. Her lesson for us is that none of this is our doing. The culprit is culture.

When I was about seven or eight, after school my dad would sometimes take me, my mum, and my younger brother to his building site. I loved going there. It was a place of enchanting, vacant expanse, littered with bricks piled high on pallets, aggregate where roads should be, and rows and rows of half-finished houses. The crane lights burned on in the early night. And an army of cleaners came in from the shadows, silent, carrying industrial vacuum cleaners, lifting tarpaulins, brushing cement dust, emptying bins.

My parents were part of that army. It turned out that the foreman used to give my dad some hours on the cleaning roster when we were hard up, which was often. He wasn't a particularly good cleaner. He wasn't a bad cleaner, either. Like most of the other tired and underpaid people there at god knows what time of night, he just wasn't especially invested ("That'll do, won't it?"). And besides, his talents were suited to doing things that made the mess, like hacking a saw through splintered plywood, or hammering down decking using his teeth as a makeshift nail dispenser.

But Mum, she was mesmerizing. I followed her all over the site, my eyes like saucers in bewilderment. How did she manage to turn the keys in the door clutching trash bags, brooms, and a vacuum cleaner? What kind of superpower did she possess to vacuum gristly floors while wiping mucky walls and shouting out instructions? Her furious, wanton thoroughness seemed miraculous from the vantage point of a child. She had no incentive to scurry like that for less than minimum wage, but she still did so, uncomplainingly. That's the thing about my mum: she truly understands that anything worth doing is worth doing properly.

There's that, and there's also the fact she's a perfectionist. Everything she does, she does with painstaking exactitude. From tending to her immaculate conifers to counting my dad's every dime, to the exacting, regimented way she raised us. Like Horney, she was a victim of patriarchy—her father an old-fashioned disciplinarian, traumatized by war; her siblings all brothers, sent to other schools, with better chances. Life would've been kinder in other circumstances— her ingenuity recognized, her exactitude rewarded. Instead, she takes injustice on herself and truly believes that she's just a bit "thick."

On the plane home from Palm Springs, I thought about how similar me and my mum are. If she were in my place, she, too, would surely be fretting. Was the talk okay? Was it stilted? Awkward? I wished I didn't harbor these doubts. I wanted to savor that moment of success, right there, lounging in a business-class cabin somewhere over the Atlantic. But every time I tried, my mind circled back to the things that signaled failure: to the audience, their gentle applause, and their crushing, seated feedback.

There's a degree of destiny to all of this. A great deal of my perfectionism—about 30 to 40 percent—is indeed inherited from my parents. And of that number, I suspect most comes from my dear mother. Her genes are my genes. We were born with perfectionism in our bones, and it'll leak from our pores in one form or another for the rest of our lives. There was no action either of us could have taken; our life scripts were embossed with the temperament labeled "perfectionist" long before we had any choice in the matter. And, oddly, there's something remarkably comforting about that.

However, although we're the same, we're also very different. Genes are an essential part of life's jagged script, but they're not the full plot. In fact, they're not even the principal protagonist. Thirty to forty percent is a lot to share, but even so, it leaves plenty for circumstances to work with. And when we talk about circumstances, as Judith Harris taught us, what we're really talking about is culture. Culture could've silenced my perfectionism, but instead it's amplified it to a screeching racket.

It's the reason I get overwhelmed in places like Palm Springs. It's the reason why, despite good evidence to the contrary, I sincerely believe I'm an impostor, completely out of my depth, with more that connects me to La Quinta's groundskeepers than those spending thousands of dollars to hear me speak. This psychology was planted first in my genes. But ever since, in exactly the way that Horney said it would, it was nourished to full blossom by cultural forces far from me, and far from my control, out there in the big wide world.

Karen Horney did most of her writing in the 1940s and '50s. Since then, the world's changed quite a bit. Competitiveness and individualism are still dominant values, and injustices like gender, class, and racial prejudice still exist. But there are new pressures, too, pressures that fall on all of us, pressures that would've made even Horney herself wince. The gaze of social media, helicopter parents, industrial-scale standardized testing, eighty-hour workweeks, yawning income, wealth and generational opportunity gaps, which are widening, and the spectacle of an unstable financial system that just seems to lurch from one crisis to the next—these are backing tracks to the preeminent age of never enough.

So let's update Karen Horney for the twenty-first century. Let's take a look at modern culture, and the unrelenting pressures to be perfect under which we're all scrupulously bound.

CHAPTER SEVEN

What I Don't Have
Or How Perfectionism Grows in the Soil of Our (Manufactured) Discontent

"The individual owes their crystallization to the forms of political economy, particularly to those of the urban market. Even as the opponent of the pressure of socialization, they remain the latter's most particular product and its likeness."
Theodor Adorno[1]

I grew up in Wellingborough, a small market town approximately one hour north of London. Quintessentially middle England, Wellingborough is a community whose peripheries roll longingly into the countryside, with boundary lines drawn by hedgerows that border acres of fluorescent rapeseed. Decades ago, it was a "buoyant" town, my father recalls. A place where Victorian terraces and workhouse cottages accommodated families of masons, clerks, and junior engineers employed at the nearby foundry. Independent businesses bristled with shoppers, the community theater regularly sold out, and pubs were filled to the brim with young and old alike.

These days, Wellingborough has a rather different complexion. The town attempts to limp on stoically as globalization, technology, and a decade of spending cuts gnaw away at its deindustrialized edifice. The independent businesses have all but vanished, along with the middle classes that once supported them. The shopping center has passed through all phases of retail life, and the market square is shrinking irreversibly, propped up by conglomerate fast-food chains, charity shops, and bookmakers. A graffiti artist has sprayed black paint over the letters "ingbo" on the "Welcome to Well█████rough" sign that juts out from the sidewalk on the artery road into town and no one's in any rush to have it scrubbed off. Most folks around here rather like the ingenuity, and understand it for the overly honest, self-deprecating humor that it is.

My father used to love Wellingborough, but he doesn't love it anymore. "It's going backwards," he keeps telling me, "and there's nothing anyone's doing about it."

In this neglected small town, as in most neglected small towns across the postindustrial West, it doesn't take much to be comparatively well off. Kids with money, kids like my high school friends Kevin and Ian, were the ones you looked up to and never forgot. On the estate where we grew up—parked smack in the middle of Wellingborough's problems—these boys had a good life. They lived in the newbuild houses bordering the estate, where no broken bottles or soiled diapers littered the streets. They traveled to school in the back of clean, presentable cars. They went package holidaying once a year to Turkey or Spain. And you spotted their parents from a mile off at after-school events because they were the only ones there in knitwear and ties.

Kevin and Ian spent several years forging their friendship by the time I really got to know them in the sixth form of our local comprehensive.

By then, they appeared to be inseparable, ferociously loyal, and instinctively understanding of each other's needs. Both spending by the grace of their dads' credit cards, dressing like walking advertisements for Nike, Ralph Lauren, and Adidas, always with the latest mobile phone, and spending free periods thumbing through *GQ* and *FHM* for the photos of watches, yachts, and mansions that, they promised each other, they'd one day own.

As I recall it, they seemed transfixed by what the other had. Lost in a battle over designer labels and the hottest new gadgets, they'd come to use material things as the yardsticks to measure themselves and other people. Their young, impressionable lives were stuck on one channel—the shopping channel—which seemed to have hijacked their wants and needs and turned them into well-trained consumers. With a slavish devotion to what was trendy, and with the means to purchase more or less what they needed to earn that all-important schoolyard cred, their worlds seemed to collide in the act of conspicuous, competitive consumption.

That competitive consumption seemed to reach something of a climax with the introduction of cars. At seventeen, Kevin and Ian hurried to pass their driving tests, and when they did so, both received brand-new hatchbacks complete with modification kits and custom license plates. I remember them darting those souped-up machines through Wellingborough's narrow streets. Stereos turned up, plates illuminated, fog lights glowing fluorescent blue against the frost-glazed road—they liked to egg each other on and got a boisterous thrill from the spectacle.

I'd watch all this going on with a certain green-eyed envy. Peering into the tinted passenger window of Kevin's hatchback, hands cupped around my eyes, I could see colorful, futuristic buttons, shiny chrome switches, and motorsport racing seats that seemed to exist in a breathtaking dimension of their own. I was transfixed. I couldn't resist slipping into one of those seats, which smelled like freshly fitted leather, Lynx

Africa, and the WD-40 Kevin's dad used to grease the door hinges. Looking back, it was evident, even then, that fast cars had given Kevin and Ian something approaching local-hero status. And the sheer awe of kids like me sitting giddy in the passenger seat was music to their ears—yet more evidence, as if it were needed, of their top spot in the social hierarchy.

For my part, the experience was rather different. Consumer culture, the one that celebrates having loads of money and stuff, taught me to be embarrassed about almost every comparison I made with these two boys. Nowhere was this embarrassment more gut-wrenching than when it came to their cars. So I lied. I told them that any day now my dad would buy me one, too. He wasn't. He couldn't. Still, I maintained the pretense well beyond the point of credibility because the very zenith of status, success, and self-worth these days is other people's recognition and approval. And what better way to win those things than by showcasing what we have?

We live in excessive times. Our economy is an unleashed, superheated centrifuge in a permanent state of expansion. To maintain its size, never mind grow, it must be continually fed newer and ever more lucrative sources of profit. Which explains why avid consumers like Kevin and Ian are so widespread. If they didn't exist, if everyone suddenly decided to ditch the throwaway commodities and settle for a "good enough" standard of living, then the plunge in demand would drive the economy into a spiraling recession. And we know what happens then.

Economists call this growth-is-everything economy a supply-side economy. "Supply-side" because the vast supply of newer and ever more exotic goods creates feverish consumer demand, and this demand creates profits, which creates jobs, and so on. Ideal citizens under this regime develop the qualities of a good consumer. They don't produce things; they buy them. Just like Kevin and Ian did with their clothes, watches, and cars, we're expected to express our personalities via a constant churn of lifestyle spending. To whet our appetites, businesses devise ingenious ways of manufacturing a public perception of unending newness and improved must-haves. So rather than popping out to get what we need, going to the mall these days, even for something as straightforward as a pair of socks, feels paralyzing with its tsunami of choices.

It's a dynamic, if wasteful, system. And to work it needs eager consumers who're willing to buy an ever-growing basket of things they don't really need. Fast fashion's choice overload is an obvious case in point. But there are countless other examples: combi fridges, espresso machines, cast-iron cookware, flat-screen TVs, sound systems, streaming subscriptions, robotic lawn mowers, multiple cars, blenders, decorative hardbacks, washer-dryers, face scrubs, smartphones that double as just about everything imaginable, candles, exotic vacations, perfumes and colognes, scented moisturizers, diet pills, treadmills, yoga mats.

What accumulates from this excess is a steadily flowing avalanche of commodities that no modern family could possibly live without. And with every passing year, more and more stuff gets added to the list. US retail sales exceeded a staggering $6.6 trillion in 2021, up from $4.3 trillion in 2012.[2] Globally, international retail sales are expected to reach an eye-watering $31 trillion by 2025.[3]

To keep that thermonuclear consumption going, not only do the products we buy need manufacturing, but so, too, do our desires for them. Hence, in the past forty or so years, the public relations, marketing, advertising, and finance industries have boomed. So large are these industries now that there's a high chance you work in one of them. And if you do, you'll know that making products feel "trendy," "cool," "hip," "shiny," "pristine," "exciting," "fresh," "luxurious," and "aspirational" is much more important than explaining their actual use value to consumers.

The all-channels bombardment of that kind of marketing-by-vibes has created a holographic culture of synthetic reality from which it's almost impossible to escape. Via carefully concocted fantasies of lives made more perfect, the hologram scrambles natural impulses of interest and desire, pointing our wants and needs firmly in the direction of anything that can be purchased. Flawless images and moving pictures of photogenic lives and lifestyles are right there in the morning news, above our heads on commutes, in the middle of football games, on billboards over highways, and sandwiched between airport departure boards. Our wardrobes, hygiene routines, grooming, ownership of gadgets and homewares, modes of transport, fitness rituals, and even diets are shaped and conditioned inside the hologram. In fact, all problems these days have a commoditized solution—even moods, sensations, thoughts, and behaviors through psychopharmacology, and friendships and relationships through subscription apps.

No wonder advertising is a $766 billion global industry, predicted to hit $1 trillion by 2025.[4] The hologram works.

Back in the 1920s, the trade journal *Printers' Ink* had no qualms admitting why advertising's self-referential illusions were so devastatingly effective: they breed insecurity. Insecurity about ourselves and insecurity about our existing life circumstances. Picture-perfect ads "make [the consumer] self-conscious about matter of course things such as enlarged nose pores, bad breath," one advertiser wrote. Another said ads exaggerate reality to "keep the masses dissatisfied with their mode of life, discontented with ugly things around them." Contented consumers, the same advertiser concluded, "are not as profitable as discontented ones."[5]

Sure, we've come a long way from the shaming posters of yesteryear (although you can still find them). But that fact notwithstanding, advertising's basic ethos remains more or less unchanged from the days when publications like *Printers' Ink* just went ahead and said the quiet parts out loud. For example, ads make me well aware of how I'm *supposed* to look. And I've no doubt that somewhere in the world there really is a perfectly groomed, chiseled-jawed gentleman peering into space while gently fondling his Rolex. Yet no matter how sharply I dress or how much anti-wrinkle cream I apply, that gentleman won't be me. Nor, frankly, will it be the great majority of men staring up at the billboard and ogling the marked-up timepiece (hate to break it to you lads).

Even mundane products are sold with an absurd level of fizzing, hysterical effervescence. And if anything, the strobe lights and glitter balls only serve to amplify the all-important implication. Think positive! (Yes!) Unlock your potential! (Yes!!) You've got this! (Yes!!!) . . . Here's a gym membership (Oh). You only need to peel back the wafer-thin facade of this age-old industry and you'll invariably find the timeless detail: not cool enough, not fit enough, not attractive enough, not productive enough without a certain brand, subscription, gadget, or commodity.

Not that every ad is like this—some try to push pay-day-loan, debt consolidation, and mortgage refinance services. But there's enough engineering of discontent going on within the great consumer hologram for it to be patently obvious that what was true about advertising in the past remains substantively true today. And once you see the deficit model by which advertising works, you can't then unsee it. Kevin's and Ian's fixation on material possessions is symptomatic of a culture that's taught them to treat the accoutrements of their existence as though they were as disposable as a casino chip—one that, in deference to advertisers, marketers, and PR people, must be continually betted away on the hottest new trends in search of a better hand.

To put it bluntly, Kevin and Ian behave exactly how their economy wants them to behave. And not just them. Billions of others living in supply-side economies are avid consumers, too—myself included. Indeed, the power of advertising is so enormous that even the most informed people have a hard time resisting vociferous and aggressive social persuasion that's working against them around the clock. Again, the hologram works, and it works with astonishing totality.

That totality is why a great majority of us struggle with self-acceptance. It's the reason we can never feel like we're ever enough. Because as long as contentment is kept tantalizingly from our reach, we're putty in the advertiser's hands, and guided by them we'll keep craving and consuming and craving and consuming in the hopeless quest for perfection in our lives and lifestyles.

And this is where the issues broaden out. In the growth-is-everything economy, discontent must forever be engineered into our lives. There's simply no alternative. It sounds perverse, but if we want to have the things we need, we're going to have to keep buying the things we don't. Healthcare, security, education, jobs—these necessities of life now depend on our continuing to trade present happiness for the promise of something more.[6] Because if we were just allowed to breathe for a moment, step outside of the hologram and discover contentment in the miracle that is our mere existence, then we'd stop craving. And if we stop craving, we'd stop consuming. Businesses would then have to close, jobs would be lost, the things we need would begin to disappear, and the foundations of society as we know it would collapse.

Popular self-help books, documentaries, TV shows, TED Talks, and wellness websites overflow with tips, tricks, and life hacks for how to overcome the all-pervasive feeling of never enough. But the illusion of agency makes me wonder: Do we truly understand how completely and utterly built-in that feeling is? Not rich enough, not cool enough, not attractive enough, not productive enough—these aren't bothersome tics that can be flicked away with a bit of self-care or positive thinking. They're systemic thoughts, or what cognitive historians call "root metaphors," which have penetrated so deeply into our interiors that we truly believe not feeling enough, or needing to constantly update and improve ourselves, are conditions of human nature.

But that's not true. The Qin dynasty Chinese or tenth-century Inuit would surely struggle to fathom what on earth go-getting, hashtag-success-trains failure-complains LinkedIn Man was blabbering on about, even if they did understand his language. The reality is far more ominous. That deficit thinking underneath our collective scramble for more—the one that holds us in a steady state of insecurity about whether we're enough—is a socially conditioned mindset that our economy needs to drill into us, and keep on drilling into us. For if we were to suddenly snap out of it, stop thinking like that, and know that our lives didn't need to be constantly updated and improved, then everything else stops, too.

The very fabric of modern society is woven from our discontent. Magnifying the many imperfections that advertisers have manufactured into existence is how we're kept in an always expanding state of super-charged consumption, and how, by extension, our economy is kept in an always expanding state of supercharged growth.

You might ask: Is this not the very same cultural dilemma that worried Karen Horney? Well, yes and no. Yes, because today's culture, like hers, opens a yawning chasm between the perfect person society tells us we should be and the imperfect person we actually are. But no because there's something quite unique to this moment. The dilemma in Horney's day was that many of the things society told people they should have, and the standards to which they were expected to be held, were out of reach for the average person. That crushing sense of lack and inadequacy was what created the inner conflict.

Our dilemma, in many ways, is more acute. We're still bombarded with messaging about what we should have and who we should be. But these days cheap imports and a bonanza in consumer credit mean a great major-ity of us can buy the things we're told we need. We don't lack, certainly not in comparison to older generations. If anything, we have access to too much stuff—more than we could ever need. And yet somehow, despite that, de-spite spending most of our waking existence swimming in the regalia of consumer culture, we're still chronically insecure and more discontented than ever.

*   *   *

I lost touch with Kevin and Ian at age eighteen when I went away to college but reached out several years later. They'd remained inseparable, loyal, and fiercely competitive—not wanting to do anything or see anyone without the other in tow. I, on the other hand, had changed beyond all recognition. So it was rather comforting to return home and find both the place and people more or less how I'd left them.

There was one difference, though. Kevin's father had enjoyed substantial success with his business while I'd been away. From a home-office consultancy, he'd amassed a mini-empire and was servicing some of the world's biggest companies. His income increased exponentially, and it showed. In just three years, Kevin's family had relocated out of Wellingborough to a gated mansion in the country, tucked away on a two-acre plot at the end of a quarter-mile-long driveway.

The short time it took for Kevin's dad to go from well-off to absurdly rich changed Kevin's life almost overnight. This twenty-one-year-old was earning substantial money in his father's company, buying a four-bedroom house, collecting multiple high-end cars, and, of course, taking up golf.

"I'm very lucky," Kevin told me as we shot billiards in his game room. I was never sure if he was reassuring himself or me. It always struck me how, as an emerging adult, Kevin would view his life with a certain embarrassment. Having grown up around scarcity, he knew how shit things could be, and he wasn't terribly good at hiding the lingering guilt of his obvious overindulgences.

But that didn't keep him from developing a certain fearlessness. When we speak of privilege, we often focus on the frills of advantage, forgetting the more basic benefit: an absence of obstacles. Kevin had little fear of anything, really, and it was evident his background had taught him that his life was more straightforward than other people's. When he spoke of being lucky, this, I think, is what he meant. In a world replete with stark inequities, he possessed that rare gift of acceptance. Acceptance of himself and acceptance of his circumstances, not needing to justify them, not needing to explain them away on a narrative arc in which his lot in life, rather like compound interest, accumulated smoothly upward and in direct correlation to effort and acumen.

Kevin knew it didn't happen like that and the acceptance of how it did happen gave him complete permission to just be himself.

The effects of Kevin's fortunes on Ian didn't appear to be rather different. Ian looked up to Kevin. He seemed to see in Kevin's lavish lifestyle the end point of his own striving. When Kevin bought a house, Ian did the same. When Kevin got a new car, Ian took out a loan to buy the equivalent model. And when Kevin bought an expensive watch or piece of jewelry, Ian stretched himself to purchase something similarly extravagant.

When Ian remarked at Kevin's birthday party that "me and Kevin have always competed," he articulated this condition transparently. The room fluttered with laughter. But it seemed to me that the competition Ian spoke of was, by this point, one-way, and had boiled down to chasing Kevin's impossible standard of living—a fantasy of material perfection akin to the rich and famous, one that seems rather typical in this have-everything age.

Chasing that ideal appeared to inject Ian's life with insecurity, especially in hard times. I remember taking Ian out one winter's evening to drink away the sting of a cruel layoff. He wasn't sad or especially angry at the shoddy way his boss had handled the sacking; he was in a disoriented state of worry, not about what had happened, but what came next. There was little wriggle room in Ian's lifestyle for a blow like this. Like most of us these days, he had a big mortgage, a car he'd just financed, and multiple credit card bills that just kept piling up. Now without a job and with few savings to fall back on, he seemed terrified of what people would think of him should he somehow fall into arrears.

He didn't because he's extraordinarily enterprising. But for a while, it was a little too close for comfort.

So there we were in one of Soho's dingy basement bars, putting the world to rights behind seven drams of scotch (which is precisely one too many). And for that moment at least, his worries melted away.

Living inside a culture of bigger and better, there'll invariably come a point when no matter how rich you are, your desires will reach the threshold of your means to satisfy them. For Karen Horney, this contradiction was more than just a material lack. It was the root of a basic inner conflict—between who we are and who our culture tells us we *should* be.

That contradiction is blurrier nowadays but no less problematic. Cheap imports have crushed manufacturing costs. And a boom in credit cards, buy-now-pay-later schemes, and hire purchase agreements have allowed a great majority of us to satisfy our numerous and ever-expanding list of cravings. When Horney was writing about "tyrannies of should" in the 1950s, US private debt was about 50 percent of the gross domestic product. Today, it's 224 percent. And although the US is a clear outlier, most other developed countries have enjoyed similar debt sprees in recent decades.

In the modern world, credit, or debt, is what we're relying on to wring new growth from advanced economies that are entering various phases of secular stagnation.

And that's fine. But generating growth via helicopter money is rather like using a sledgehammer to crack a nut. The amount of magicked-up cash showering down on the modern economy is simply astronomical, and with every zero added to the spreadsheet comes ever-diminishing returns. According to economist Tim Morgan, total world debt increased by $55 trillion between 2000 and 2007, while the GDP increased by just $17 trillion. Stripping out interbank debts, that's about one dollar of growth for every two dollars of new debt. Morgan then followed those calculations through to 2014. And when he did so, he discovered that world debt increased by another $50 trillion, but GDP increased by just one dollar for every three dollars borrowed.[7]

If Morgan's numbers are right, then before long the amount of money needing rained down to eke out more growth is going to be so enormous that you don't have enough helicopters. Rather than accept that fact, we go on furiously humping the credit pump to inflate a bloated economy. There's simply no "plan B." Should recession strike, as it seems to do a lot these days, we just slash interest rates and fire up the printers. Corporate losses are backstopped, failed banks get bailed out, and after a period of intense and serious reflection, in which men in suits vow to never let it happen again, stocks rip, bonuses soar, house prices—already on a moonshoot—go into hyperdrive, and the average paycheck buys a little less than it did before.

In this suspended-by-credit, supply-side, growth-at-all-costs economy, that's a "recovery."

Still, so long as we keep consuming, does it matter that the ever-expanding pile of debt we're taking on to do so isn't at all sustainable? It certainly doesn't seem to. After all, thanks to the opening of financial markets, our lives and lifestyles really can be made more perfect, more extravagant, packed with gadgets and technological wizardry, elaborate cookware and appliances, bigger and more powerful SUVs, furniture, and increasingly ginormous houses—forever—even if our wages do stagnate.[8] Ian's buy-now-pay-later self-improvement project is perhaps an extreme example, but it's far from unique. In fact, it follows a well-documented pattern of shifting attitudes in the past few decades.

For example, when people in the 1970s were asked what the good life meant, they tended to respond with things like a happy marriage, children, a fulfilling job, or doing something that improves society.[9] When the same question was posed to people in the 1990s, they responded with things like a vacation home, a new television, trendy clothes, and generally loads and loads of money.[10] Fully 80 percent of Americans born in the 1980s report getting materially rich as among their most important life goals. This is a figure that's up almost 20 percent on those born in the 1960s and '70s.[11]

With these material wants, and now the finance to satisfy them, you'd think we'd be happier. But as Ian's story shows, it's not quite that simple. American economist Richard Easterlin's classic research on the impact of wealth on people's well-being is clear in its conclusions: more money and stuff does not equal more happiness. His analyses consistently reveal that once a country reaches a certain threshold of affluence, additional affluence is not matched by gains in people's well-being.[12] The same story is apparent at the level of income. Despite incomes in the US having soared between the 1940s and the 1990s, the general level of happiness that Americans reported over that period remained more or less unchanged.[13] About $100,000 a year seems to be sufficient. After that, well-being plateaus, and with every additional dollar we don't seem to get any happier.[14]

This paradox, in which surplus wealth is weakly linked to happiness, is known as the Easterlin paradox. And the textbook explanation for it is something called status anxiety. Status anxiety isn't the fear that we don't have enough money or stuff—it's the fear that we don't have enough money or stuff compared to other people. That we're not, to put it colloquially, keeping up with the Joneses. This anxiety is extremely widespread these days and is neatly embodied in Ian, who can never feel content next to Kevin despite purchasing his way through more goods and services than most could mention.

"Wherever and whenever we are excessive in our lives it is a sign of an unknown deprivation," writes British psychotherapist Adam Phillips. "Our excesses are the best clue we have," he says, "[of] our own poverty and our best way of concealing it from ourselves."[15] He's right. Despite every cent we throw at it, the inner poverty we feel—the lingering sense of never enough—can't be shaken with throwaway commodities. Because it's not about the commodities. It's about feeling never enough for our purchasing to have an end point, or to begin investing in ourselves, or be recognized simply for who we are.

Then again, feeling inadequate and unloved is sort of the point of our economy. It has no concern for our happiness or contentment or fundamental needs for purpose and social connection. Quite the contrary. It's expressly designed to manufacture insecurity so as to prevent the idea that we could ever feel enough from taking seed. This system's priority is—will only ever be—growth and how to generate as much growth as possible in the shortest possible time. Left to its own devices, it'll discard all other considerations so that eventually our existence consists purely of medicating shame-based fears about what we lack with a material remedy.

Growing up, consumer culture, and the spectacle of other people's consumption, taught me to be ashamed of every aspect of my life that didn't match up—which was just about all of them. And I'm not alone in having that deficit thinking drilled into me. "Every single person I've interviewed," says influential professor Brené Brown, "spoke about struggling with vulnerability" and "shame-based fears" of not being enough.[16] All of my students speak of exactly the same struggle. As do a great majority of my family and friends. Shame is the reason we're seeing those surging levels of socially prescribed perfectionism. "I'm not perfect enough" and "everyone expects me to be perfect": that's the inner dialogue of a new generation molded in the image of supply-side economics.

✳   ✳   ✳

Socially prescribed perfectionism is something of an inevitability inside an economy reliant solely on growth. And although that means it's unavoidable, there are things we can do to help us lead a more contented and purposeful life. The most important of these things, to my mind, is self-compassion—the permission to accept yourself.[17] We all have imperfections. When they get picked on or exposed, when ads paint them as reminders of our shameful interiors, our instinct is to listen and loathe them. We react as if something is terribly wrong with us.

"I'm not enough," we tell ourselves. "I should be fitter, happier, cooler, prettier."

Kristin Neff is perhaps the most forensic self-compassion researcher. She draws a distinction between self-compassion and self-esteem. Although self-esteem can build up a positive self-image, Neff says, research shows that such a self-image can be brittle and easily broken.[18] Self-compassion, according to her, works instead on building self-clarity. Self-clarity means reflecting on how we care for ourselves. Rather than measuring our worth by what we have or how we appear, it focuses on our thoughts and emotions. It's an inner dialogue that essentially goes: "No matter what happens, no matter what anyone else says or does, I'm enough, and I'm going to care for myself with kindness."

Research shows that people who're higher in self-compassion have fewer self-presentational concerns, feel less need to be perfect, and report more body appreciation than those who are lower in it.[19] These people also cope far more adaptively with stressful situations, brood and ruminate less, and tend to report fewer mental health problems such as anxiety and depression.[20] All of which sounds like a healthier platform from which to navigate the modern world than the one we're expected to start off from: insecurity and discontent.

So instead of letting self-esteem desert you when you need it the most, make a promise to be kind to yourself. That means, as Neff says, taking ownership of your imperfections, recognizing your shared humanity, and understanding that no matter how hard your culture works to teach you otherwise, no one is perfect, and everyone has an imperfect life. If you can commit to doing those things, then you can, slowly and at first unevenly, start to shut out the shame you're supposed to feel. Keep at that self-compassion and, over time, as Neff's research shows, shame, rumination, and appearance concerns will feel less and less intrusive.[21]

We are who we are: the rickety lump of imperfection that we go to sleep with every night. Embracing those flaws, being kind to ourselves, and recognizing that to be human is to be fallible is the equivalent of taking a sledgehammer to perfectionism. Keep practicing self-compassion whenever this world tries to defeat you. Because no matter what the advertisement says, you will go on with your imperfect existence whether you make that purchase or not. And that existence is—can only ever be—enough.

★   ★   ★

One of the things I'm often asked is whether perfectionism is a middle-class craze born of relentless expectations to excel. That's part of it, and we'll talk about those expectations later. But growing up in Wellingborough, knowing what I do about how the other half lives, I feel well placed to answer that question with a resounding no. Every last one of us in the modern world is a consumer. And none of us, regardless of class, is immune to the perfectionistic fantasies that are the rocket fuel for this economy.

I don't have any data to back this up because the only perfectionism scores we can reliably track are from college students, who, in the specific material we've gathered, tend to have characteristics of the middle class. But I do have the evidence of my eyes and ears, and it tells me that wanton discontent is conditioned at every single level of society. Perhaps more so among those farther down the social ladder, if you consider that they start life with far less means to attain this culture's ideal of the perfect life and lifestyle.

Which is why I've described Kevin and Ian. I believe their encounters with the modern world are typical enough to be illustrative, as are their emotional responses to it. The growth imperative of supply-side economics is a simple fact of modern life. It means advertisers, marketers, and PR people must dream up newer and ever more inventive ways of keeping us in a holding pattern of insecurity—forever. We're not meant to be content in this world any more than a puff of Chanel is meant to turn us into an impeccably toned, scantily-clad model marauding through a moody forest clutching a pickax. "Everyone expects me to be perfect!"—that's simply what it feels like to live inside an exaggerated hyperreality of limitless perfection.

Socially prescribed perfectionism, then, is the emblem of consumer culture. The defining social character type of a citizenry who're never allowed to step outside of the hologram and feel like they're enough. And if you thought the insecurity manufactured by analogue advertising was problematic, wait till you hear about social media.

CHAPTER EIGHT

What She Posted
Or Why Social Media Companies Thrive on Pressures to Be Perfect

"We make more money when people spend more time on our platform because we're an advertising business."
Adam Mosseri, Head of Instagram[1]

In the beginning we had friends. We could "friend" the people in our class, have a relationship status with whoever we were dating, create clandestine splinter groups, list events, and even send messages. Our profile had something called a "wall," which was a freely editable textbox that everybody could see (but few updated). "Poking" was an option, although nobody knew what it meant. The main attraction, it seemed to me, was "tagging," which we mostly used to tag our friends in the most embarrassing photos we could find from the night before.

This was early-days Facebook, and it was an exciting place for credulous college students like me. We used it to poke fun at our friends, laugh about drunken antics, and catch up on who went home with whom. It was a social network in the truest sense of the phrase—solidifying community, greasing the wheels of offline friendship.

Somewhere around 2006, however, that all changed. Facebook opened its doors to the general public, and our parents, grandparents, uncles, and aunts flocked to the platform. In just a couple of short years, the in-jokes started to disappear along with the embarrassing photos that spurred them. And in their place, post after post of amusing cat videos, motivational memes on shooting-star backgrounds, and ads, loads and loads of ads.

And yet, despite the college fraternity protests, Facebook's opendoor policy proved stunningly successful for its owner, Mark Zuckerberg. It helped him build a huge global user base, then use that clout to eat up competition like Instagram and WhatsApp before rebranding his suite of platforms as Meta in 2021. By then, Facebook—or Meta—had gone from no revenue and 10 million users to $117 billion revenues[2] and almost 4 billion active users.[3]

One of those users is Sarah.

I dated Sarah briefly in the sixth form of my local high school. Back then, she was well known, not just in the part of town where we grew up, but in many of the surrounding areas. In modern vernacular, I suppose you'd say she was something of a local influencer—that's how people got to know her—always visible in Wellingborough's hot spots, dressed in glittering outfits, hair perfectly curled, handbag heavy with brushes, foundation, and mascara. At eighteen, Sarah left our little town to find more excitement in the next one over. But we kept in touch.

She's doing well. After leaving Wellingborough, she got an office job at a construction firm and worked up to middle management. That's where she met her husband, Geoff, a tattooed, muscly plasterer of several more years. Their marriage happened at sunset somewhere off the coast of Thailand. They have two children, Becca and Alfie; she drives an Audi, him a BMW; and they live in a detached house on a new-build subdivision located in a leafy suburb about forty minutes from her parents.

I know all this because Sarah shares a great deal of her life on social media. Posting fresh content, commenting, liking, and sharing most days, she has been well and truly sucked into Facebook's platforms. The company's technologists have escalated social comparisons from occasional to nearly constant. And they've globalized them, too. Where once it was just Wellingborough's teens Sarah compared herself to, now it's millions of photogenic influencers. She follows a great deal of them, and if she isn't posting pictures, videos, or stories herself, she's scrolling through theirs.

Sarah's social media use is not unusual. Nowadays, rather than pokes and tags, users like her are attuned to metrics that have a running total, like follower counts, the number of likes a post gets, or the number of shares a post generates. There was a precious moment in history when social media users would log on with a certain trepidation about what they'd been tagged in. Now we fear the opposite. Without likes, mentions, or shares, we worry that we're being ignored or discounted, as worthless as an unwanted item of clothing gathering dust on the shop floor.

The apps work on this deficit model. That's why a great majority only share content after it's been carefully retouched. We've learned that this boosts metrics, and metrics are the validation tokens we need to clear the debt in our checking accounts of self-esteem. Sarah's profile is a case in point. Her stories feature exciting, exotic adventures. Her wall pulses with square after square of pixelated perfection: touched-up selfies, filtered vacation snaps, angled gym shots, cuddly couple pics. It's a telescope into the ideal life that Sarah, and millions like her, want other people to see.

But nobody's life is *that* perfect. We have chaotic moments, periods of elation, flashes of tragedy, promotions, layoffs, health scares, and heartache. And in the empty spaces between this drama, our lives simply go on. Nothing exceptional, nothing out of the ordinary. Just the humdrum, everyday routine.

Thomas Curran

The tension between our picture-perfect online lives and the more mundane reality poses important questions for all of us sculpting our lives with the airbrush of social media. Can contentment ever be truly realized in the pursuit of likes, shares, and mentions? Can durable relationships ever be forged through the prism of pixels? Can secure self-esteem ever be built on the backs of fire and applause emojis?

If I could state our dilemma more concretely, it's that social media has finished the job that consumer culture started way back when the supply-side revolution first took hold of our economy. While billboards, magazines, and television ads are adept at creating holographic images of limitless perfection, there's simply no parallel to social media. The platforms lay bare what this economy looks like in its purest incarnation: an unregulated bear pit where users themselves create the glittering content, which algorithms aggregate, and then mirror back on those same users to generate an aura of inescapable insecurity. Behind our backs, these algorithms feed on our insecurities—their notifications keep us hooked on the next hit of electronic validation. And then, when you're at your most vulnerable—*bam!*—an ad appears with the perfect remedy.

More than 2 billion people log on to either Facebook or Instagram each day. And since everyone's there, everyone feels obliged to show up. We compare with each other, our profiles invite the mimicking and rivalry of our followers, and their profiles, in turn, invite ours. Every time we click on the app, we're introduced to an unwinnable popularity contest that creates a suffocating atmosphere of digitally enhanced perfection. An atmosphere in which no one user, regardless of how liked, followed, or acclaimed they might be, can ever feel enough.

And there's that feeling again.

Facebook says it provides innovative tools to connect us with our friends. But those of us who used it from the beginning know that's not true anymore. Sarah, and the millions like her, are ample evidence that social media has evolved and changed into something altogether different. When you strip it down to its algorithms, when you really get to the nub of what social media is these days, you'll find nothing more than an advertising device. And like all advertising devices, it's doing exactly what a supply-side economy needs it to do: stuffing us together in a jar, shaking us vigorously, and opening the lid over a bewildering array of targeted ads.

Even so, we should talk about social media. Because as advertising devices go, it's a devastatingly powerful one, with tremendous potential to exacerbate epidemics of perfectionism.

From the get-go, we should be clear about one thing. When we talk of harm in social media, we're mainly talking about the dominant visual platforms, namely Instagram and TikTok. Instagram, in particular, was created to stoke social comparison, and follow-on platforms work on more or less the same basis. Via highlight reels, videos, and stories, these platforms expose us to curated lives, promote celebrity content, push hot new influencers, and simulate unrealistic health and beauty ideals. "People use Instagram because it's a competition, that's the fun part!" a former Facebook executive said in a leaked memo. Another employee added, "Isn't this what Instagram is mostly about? The (very photogenic) life of the top 0.1%?"[4]

Maybe it is, but those kinds of impossible standards leave their mark on young, impressionable users. They ask them to continually measure themselves against an algorithm that just keeps serving up walls and walls of curated hyperreality. And those comparisons are the gateway to dissatisfaction with existing life affairs, discontent with one's self-image, a need for perfection, and the depression, anxiety, and suicidal thoughts that come with it.

We know this is true because Facebook's own research says so. In 2021, Frances Haugen, a former Facebook product manager, leaked findings from an in-house "mental health deep dive" to the *Wall Street Journal*.[5] The deep dive was a triangulation of research methods—focus groups, surveys, and diary studies—that Facebook carried out somewhere between 2019 and 2020. They were concerned about how Instagram impacted teens and wanted to know what effects it had on their mental health.

The conclusions were alarming. So alarming, in fact, that Facebook didn't choose to distribute them publicly. It's only down to the astonishing bravery of Haugen that we even know the research exists. "We make body image issues worse for one in three teen girls," said one slide from a leaked presentation deck. "Teens blame Instagram for increases in anxiety and depression," said another slide. "This reaction was unprompted and consistent across all groups."[6]

Not only that, but the leaked slides also reveal startling data on the way Instagram makes young people view themselves. One chart shows that about half of Instagram users feel the platform amplifies pressures to look perfect. Another reveals that about 40 percent of users say the platform makes them worry about not appearing attractive enough, wealthy enough, or popular enough. But perhaps the most disturbing slide of all was the leaked bar chart on thoughts of suicide. According to that, 6 percent of US teens and a staggering 13 percent of British teens told Facebook's researchers that spending time on Instagram was one reason why they felt like they wanted to kill themselves.[7]

Psychologist Jean Twenge's in-depth research echoes Facebook's findings. In a recent analysis of three big American samples, she discovered that the correlation between social media use and mental distress was substantial.[8] People who used social media a lot were roughly two to three times more likely to be depressed than those who didn't use it at all. This link, Twenge says, is larger than links between mental health and "binge drinking, early sexual activity, hard drug use, being suspended from school, marijuana use, lack of exercise, being stopped by police or carrying a weapon."

Author Donna Freitas's research goes deeper.[9] Her interviews with young social media users tell of a generation besieged by social comparisons and preoccupied with a hypervigilance for other people's approval. Their stories show how young people who are online feel they must always appear to be happy, achieving things, and living their best lives. Social media "gives this false image that you're living a perfect life," one young person told Freitas. "You don't want people to see you at your low times, you want them to see only the good times so that they go: Wow, I want to live like them!"

My own research reveals similar patterns, albeit not at the scale of Twenge's or Freitas's. In one study, we asked teen girls whether they compared themselves to others online.[10] More than 80 percent said they did, which was bad enough. But of that number, fully 90 percent said they compared worse or much worse than other people, and those negative comparisons were linked to higher depression and lower body appreciation. Worse, we also asked girls to report their socially prescribed perfectionism. And guess what? Girls high in socially prescribed perfection had especially high depression and especially low body appreciation after making a negative social comparison.

Here's how that relationship unfolds. A teen girl is flicking through Instagram. Suddenly, she sees an image of an influencer. That image has been cherry-picked from a great many alternatives and retouched in several ways, but this, to the girl, is irrelevant. She's transfixed, she makes a snap comparison, and in an instant feels decidedly worse about herself. That's bad enough, but the more socially prescribed perfectionism she has, the more this comparison will generate depression and body image concerns. This is exactly the type of aggravated vulnerability that we discussed in chapter 3.

Jean Twenge thinks this link between social media and mental distress is due mostly to smartphones.[11] She makes her case on the back of many data sets, including her own, which show that youth depression and suicide began skyrocketing around 2008. Incidentally, 2008 was also the year socially prescribed perfectionism skyrocketed, too. And

Thomas Curran

when you add to these trends the release of Apple's first iPhone in 2007, there is indeed a compelling correlation.

That correlation certainly passes a few smell tests. After all, smartphones give us absolutely no respite from the noise of social media. They link us up all day, every day, and penetrate social comparison into parts of life that were hitherto untouched. With them by our sides, apps like Instagram and TikTok are right there first thing in the morning and last thing at night. We idly scroll through profiles on the sofa and in the bath, during the commute and at the gym. In what used to be meditative moments, where we could breathe and think, now we swipe and compare.

Smartphones made social media ubiquitous, and that ubiquity, according to Twenge, is what makes it so damaging.

And this makes perfect sense. So why, then, does it feel like something's missing? "It's Facebook! It's Instagram! It's TikTok! It's smartphones!"—these are satisfying headlines. But you'll notice how conveniently laser-focused they are. Like a finely tuned precision bomb, they're targeted enough to damage specific companies, but not targeted enough to knock over the infrastructure that built them. Blaming smartphones for social media's ills is fine, and there are certainly grounds for it. But doing so leaves intact and untouched the economic infrastructure that dictates the way social media companies write their algorithms in the first place.

Which brings me to something else that happened in 2008, something that's got nothing at all to do with smartphones: Facebook made an advertising executive it's chief operating officer.

In the halcyon days of early Facebook, the platform was a lot of fun. But sadly, it wasn't turning much profit for Mark Zuckerberg. For that to be the case, Facebook needed to get people interacting on the platform—clicking on profiles, flicking through updates, messaging each other, all while passively ingesting ads. That's why, in 2008, Zuckerberg brought world-renowned advertising executive Sheryl Sandberg to Facebook. Her job? To turn its users into consumers.

The changes Sandberg made were those a supply-side economy needed her to make. Facebook couldn't stand still. It had to grow, at any cost. And to do that it needed to diversify its revenue streams in the pursuit of new and ever more lucrative sources of profit. Thus Sandberg did what any good COO should do. She turned Facebook into an advertising business that used its vast troves of personal information—ages, locations, interests, sexualities, likes, clicks, and so on—to sell targeted ads.

"We're proud of the ad model we've built," Sandberg told Facebook's first-quarter earnings call in 2018. "It ensures that people see more useful ads, allows millions of businesses to grow, and enables us to provide a global service that's free for all to use."[12] That may be true, but Sandberg's definition of "useful" is euphemistic, to say the least. Few ads sell useful things—most are discretionary. We don't need them; we've just been convinced they'll plug the holes that advertisers have punched.

The ads Facebook sells are no different. Calling them useful is like thanking the arsonist for handing you a hose as your house flickers in flames. And under Sandberg's watch, the company learned that Instagram is especially well placed to light fires. With its global reach and enormous, impressionable user base, Instagram can invite young people to measure their own lives against walls and walls of models, fitness bloggers, lifestyle coaches, and influencers.

No wonder young people struggle with feeling enough. Like the age-old tactics of analogue advertising, social media companies can generate the insecurities—about what we don't have and how we don't appear—that are catnip for targeted ads. And over the years, they've honed their algorithms to predict the types of ads we're likely to click on with eerily high accuracy. So high, in fact, that there's widespread panic that social media companies must be listening to our conversations. For Sandberg, investment in these kinds of technologies was an inspired strategic decision, and because of it, Facebook (now Meta) has increased its advertising revenues exponentially since 2009, to almost $115 billion today.[13]

Facebook, or Meta, likes to dress this part of its business model—the profitable part—in euphemisms. But a confidential document recently seen by the *Australian* says the quiet bit out loud.[14] Facebook, it reads, can offer advertisers the chance to target millions of young users when at their most vulnerable, such as when they feel "stressed," "defeated," "overwhelmed," "anxious," "insecure," "stupid," "silly," "worthless," and like a "failure." Their algorithms can even pinpoint moments when young people "need a confidence boost."[15]

Facebook has confirmed the authenticity of this document, but denies it offers "tools to target people based on their emotional state." Which is odd, since research conducted in 2021 by *Fairplay, Global Action Plan,* and *Reset Australia* shows that Facebook is still monitoring and targeting teens for ads.[16] "Facebook is still using the vast amount of data it collects about young people," the organization writes in an open letter outlining its findings.[17] And "this practice is especially concerning," they go on, because it might mean "weight loss ads served to teens with emerging eating disorders, or an ad being served [when] a teen's mood suggests they are particularly vulnerable."

Although Instagram is the main culprit, other platforms work off of similar business models. For example, some TikTok influencers are sharing checklists of mental health conditions like ADHD, anxiety, and depression.[18] This trend has aroused the interest of predatory companies who're teaching young people how to self-diagnose their mental health problems. And when they've done so, yep, you guessed it, they're selling them costly treatments as solutions.

Sure, we can point to smartphones and say, "That's why social media harms teens!" But this charge doesn't help us understand why Facebook wouldn't hear the gravity of its own research, or why, despite all the evidence of harm, the industry as a whole is so vociferously resistant to change. To understand that we need to listen to the insiders. According to one Facebook researcher, nobody at the company wanted to act on their findings because the necessary changes would stand "directly between people and their bonuses."[19] I don't think there's a more succinct explanation for why we are where we are than that.

And you know what? I can't get upset at Zuckerberg, Sandberg, or anyone else in positions of influence over what social media's algorithms do and don't target. They're managing their businesses and going about their lives exactly as they're supposed to. When social media connects us to those in our communities, it has tremendous human value. But if we insist on living inside an economy that needs to grow more than we—the people—need to feel connected and secure, then we can't be outraged when executives ultimately put profits ahead of providing something truly life enhancing for their users. That's a question of priorities, and the types of priorities we've chosen to privilege.

If we could just bring ourselves to confront that reality, then the obvious question is, why should Facebook's business model be any different from all the others in this economy? Why should it care about us? Facebook, Instagram, TikTok, and all the other platforms like them weren't plucked out of thin air. They were selected by the supply-side economy, which, having squeezed every last drop of profit out of analogue advertising, needed a bigger, more global, more manipulative tool to keep us consuming.

A great deal of our modern-day obsession with perfection is undoubtedly due to the omnipresence of social media apps. But it would be a mistake, I think, to conclude from this that if we were to shut down the apps tomorrow our obsession with perfection would disappear. The economy, which needs our constant attention and spending, would just find another way to keep us doubting ourselves and wanting more. You can't cure the disease by treating only the symptoms.

★   ★   ★

The question is: How on earth do you navigate social media in a way that avoids its predatory elements?

That's a tricky question to answer, since the most fail-safe escape route is by far the hardest: refuse to engage. Research shows that reducing social-media-based smartphone use for just an hour a day significantly decreases symptoms of depression and anxiety and increases happiness and health.[20] Why? Because digital moderation allows us to allocate the time saved to other activities, which enliven our lives.

That's not to say social media can't be healthy. It's just to say that it should be used in moderation and for the right reasons: community, shared interests, and helping us to facilitate offline relations.

So try, where you can, to replace time spent on the apps with time spent offline. Step outside into the animating forces of nature, ideas, art, and social and political causes. Just marvel at the wonder of life, this lonely planet, and all the magnificent people, plants, and creatures that inhabit it. Certainly, that sounds far more inviting than the company of advertisers and photogenic influencers.

Indeed, time immersed in the wonders of the real world—breathing them in, listening, learning, and caring—is infinitely more joyous than anything we can airbrush into existence. It makes us instantly at one with our humanity. It draws us closer to ourselves and our environment. It stops us from viewing everything and all around us through the lens of a camera. When we and our environment are not opposed, when we're on an equal plane, the urge to introspect on what we're (not) doing or what we're (not) capturing quickly evaporates. We become grounded and intimately appreciative of life for the incomprehensible miracle that it is.

All of which is why sometimes it really is okay to put the phone away and just be there, in the real world, with all of yourself and all of your feelings instead.

That time offline—with other people and in the outside world—has countless benefits for our physical and mental health. Research shows that roaming outside, especially in new places, contributes to enhanced well-being. For example, in a recent study, psychologist Catherine Hartley found that the amount of wandering people do in new areas on any given day correlated positively with how happy they were later on (and not vice versa).[21] Other benefits of getting out there in nature include, according to one extensive review, "improved attention, lower stress, better mood, reduced risk of psychiatric disorders and even upticks in empathy and cooperation."[22]

But most important, time offline is also essential to breaking through perfectionism. Because out there in the real world, with real people and real sensations, is a place chock-full of reminders that away from the hyperreality of social media, and beyond the brute indifference of a faceless following, we do matter, and we matter rather a lot.

In 2015, Instagram influencer Essena O'Neill did something that sent shock waves through her industry. She left the platform in disgust, explaining that the dozens of carefully staged, well-lit, spotless shots of her slim, toned, and cheery self were all corporate-sponsored, vetted, and retouched to maximize likes and shares. Just before leaving, O'Neill wrote little notes for her followers in the caption spaces underneath her photos. In them, she described the anxiety-ridden experience of being an influencer: waking at dawn, far from home, posing for several hours only to leave with one or two shareable shots out of many hundreds. In not one of her photos was she happy. It was all a charade.

As well as the notes, O'Neill also posted a video on YouTube.[23] Facing her webcam, she's tired and visibly upset. You get the impression that this has been tossing around in her conscience for some time. "Social media is a business," she says, "and if you don't think it's a business, you're deluded." Looking into the lens, she tells viewers straight-up: if you're following someone and they've got lots of followers, "they're promoting products, they're paid."

"Everything I was doing," she says, "was edited and contrived, to get more value, and to get more views."

It's an uneasy watch, especially when O'Neill talks about the psychological toll. She explains, "I let myself be defined by numbers . . . The only time I felt better about myself was with more followers, more likes, more praise, and more views." And then, puff, gone in an instant, as if the attention didn't mean much, as if it never mattered at all. Irrespective of how high O'Neill's numbers soared, "it was never enough," she says, holding back tears. She was living her childhood dream, but found herself trapped in a nightmare of impossible expectations. "I don't want to say I was depressed or had anxiety . . . but I definitely had all the symptoms times a billion.

"When you let yourself be defined by numbers, you let yourself be defined by something that's not pure, that's not real." O'Neill says she spent her childhood "wishing I was this perfect person online," and then spent her young adulthood "proving my life on social media, perfecting myself enough to be that person." It was an exhausting existence. "Everything I did each day was to be that perfect person online," she explains. "There were shoots, style pictures of what I was eating, carefully edited videos on YouTube. I did everything in my power to prove to the world that, hey, I'm important, I'm beautiful, and I'm cool.

"Is that life . . . taking pictures just to get likes and compliments?" she asks. "It's not life and it's not what's making you happy."

Not every young person uses social media like O'Neill did, but enough to make us incredibly nervous. Over a third of elementary and almost half of high school students say that social media is why they feel compelled to look perfect in every possible way.[24] And according to one recent poll, a staggering 90 percent of young Americans say they'd be an influencer if given a chance.[25] Their thirst for online recognition is why we should listen carefully to what O'Neill's got to say. Because she's saying, in essence, that using social media's digital validation tokens as props for self-worth has terrible consequences. Even for—especially for—those who make it to influencer stardom.

I don't know if Sarah ever followed O'Neill. But she certainly possesses the digital hallmarks of O'Neill's past life. Inside all that filtering and airbrushing, all those photoshopped images of her living her very best life, there's a profile that tells a now-familiar story. A story about how social media exaggerates reality. A story about how competition for likes, mentions, and shares force us to embellish and conceal. A story about how our lives can be shared and reshared around the globe. And a story about how all those images of photogenic perfection make it simply impossible to accept that, in the end, we're just human.

Whenever I visit Sarah's profile, and the great many like it, I think about Essena O'Neill. And then I remember Karen Horney. I wonder what she'd have made of social media. Because no doubt about it, she'd have had plenty to say. I imagine her sitting low in her favorite chair, smoking a cigarette, nursing a large glass of red wine, and cracking a wry smile. You could draw a straight line from her observations of cultural contradictions in the 1950s to the present moment. It's as if she could see social media coming. As if, somehow, she knew this was how a nascent, aggressive consumer culture would eventually shake itself out.

Even so, she'd surely marvel at social media's absolute power. She'd say social media presents us with the age-old dilemma of never enough—but puts it on a level far beyond anything we've ever seen before. The platforms, which are addictive by design, invite us to measure ourselves against the impossible criteria of perfection. And they do so in the most manipulative way possible, by making us putty in the hands of advertisers.

If she were alive today, Karen Horney would've made us feel less weird about this moment. She'd have taught us how social media platforms prey on our imagined imperfections, how they make us question ourselves, and how they cynically divide us with inner conflict. She'd help us feel less alone, too, by teaching us that the reason we feel never enough inside social media is the same reason we feel never enough outside of it. There's our economy's morbid dependency on competition and growth, and there's the all-channels social persuasion—advertising—which brings that competition and growth into being on the backs of our discontent.

We have plenty of evidence for this, and I've presented quite a bit of it in the last two chapters. But we mustn't stop here. If we really want to understand why perfectionism—and socially prescribed perfectionism in particular—is rising so rapidly, we'll need to spread our gaze wider than advertising. Because a supply-side economy not only requires us to question what we have, and how we look, but also, as well, to question whether we're doing enough to merit our place in the social pecking order.

CHAPTER NINE

You Just Haven't Earned It Yet
Or How Meritocracy Has Set a Standard of Perfection in School and College

"Perfectionism is the emblematic meritocratic malady."
Michael Sandel[1]

Where I come from, it's rare for kids to make it to the academic elite. Or any elite, for that matter. According to the UK government's Social Mobility Commission, just one local authority in the whole of the UK has worse social mobility than Wellingborough.[2] Policy makers call my hometown a "cold spot." Which I suppose is a polite way of saying, "If you're born here: good luck!"

You don't really need a fancy commission to tell you this. Most of the kids I went to school with, and I include myself in this, were not especially ambitious in an academic sense. Not because we weren't smart or resourceful, but because we could see the evidence of our eyes and ears: the prefabricated school building being ground into disrepair, burned-out teachers so exhausted they spend entire classes simply reading textbooks verbatim to blank-faced students, parents with no time or energy to help with studying or homework.

None of those things injects you with enthusiasm for studying. Few of my school friends went to university; most moved straight into the world of work. If I were to guess, I'd say perhaps one, maybe two others in my entire high school class of two hundred have a master's degree.

Real expertise, so it's said around here, is acquired from the school of life. Partying till the small hours at Club Life, then manning a checkout at 8:00 a.m.; drilling holes through the water pipe and plugging it with grout; or getting deafened by a chorus of *Wheeeeey*s after tripping arse-over-tit on the scaffolding. It's not learned from the pages of a dusty textbook, and certainly not from the high-minded thoughts of a bearded professor. Ask Sarah, Kevin, Ian, or anyone else I went to school with why they didn't go and get a degree, and these are among the reasons they'll undoubtedly recite.

Deep down, much of me agrees with them. We working folk have a built-in antipathy toward the well-educated. The moral judgment of modern society is that those at the top deserve their position, and those at the top are almost always well educated. Every time our betters tell us that we just need more schooling, what they're really saying is: your struggles are not our failures, they're yours. "If you don't have a good education," Barack Obama once told students at a New York high school, "it's going to be hard for you to find a job that pays a living wage."[3]

Britain's own liberal pinup, Tony Blair, had a similar message: "Education, education, education!" And to be fair to both him and Obama, these men backed up their rhetoric with some pretty hefty investment. I'd never once considered university until Blair's great education thrust presented itself in the form of various incentives to keep studying. They've been cut away now, along with most other forms of social support under that most suspect of guises: austerity. So I guess you could say I was one of the lucky ones. Despite the terrible grades I made back then, and despite no college fund or parental support to draw upon, I could still take up a place at the nearest teacher-training college.

And for that, I was over the moon.

I'm not so sure I'd be able to make the same choice now. In fact, I'm quite certain that if I were born in the 1990s or 2000s, I wouldn't have made it as far as I have. These days, fewer than 2 percent of graduates from families in the bottom fifth of the income distribution end up ascending to the top fifth of the income scale.[4] Granted, that's an ambitious leap—but even smaller climbs are rare. In a recent study, just one in ten working-class graduates were found to have risen more than a quintile on the social ladder.[5] These statistics sit alongside a broader trend of downward mobility among all graduates, and young people more generally, who must study for longer, work harder, and earn more money than their parents just to have the same standard of life.

In the land of the American Dream, poor Americans must climb a social ladder with one of the lowest rates of upward mobility of any developed country.

"No matter what your educational background is," American economists Michael Carr and Emily Wiemers told the *Atlantic*, "where you start has become increasingly important for where you end." Using data from the US Census Bureau's Survey of Income and Program Participation, Carr and Wiemers showed that, in recent years, the general amount of social movement among young people is in reverse. "The probability of ending where you start has gone up," Carr said, "and the probability of moving up from where you start has gone down."[6]

We're told to work hard at school. But we're rarely told why, in 2023, an undergraduate degree feels like the new high school diploma. Or why, outside of the Russell Group and Ivy League, education offers increasingly little to young people who study diligently and still find, once they graduate, that there are simply no jobs out there or that the jobs that do exist are insecure and poorly paid. It's a confusing discovery. And it's made even more confusing by the prevailing logic that says education is the great social leveler—the majestic cruise liner—which will carry all who buy a ticket safely across the gulf of class.

Maybe it was different in the past. Maybe education really *was* the escape hatch out of hardship. I don't know. What I do know is that nowadays the prevailing logic underneath the great education thrust feels increasingly difficult to square against cold, hard reality. Because in any distribution of income, particularly our highly skewed one, there can only ever be one top percentile. And most won't be in it. So if you don't increase wages across the board—and the average American's real wage has about the same purchasing power it did forty years ago[7]—then all you're doing by churning out more and more indebted graduates is stuffing them into the squeezed middle and slicing their share of the college premium thinner and thinner.

I was in my final year of college when I finally figured that out. I could feel the pinch as my landlord jacked up the rent for the second time in as many years. I browsed recruitment websites and read the criteria for entry-level jobs in bewilderment. And I watched in horror as the debt I was accruing spiraled upward, and just kept on going.

At which point it hit me: *I'm going to need to work hard in this world just to maintain the modest standard of life I already have.* And I also realized something else: if I want to climb the social ladder, I won't just have to lift myself above people way smarter and far more privileged, I'm also going to have to lift myself above an economy ill-equipped to accommodate the number of graduates it produces. Life's one big race, and I felt already defeated.

If I'd had like-minded friends to share these feelings with, they might not have been such a handicap. But living in a competitive world, in the hypercompetitive amphitheater that is the modern university—not wanting my background to define me—and feeling generally inferior to everyone else, I could only develop an urgent need to secure my future by striving after better-than-average grades. Psychologists call this single-mindedness "identity foreclosure," which happens when we're completely fixated on narrow goals imposed by strict pressures in the outside world. As my own identity foreclosed around academic metrics, my entire self-worth became tied to how strenuously I could strive for them.

That's a completely draining way to live. But with a fair wind, it can propel you quite far. After excelling in my undergraduate degree, I went on to write a master's thesis in sport psychology before making it into the doctorate program at the University of Leeds. There, I continued to justify myself with the currency of work ethic. This was a period of my life when I wasn't really in the driver's seat, so to speak. I was a passenger in a speeding vehicle meant to turn me into a perfect student.

I was defensive and confused. I didn't know who I was or what I truly wanted. Why was I here, of all places? Was I still the kid from Wellingborough, penniless and late to mature, cupping my hands on car windshields and bursting with excitement at the sight of a glowing start switch? Or was I a chin-stroking, cardigan-wearing intellectual who'd begun attending seminars on structural equation modeling? I knew in my bones that I wasn't who I was trying to be. But I also knew that if I was going to survive a toxically competitive culture that celebrates overachievement and credentialized success, I had to fake it to "make it."

In that period of my life, the guilt and shame of not working enough was suffocating. And it made me do absolutely everything I could to ensure that every waking hour was spent reading, writing, and studying. As soon as I began my PhD, I made sure I was the first in the office and the last to leave. I regularly did eighty-hour weeks and let everyone know about it. I sent conspicuous emails to my supervisors in the early hours of the morning and last thing at night. I wrote a thousand words of my thesis on Christmas Day and was rather proud of it.

Wrapped in an obsessive need to excel, I left a trail of destruction. I moved myself away from people, became irritable, and hyperaware of other students' successes and failures. The social disconnection on top of the self-imposed pressure did silent damage to my mental and physical health. That damage gave way to a low-level depression that would later explode into generalized panic.

Rather like a sleeping volcano being suddenly awakened, my dormant perfectionism took it's time to finally erupt. But right there, trying to survive the selective hotbed that is the elite university, with heartache and life stress going on in the background, and a paralyzing sense of inferiority accompanying me everywhere I went, I was unquestionably a fully-fledged, card-carrying perfectionist.

And in one way or another, I'll spend the rest of my life living with the consequences.

We must overconsume and overwork, everywhere and all the time, because we live in an economy that depends on superheated growth. The upshot of that imperative, as we explored in chapter 7, is an unrelenting blitz of cultural conditioning in which every flat-screen TV, smartphone, billboard, and poster tells us that life's one big party, there's a product for everything, and your life can always be upgraded and made more perfect.

What I didn't mention, however, is that tucked away in the small print on the flip side of that party's invitation is one important clause: nothing comes for free. The balance must be cleared. Yes, you can and should have it all, in perpetuity, and with no limits. But goddamnit, you've first got to "make it" and earn your right to pay for it.

Work ethic, competitiveness, and personal agency—these are the foundational belief systems upon which supply-side economics depends. With them writ large, so the theory goes, we get a tidal wave of economic activity and, with it, a continual flow of better and cheaper products and services. This is also morally correct because the difference between surfing and drowning in that tidal wave depends on the individual. If you're poor, down on your luck, worn-out, or just feeling a bit low, that's your fault—your responsibility to fix. Everybody is accountable for themselves, and they're free to have anything they want, be anybody they want, so long as they work hard enough.

Now some believe that young people aren't aware of modern society's hard-work clause. Or, to be more exact, that they haven't been made aware of it by coddling parents, teachers, and professors, who shield them from the slightest inconvenience or discomfort. Such a belief isn't without evidence. As finals approach and pressures ratchet up on my stressed-out students, it's not completely unheard of to get the odd email from a parent asking me to give their delicate petal an extension this one last time.

But that's far from widespread. In fact, in my experience, those kinds of requests are actually rather rare. Most young people are acutely aware of the hard-work clause. And they're made aware of it because we live in a culture that dresses success and failure—high class and low class—in the moral fabric of merit.

Under this regime, which we call a meritocracy, you're expected to always prove yourself a someone of worth. The rules are quite clear, and they're mercilessly drilled into you from childhood. Work hard, amass a tranche of credentials, preferably academic certificates, degrees, accreditations, and so on, and then sell them in the job market for the maximum possible price. The higher the value of your credentials, the more money you make, and the more money you make, the shinier new things you can buy to mark your status.

To the best and brightest go the spoils—now, who could argue with that? And I suppose, for well-to-do, educated professionals like myself, meritocracy very much feels right and fair, granting us, as it does, all sorts of juicy rewards and fancy statuses. But not everybody ends up on the winning team. In fact, as the apex of society narrows, most will lose out. And for those "left behind," as we euphemistically call them, meritocracy's repercussions are rather different. They include, among other indignities, having your pay cut year after year, drowning in debt, losing your tenancy, or surviving on minimum wage.

"To the injury of struggle," writes philosopher Alain de Botton, meritocracy adds "the insult of shame."[8]

But here's the thing: it's not real. All of that shame is summoned in pursuit of a sham. Rather than a vehicle for social mobility, meritocracy is actually just a social pacifier; a neutering agent, one that staves off a full-throttle class revolt by sanitizing what would otherwise be grotesque gaps between the rich and everyone else.

Here's how that works. The elite can stand on the winner's podium and spray champagne into each other's faces on account of their wealth and status. They own and earn more because they *deserve* more. By the same token, the just-deserts defense means they can also pretend they had no role in loading bowling balls onto the scales of wealth and power in their favor. We live in a meritocracy; the elite earned their spot at the top table. And they can damn well make certain that their offspring sit right next to them, feasting from the same bounty, while an undeserving majority fight among each other for the scraps.

According to Oxfam, about a third of elite wealth comes from inheritance. Another third comes from connections to government. And most of the rest comes from skimming rents from assets—commodities, financial instruments, property, and so on.[9] Money, quite literally, breeds money.

The undeserving majority, for our part, will swallow a doctrine that calls encased privilege "merit," so long as it provides a grand narrative that tickles the temporarily embarrassed billionaire within us. One day, we tell ourselves, the hard work will pay off. We live in a meritocracy; you can earn your spot at the top table if you try. We're not coddled and we're certainly not work-shy. If we're complaining, it's probably because we're figuring out the sham, and wondering why we've put so much of ourselves into a rigged economy that's giving us less and less back.

Soon, meritocracy will run out of real-world evidence to defy, and more and more of us will start to see it for the inequality smoke screen that it really is. In fact, the ripples of social unrest reverberating around the West—Brexit, Trump, Le Pen, Meloni, and so on—suggest that's already happening.

Yet more urgent than social unrest is the untold damage meritocracy is doing to our psychology. Because that damage affects everyone, including—perhaps especially—the better-off. Comforting stories about how you can lift yourself up by your bootstraps undoubtedly make for rousing speech fodder. But their narrative arcs only bend to a satisfactory end point if people can see and experience opportunities to ascend. Otherwise, those stories might as well be cruel jokes played on a new generation who're waking up to the fact that they're the punch line.

For the first time in living memory, young people are downwardly mobile. Under its top-heavy weight, their economy teeters on the brink of collapse, government is out of the picture, and there are fewer opportunities out there, with more obligations—particularly debt. Against this background, meritocracy seriously backfires. Because rather than liberating us to rise up the social ladder, it traps us in a breathless state of relentless striving, pursuing an idealized standard of life that's getting more and more impossible to attain.

★   ★   ★

Before we get into meritocracy's relationship with perfectionism, I should clear one thing up. Although very much in the grip of advertising's perfectionistic fantasies, the people I grew up with, people like Sarah, Ian, and Kevin, are not, as a rule, gravely wounded by meritocratic pressure. Indirectly, perhaps, since they can be looked down on by a certain type of professional for not having the wherewithal to get a degree. But when it comes to the full-throttle academic sorting machine, they're largely spared the more aggressive excesses of meritocracy's toxic competition. The people most affected by that are the descendants of the well-educated and wealthy who primarily come from the middle and upper echelons of society.

I know this because I myself experienced the full force of meritocratic pressure as soon as I grew away from the working-class community in which I was raised. In the course of my journey between leaving Wellingborough and landing at the London School of Economics (LSE), age thirty, as a moderately successful prof, I've become a fully paid-up member of the credentialized middle class. And what I've witnessed from this outpost has shocked me. The young people I teach, most of whom are from affluent families, experience intolerable pressures to excel, which start almost as soon as they're out of the cradle. By the time they meet me, they truly believe that meritocracy is akin to natural selection, and that belief is only reinforced when they make it to a top-ranking university and mix with the very best of the best.

But "making it" is just about all they're doing. In 2018, an American charity called the Robert Wood Johnson Foundation did an audit of youth well-being.[10] Against a backdrop of rising mental illness, they wanted to know the most pressing factors that were continuing to undermine young people's health and happiness. The typical things we associate with disadvantage invariably cropped up, like poverty, trauma, and discrimination. But there was another risk to young people that researchers saw over and over again, one that this time afflicted more advantaged youth.

That risk? Excessive pressure to excel.

For young people in education, of course, this means pressure to excel in school. In America's big-city schools, over one hundred tests are administered between prekindergarten and the end of twelfth grade.[11] And just in case that isn't enough pressure, some school administrators make the test results public and openly viewable online for young people and their parents to compare.[12] Talk about toxic competition. Almost from the moment they pass through the school gates, young people are exposed to unrelenting assessment pressures that invite performance anxiety, rivalry, and a general dependency on metrics for their self-worth.

To ensure students make the grade, teachers routinely ask them to do anywhere between two and four hours of homework a night. Five hours, in some US districts, isn't unheard of.[13] Teachers prescribe this amount because (1) students need it, (2) parents demand it, and (3) schools are judged on their college acceptance rates. If teachers don't push their students, they risk losing spots at elite colleges, which isn't just a bad look for them; it's a bad look for the school, too.

Never have the stakes been higher than they are today. Over the past two decades, the average elite college admission rate has plunged from 30 percent to less than 7 percent of all applicants.[14] About 75 percent of high school students, and around half of middle school students, say they often or always feel stressed by schoolwork. More than two-thirds say they are often or always worried about getting into their preferred college.[15]

This stress is echoed in research conducted by American psychologist Suniya Luthar. Her surveys find that school pressures create emotional distress and that this distress is found most acutely in more affluent teens—the ones who're most aggressively primed for elite colleges.[16] She's also observed that these teens show higher rates of drug and alcohol abuse than less-advantaged contemporaries and suffer depression and anxiety at rates of up to triple those of matched peers. Sociologist Daniel Markovits puts their predicament plainly: "Where aristocratic children once reveled in their privilege, meritocratic children now calculate their futures—they plan and they trim, through rituals of stage-managed self-presentation, in familiar rhythms of ambition, hope, and worry."[17]

Socially prescribed perfectionism is rather emblematic of this meritocratic malaise. Via endless assessments and tests, and a knock-on process of very public sifting, sorting, and ranking, young people are being taught to understand that the excessive pressures built into meritocracy are simply the natural order of things. Whether they like it or not, they must continually benchmark themselves against others, and understand that there's always more studying to do, higher goals to set themselves, and extraordinary grades to shoot for. That culture of excellence makes you reliant on the outcomes of your striving, and, ultimately, it means you come to define yourself in the very strict and narrow terms of straight As and nothing but straight As.

Research seems to support the idea that recent generations are increasingly benchmarking themselves against perfection. For example, a 2017 survey of Canadian youth found that 55 percent of elementary school students and 62 percent of high schoolers said they needed to be perfect in their schoolwork.[18] Another Canadian study by psychologist Tracey Vaillancourt went further. She tracked high school students' levels of perfectionism over six years and found that about two-thirds of students have at least moderate levels of self-oriented and socially prescribed perfectionism. Those levels are high enough, but Vaillancourt's data shows that they go even higher as students move toward the critical phase of college selection.[19]

The conclusion we must take from this data is that the school system is teaching young people that perfect grades are not only desirable but absolutely necessary if you want to make the college cut.

By the time these remarkable young people reach me at university, they've survived the school sorting machine. But they've emerged stunned, wounded winners. They vibrate tension like a tightly coiled spring and their deep-rooted fears of failure are just as visible as their eclectic fashion choices. If they were hoping for some respite, they're about to be bitterly disappointed. All the grading, sifting, ranking, competing, and comparing they've endured in their prior school years doesn't magically disappear once they step foot on campus. It ratchets up.

"Having fomented and rewarded achievement mania by their admission policies," American philosopher Michael Sandel writes in his book *The Tyranny of Merit*, "elite colleges do little to dial it back."[20] On the contrary, they positively boast about it. Student organizations, school administrators, departments, and even faculty sing about low acceptance rates. My university's undergraduate prospectus advertises it matter-of-factly. "LSE is a highly competitive institution," it reads. "In 2021, we received approximately 26,000 applications for roughly 1,700 places. This fierce competition means that every year we unfortunately have to disappoint many applicants."

Unintentional though it may be, such hubris trickles down. And it creates a curious campus culture whereby students feel compelled to give the impression they're smashing it effortlessly, even though, behind closed doors, they're working like crazy. And not just at LSE. Talk to any professor, counselor, or college administrator at any other elite institution and they'll tell you the same story. A recent study at Duke University, for instance, found that students felt pressure to be "effortlessly perfect"; that is, smart, fit, cool, attractive, and popular—all without breaking a sweat.[21] At Stanford, they call this facade "Duck Syndrome," because a duck always appears to glide serenely over water, while underneath, it frantically paddles.

The cause of all that frantic paddling is almost always anxiety about grades. This worry is a hangover from intensive school testing, but it gets worse at university. Here, the pool of competitors is not simply the people you grew up with—it's a bunch of elite overachievers who're concentrated at the upper end of the academic distribution. Everyone's exceptional, so everyone's acing their tests. And since there's no escape, the general aura of exceptionality creates a pressure-cooker atmosphere where even objectively high grades can feel decidedly disappointing.

If an alien descended to earth from the planet Zog and was tasked with designing a clearinghouse to churn out perfectionists, they'd be hard-pressed to design a better one than the modern-day university. The data we discussed in chapter 5 shows exactly the extent to which college students are feeling the social pressure to be perfect. But we don't need data to see this. Students ooze perfectionistic concerns from their pores. Some of my students are so paralyzed by anxiety that they can't even bring themselves to open their report cards for fear that one bad result will ruin their dreams of a perfect future.

As far as I can tell, elite colleges are not showing much effectiveness in dealing with the immense pressures felt by their students. Many institutions furiously pour water on the hottest pressure points, but can't put out the fire. A recent UCLA survey of freshmen found that the proportion of students who feel overwhelmed has soared by more than 60 percent since the mid-1980s.[22] Another survey by the American College Health Association found that university students reporting overwhelming anxiety rose from 50 percent in 2011 to 62 percent five years later.[23]

In the UK, we have similar problems. Recent research by the Mental Health Foundation found that a staggering 74 percent of eighteen- to twenty-four-year-olds feel overwhelmed, unable to cope with pressures from their outside environment.[24] UK universities, like those in the US, are experiencing increases in students dropping out.[25] And for those who simply want to take a break, stress is exacerbated by policies that make reenrollment unnecessarily difficult (not to mention costly). Perfectionism isn't just embedded in the principles and practices of the modern-day university, it's etched into the mindscape of a student body that must attempt to navigate the deeply embedded cultures of exceptionalism, fear of failure, and toxic competition.

It's tempting to tell young people to dial back the pressure, to forget about the grades and focus on their development and growth. Those are indeed useful pieces of advice. But inside an education system where exceptional grades are all-important—quite literally the difference in life chances—telling young people to dial it back a bit is like asking someone who's taken a fastball in the nuts to ease up on the profanities. There's simply no other action to take: students must strive relentlessly and with ever more tension just to stand still (never mind succeed). What they need isn't instruction on how to navigate overwhelming pressure to excel with more grit, resilience, or growth mindset. What they need is to be educated under a different set of rules altogether.

And despite everything I've just said, those rules should absolutely be rooted in meritocracy. A diverse, lively, and flourishing society requires a path for each and every young person's skills, talents, and ingenuities to blossom. But that's not what we've got, is it? We've got a Darwinian-style *Hunger Games* for the affluent, and the great American Dream™ Trojan horse rolling in behind for everyone else. Rather than that sham meritocracy, we could have a true meritocracy, in which every child has the freedom to be well-educated and choose for themselves a meaningful path in life—whatever that might be.

Schooling under that more enlightened set of rules wouldn't be there to sort, sift, and rank us for the marketplace, but rather to give us all—no matter our starting point—the tools to live dignified and responsible lives of our own choosing. For this to happen, every school needs to be adequately resourced, and teachers must be paid fairly, so they can provide an excellent standard of education across the board. The focus should be on development, exploration, and learning, and it must reduce the exam burden to avoid specious definitions of excellence, like grades, sets, and rankings, impacting the way children view themselves—especially in the early years.

Finland has a model of what this kind of schooling looks like. Finnish children don't begin formal learning until they're seven. Before then, in kindergarten, they're allowed to just play, explore, and create. When they get to high school, Finns spend half as many hours in the classroom as American students. They get fifteen minutes of recess every hour. They have zero standardized tests except for the reading, mathematics, and science PISA assessments. And yet, despite that, they still outperform American students on every single metric.[26]

Finland is evidence, if evidence were needed, that schooling doesn't have to be a hotbed for perfectionism. It can be far less all-consuming, stripped of all but the most essential tests, and still equip children with the skills they need to make meaningful contributions to their society.

This structural focus on learning and development over outcomes and metrics must also extend to universities. The modern university measures absolutely everything: entry fees, student attendance, grades, both formative and summative, student to staff ratios, teaching scores, student satisfaction, student spend, research output, research quality, impact, and diversity. In recent years, there's even been a trend to base university rankings, in large part, on the salaries that graduates can command. It's got to stop. Universities are not soccer teams jostling for league position. They're institutions of education. They exist to create, transfer, and share knowledge. And access to that knowledge should be a fundamental right, meaning free, as it is in Europe.

There also needs to be far more access and far less pressure. Admission should be less competitive and the experience less all-consuming, even at the "elite" schools and universities. In expanding enrollment, institutions must broaden their intake so that no student is displaced as the numbers in lecture halls rise. That might sound costly to finance. But it's important to view these expansions as an investment, not a drain. Spending on widening opportunities for education more than pays for itself over the long run through the contributions to society made by well-educated people.

Indeed, a well-educated population at every level of the social strata is a thriving one. The more brilliance and diversity a society has in art, science, thought, and vocation—in its philosophers and chemists; its painters, engineers, and builders; its computer programmers and teachers—the brighter its tapestry. Marketize education, neglect it, or worse, make it only for those who can afford to pay, and everyone suffers. Higher education, in so many ways, is the ultimate social leveler. And if we manage it correctly, we can have a broad-based meritocracy that doesn't put unrelenting pressures to excel on the students fortunate enough to "make it"—pressures that ratchet up the higher they go.

The entire sector, in other words, requires a root-and-branch make-over so that you don't have to be extraordinary or rich to get special treatment. When education institutions are stable and properly funded, each and every student gains control over their lives and control over the outcomes of the decisions they make. That control provides a platform from which to find meaning in life and to develop our gifts in ways that are true to ourselves and most useful to others and society as a whole. Put simply: education in a true meritocracy doesn't require young people to be perfect. It only asks that they have a passion and free-ranging curiosity to take them in a forward direction, toward goals that are truly theirs to decide.

★   ★   ★

Whenever I see my students struggle with pressures to excel, I see myself. I see their carefully concealed frenetic paddling because I did that. I feel their crushing requirement to churn out higher-than-average metrics because I felt that. And I can relate to their desperate attempts to secure a better future by lifting themselves above others because that was my motivation, too. Every student who knocks on my door gets an empathic ear. But empathy is not enough.

Young people emerge from school primed with pressures to excel. And they arrive at college only to have those pressures amplified by intense competition and a culture of rugged exceptionalism. Some say that's a perfect storm for perfectionism, self-image related disorders, and mental distress.[27, 28, 29] I think it's worse than that. A storm suggests we can see the danger coming, or at least know when we're in the eye of it. Meritocracy is different because it has this all-pervasive, ubiquitous reinforcement from our culture, which means that its wrecking power is largely concealed from its sufferers, who are, paradoxically, also its most ardent disciples.

Try to imagine a president or prime minister who doesn't seem in a state of ecstasy talking about meritocracy. Our journalists, political commentators, and economists praise it. Our business leaders and sports stars credit their successes to it. Entire films and television series are made about it. And out there in cupcake suburbia, parents are drinking from the meritocratic cup, which is why they so enthusiastically pack their kids off to college.

Part of the endurance of this folklore is that it cuts across all classes. Meritocracy is a grand narrative that basically says we're a collection of freedom-loving individuals, with the implication that, no matter where you start in life, you can be the next Jeff Bezos or Richard Branson if you try. There isn't inequality, only individuals competing with one another, and some have done better than others because they've worked harder.

Deep down, we know that's not true. But we can't commit the blasphemy of admitting the game's rigged. That in the grand scheme of things, your work ethic might not matter much these days; that if you're young, poor, and with no intergenerational wealth to call on, it might not matter at all. And we can't admit to those realities because doing so would look absolutely terrible for the system and all the many influential people who continue to champion it.

So to preserve meritocracy's image, it's vital that we keep up the pretense that my high school classmate Conor, who was raised by an alcoholic single mother in half a subsidized house on the most violent estate in town, has an equal chance in life as expensively educated George, who was bought every advantage money can buy and is tutored evenings and weekends for the highest possible grades.

And we're keeping up that pretense rather well. Because despite the widening opportunity gaps that exist in modern society, despite every indicator of social mobility pointing in the opposite direction, the proportion of people who *still* believe hard work determines success has risen by more than 10 percent since the 2008 financial crisis.[30]

It's not that we aren't angry about our efforts being met with deteriorating living standards. It's just that we're conditioned to deflect frustrations with the system onto frustrations with ourselves, so that the real culprit, inequality, can remain safely concealed behind meritocratic mythology.

Meritocracy is dangerous precisely because it isn't a storm. It's a mirage, and we run headlong into it wide-eyed and clapping with glee.

One final caveat, since it's important. When I say meritocracy puts the heaviest burden of perfectionism on those in the middle and upper echelons of society, I'm speaking of course in the aggregate. These people make up the vast majority of elite college intake (around 95 percent, to be exact). Few, if any at all, are able to truly escape meritocratic pressures to be perfect. But that doesn't mean people from poorer communities aren't also affected. Indeed, about 5 percent of the annual Russell Group intake comes from poor families (2 percent for Oxford and Cambridge).[31] And although small in number, these talented souls arrive on the hallowed campuses to take up the meritocratic challenge alongside everyone else.

However, they're hugely exposed. Not only must they run the same loaded race as everyone else, but they've also got far fewer resources to draw on and many more obstacles to overcome. Even if they do manage to navigate it all successfully, they still have an uphill task, since working-class professionals are paid, on average, about sixteen percent less than their contemporaries *in the same jobs*.[32] Over time, both of those things—overstriving and still feeling defeated—take a psychological toll. Certainly, my own struggles with perfectionism stem in large part from a need to overachieve, in compensation for social and economic forces that are working against me around the clock.[33]

And here's the thing: as poor kids go, I'm relatively privileged. I'm a millennial. If I were a member of Generation Z, my financial future would seem more uncertain. According to Deloitte's Global 2022 Gen Z and Millennial Survey, a third of Gen Zs are worried about the cost of living above every other concern, 45 percent of them live paycheck to paycheck, and over a quarter doubt they'll be able to retire comfortably.[34] Those are gloomy numbers. But just look at the state of our economy and tell them that pessimism isn't warranted.

I'm also a white, heterosexual male, and a British and Irish citizen with no life-altering medical or disability issues. None of which makes me extraordinary; I just had the great good fortune to be able to make sacrifices and do all that overstriving without anyone, or anything, holding me back. For under-represented groups, people with disabilities, and women from poor backgrounds, the gulf they must bridge is wider still and littered with all sorts of additional obstacles, such as discrimination, caregiving obligations, and stereotype threats.

A rigged meritocracy, much like this one, makes life uncertain and insecure for all people. But it's even more uncertain and insecure for those who start the race furthest behind.

Meritocracy makes life incredibly tough for all people who take on the challenge of making it in modern society. But it's even tougher for those who are poor, or queer, or disabled, or aren't white.

I suppose I would sum it up like this. When the educated professional meritocrats took over the liberal parties around the early nineties, and that distinctly meritocratic brand of inequality started really lifting off, it was quietly understood that this system would cause misery and despair for those it "left behind." They were the undeserving lower orders whose struggles were an unflattering reflection of their lack of smarts, or laziness, or both.

That such people happened to be disproportionately from underprivileged and minority backgrounds was unfortunate for the meritocrats, who cried big tears of sympathy. But those tears never extended to doing something genuinely meaningful to address such structural inequities because that would mean tearing down the ring-fenced gates of opportunity, letting other people share in the nation's prosperity, and, in doing so, tacitly admitting to their own role in the meritocratic sham. So instead of doing that, their response, instead, was to throw a few grants at gifted kids from poor backgrounds and call it a level playing field.

So here we are; an army of well-off kids and a smattering of poor kids jostling for elite positions in the great modern meritocracy. It's tempting to view this state of affairs as extraordinarily self-serving for the victorious meritocrats. And, of course, it very much *is* self-serving. But what they didn't envisage, what they couldn't possibly see coming, was that their meritocracy would ultimately cause misery and despair for them and their offspring, too.

No one wins. Everyone loses compared to what life could be in a fairer society, under a true meritocracy.

Young people who get up the courage to point this out are often maligned as fragile snowflakes. Journalists, politicians, and even certain professors line up to label them mollycoddled, overindulged, and work-shy. I think these are cruel and disingenuous slurs committed by people who frankly should know better. Students and young workers slogging forward under meritocracy's yoke aren't snowflakes. They're brave but battle-scarred survivors of a hyper-competitive society, with its unnecessarily brutal sorting machine, which is pressurizing them to bursting point.

Sooner rather than later, we're going to need to face up to that fact. We're going to need to recognize that the impossible expectations meritocracy is building into schools, universities, and the wider economy are overwhelming young people and luring them helplessly into the tentacles of perfectionism. And we're going to need to ask ourselves: How much more of this are we prepared to put our children through?

The education system is indeed the most influential channel through which the gospel of meritocracy is passed on to young people. But it's not the only channel. Parents preach the good news, too. And that leads me to something else we haven't discussed yet: What exactly is the role of parents in all of this?

CHAPTER TEN

Perfectionism Begins at Home
Or How Pressure to Raise Exceptional Kids Affects How We Parent

> *"The child does not meet society directly at first, they meet it through the medium of their parents, who in their character structure and methods of education . . . are the psychological agents of society."*
> **Erich Fromm[1]**

The FBI called their investigation "Operation Varsity Blues." A multiyear, coast-to-coast probe, it exposed a sophisticated network of America's super-elite—celebrities, CEOs, financiers, and lawyers—who'd conspired to fix their children's admission to Ivy League colleges. Californian entrepreneur William Rick Singer masterminded the racket. Wealthy parents paid Singer anywhere between tens of thousands and millions of dollars to guarantee an elite college placement for their offspring.

Singer's scheme was elaborate. He first set up a charity to hide the money his clients paid him, and then made good on his guarantees by concocting two frauds. One involved straightforwardly paying surrogate exam takers to take college entrance exams. The other involved befriending and paying off college administrators and sports coaches to recruit his clients' kids onto varsity teams. It was the perfect ruse for a society knee-deep in meritocratic inequality. The frauds Singer perpetuated secured Ivy League access for the already superrich, but they did so while creating the all-important impression that his clients' children made it under their own steam.

In 2019, as the FBI began to unveil the true extent of Singer's operation, attention invariably turned to the parents. Their actions scandalized a public who'd themselves spent enormous amounts of anxious energy worrying about their children's chances of making it to the Ivy League. Journalists thrust cameras in the offending parents' faces. Netflix even produced an award-winning serialization of the entire affair. "They're criminals!" headlines roared. "How entitled can you be?" news anchors asked.

Certainly, those headlines are warranted. But again, you'll notice how conveniently laser-focused they are. While everyone's busy pointing at the culprits, the reasons Singer's services existed in the first place go largely overlooked. And I'm not sure there's a more illustrative example of how meritocratic pressures have warped all sense of perspective than "Varsity Blues." The scandal highlighted many societal fractures, but perhaps most vividly, it exposed the high watermark of parental hyperventilation in a lopsided economy fixated only on money and merit.

When Judith Harris, the trailblazing child development theorist, said that parents don't matter, she didn't mean they don't matter. She meant they don't matter in the way we think they matter. The values parents communicate can powerfully shape the type of people their children become, but that doesn't mean those values are theirs in the first place. Parents are rather like society's psychological agents—acting as intermediaries to pass on its dominant values through the ways in which they raise their offspring.

And no prizes for guessing the psychological agents of meritocratic culture: helicopter parents. These are mothers and fathers who're hyperpresent in their children's lives, especially when it comes to education. They direct and redirect, push and pull in an anxious, nagging, assertive way, leaving little to no opportunity for the child to pursue individual interests. The parental labor involved in helicoptering is often tireless. Its aim? To ensure their child's success in a highly competitive meritocracy.

The rise of helicopter parenting can be evidenced in many ways. But perhaps the most visible signs are shifting parental priorities and values. Between 1995 and 2011, for example, the importance American parents placed on hard work as something they wanted their children to display increased by almost 40 percent. And it's clear where that hard work should be channeled: education. Since the mid-1970s, the time parents have spent doing schoolwork with their children has increased by a staggering five hours a week.[2]

More time allocated to schooling invariably comes at the expense of other activities. The amount of time American children spend playing with their parents has decreased by 25 percent since the early eighties.[3] And since the early nineties, US parents have reallocated over nine hours per week from play to nonplay activities, such as studying for tests or doing homework.[4] The underlying message broadcast to any child with a halfway decent antenna is that some activities are worthy of parental time (schoolwork), whereas others are not (play).

Not surprisingly, these changing values have sprung up in a tumultuous period in which educational pressures are rising rapidly. A recent survey of over ten thousand US college students conducted partway through the COVID-19 pandemic found that young people reported far more stress about school than before the pandemic. Students cited grades, workload, time management, lack of sleep, and college fears as triggers. But the biggest source of stress, according to young people, was their parents' achievement expectations. Fifty-seven percent of young people said that expectations did not drop during the pandemic, while 34 percent said they actually increased.[5]

Economists Garey and Valerie Ramey think that this overparenting is part of a wider "rug rat race." Parents are cracking the whip of work ethic, becoming fixated on educational outcomes, and engaging in more surveillance because they're responding to societal pressures. More and more worrywarts hover anxiously, creating a culture of panic. The Varsity Blues scandal was perhaps the crescendo of this particular echo chamber, which got so out of hand that affluent parents went to criminal lengths to gain an advantage for their already advantaged kids.

Not that this specter is evident everywhere. In other countries like Sweden and Norway, where inequality is low and social mobility high, it's hard to imagine there'd be much demand for Singer's services. Less than 15 percent of parents in those countries, when interviewed, mention hard work as a quality they value. These mothers and fathers would rather leave their kids alone to carve their own paths. Indeed, unlike parents from the US, Canada, or the UK, Swedes and Norwegians give children time to develop their own thoughts, feelings, and interests; exercise their own imagination; and express themselves in whatever ways they see fit.[6]

Helicopter parents may seem normal in countries like the US, Canada, and the UK, but its only under very specific economic conditions that you find helicopter parents in heavy measure. And that's because under those specific conditions, the mania is inevitable and completely understandable. No British or American parent in their right mind would want their child to grow complacent right now. Not when school pressures are rising, not when elite college acceptance rates are plunging,

Thomas Curran

and certainly not when gaping inequalities mean more and more young people are falling behind. Helicopter parenting under these pressures isn't a choice; it's a necessity. Moms and dads hover anxiously to make it clear that success in school is absolutely essential, not because they want to, not even because they think it'll be healthy for their child, but because their better instincts must be suspended for the instincts they learn inside a meritocracy.

What, then, are the consequences of all this helicoptering? And is perfectionism one of them?

★ ★ ★

Children need—and seek—attachment with their parents. But helicopter parents can inadvertently make attachment more difficult for a couple of reasons. First, because helicopter parents tend to be overly concerned with the consequences of failure and, second, because they tend to set standards that are more advanced, and more mature, than their child can comfortably achieve. That kind of parenting subtly communicates to children that they mustn't slip up. And also, at the same time, that they're never quite good enough to win their parents' full, unqualified approval.

Not that all parents are like this, of course. But we do know that, in the aggregate, parental expectations are starting to soar so high that young people are interpreting them as requirements to be perfect. How do we know? Because in a 2022 research paper published in *Psychological Bulletin*, Andy Hill and I documented it in a couple of studies.[7] In the first study, we aggregated correlations between excessive parental expectations—or expectations children cannot meet—and socially prescribed perfectionism to see if there was a link. And in the second study, we retrieved thirty years' worth of American, Canadian, and British college students' perceptions of excessive parental expectations to see if they were increasing over time.

Crunching the numbers, we found that parental expectations were indeed positively correlated with socially prescribed perfectionism, and the correlation was very large indeed. So large, in fact, that almost half of the variance in socially prescribed perfectionism was explained by parental expectations. Positive links with self-oriented and other-oriented perfectionism were also observed, albeit to a lesser degree.

We then strung out thirty years' worth of data on college students' perceptions of parental expectations in much the same way we did for perfectionism in chapter 5. And when we did so, we found that parental expectations were rising sharply. The extent of the rise can be seen in the figure below. In raw units of the measurement scale, there's been an almost 9 percent increase. But that doesn't tell the full story. Because in relative units of birth cohorts, there's been a whopping 40 percent increase, which basically means that today's average college student reports scores of parental expectations that are so high they would've been around the seventieth percentile of scores in 1989.

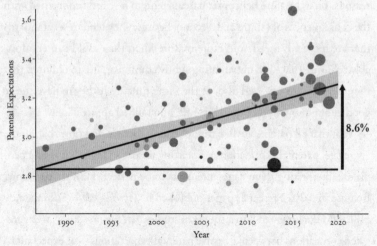

College students' excessive parental expectations scores plotted against the year of data collection.

Note: Black circles are the US data points, light gray Canada, and dark gray the UK. The data points are proportional to the number of students giving their data in each study (more students equals bigger circles), and the best-fitting line for the relationship between parental expectations and time is plotted through them (the gray shaded area around the best-fitting line is the error in the prediction).

It seems plausible, therefore, that increasing parental expectations are likely to be one reason why socially prescribed perfectionism is rising among young people. And I'd like to elaborate a little more on why that's the case. More than advertising, social media, schooling, or college pressures, parents are extremely proximal and directly influential agents of perfectionism. Children will be aware of their parents' expectations, and whether those expectations are perfectionistic, almost from the cradle. As they grow up, repeated exposure to high and excessive expectations will invariably be interpreted as a need to be perfect.

But it's important to state that the problem of excessive expectations goes deeper than simply internalizing parental standards. Childhood is a vulnerable period. Each step a child takes in attempting to make sense of their world is fraught with the risk of criticism or rejection. Even the most unreservedly loved child is sure, at some point, to find themselves painfully exposed when something goes wrong. There's nothing inherently wrong with high expectations; the problem comes when expectations are relentless, too high, and pitched at the extreme of children's ability to meet them.

Parental standards, and by extension parental approval, are always just out of reach for the child under this kind of rearing. If they manage to accomplish something extraordinary like straight-A grades, the parent will be pleased. But in this culture, with meritocratic pressures the way they are, that same parent must still subtly defer full approval and continue urging their child to keep going—to keep "doing better."

That's tough for the child. Because no matter how hard they strive, it's not enough. What the child gets is not acceptance per se, but the promise of eventual acceptance on the condition that they keep reaching ever higher. The helicopter parent, in this respect, keeps their child straining on tiptoe, fearing the consequences of failure, and creating an inadvertent but nonetheless problematic dependency on their parents' elusive approval. When the child falls short, as they invariably will, they'll feel shame because their failure tells them that they're not worthy of their parents' good regard (or anyone's regard, for that matter). And shame is the main reason why excessive expectations are so tightly connected to socially prescribed perfectionism.

Now I should add, since it's important, that in very specific circumstances, for example when a child has knowingly misbehaved, withholding approval is not always a bad thing. After all, the spectacle of overindulged, shameless children is almost as awful as shame-ridden ones. But the withholding of approval that may come in small doses as part of "healthy" parenting manifests in megadoses when parents hitch their approval to standards so high that children can never meet them. It's a tricky line to tread. Small, intermittent, individual doses of disappointment are fine, and almost certainly too innocuous to be problematic. But the cumulative effect of many such disappointments, persistently expressed and stacked one on top of the other, is perfectionism.

We parents are also children inside, and we must remember that. We, like everyone else, live nervously under the watchful eye of a society fixated on money and merit. When we talk about helicoptering, we're simply talking about parents doing their level best to navigate a bad situation in the only way they see possible. If parents really are setting the stage for their children's perfectionism, they're doing it inadvertently, for reasons outside of themselves, and through no fault of their own.

But that doesn't make what's happening any less real. And what's more, it's not likely to stop here. Perfectionism, quite literally, runs in families—first via genes and second via child-rearing strategies. That presents a serious problem, because as young people become more perfectionistic, they're going to raise more perfectionistic children, who'll themselves raise more perfectionistic children. And so on and so on. We have to recognize what's going on here. And we have to do all we can to break the intergenerational cycle.

*　　*　　*

Can we break the cycle? In this culture, at this moment in time, that's a tough question to answer. But research offers some clues. One is to provide a constant source of warmth and protection. The world is a tough place and kids are impressionable creatures. They're bombarded with wayward pressures from advertising, popular culture, social media, and their peers. When they succumb to these pressures, as they invariably will from time to time, let them know, enforce some consequence if needed, but listen to them. Always. Talk openly, acknowledge their emotions, and respond with empathy and understanding. Research shows that this warm approach to parenting is negatively correlated with perfectionism and perfectionistic tendencies in adolescents.[8]

Warm parenting also means avoiding the withholding of affection. So love your children *unconditionally*. Just keep loving them. All the time. Children who say that their parents' love and affection isn't tied to achievement or compliance tend to have low levels of self-oriented and socially prescribed perfectionism.[9] They also report lower self-presentational concerns and are less likely to conceal their imperfections from those around them.[10] That's permission right there to go ahead and tell your kids that they don't need to justify themselves to anyone or anything. They're worthy of your love and affection—they matter in this world—simply because they exist in it.

This also means educating them in the lessons of fallibility that their culture will not. Use setbacks and failures as learning opportunities, which teach kids that life has consequences, that we all fail from time to time, and that failure is nothing to fear. Try not to shield them from uncomfortable situations they're likely to find challenging (but be humane about it). Let them sit with that discomfort, at least for a little while. Remind them that no one is perfect; sometimes, for no good reason, things don't pan out the way we planned, and that's okay. There's always next time. Support them in working through disappointment rather than around it. Help them, but don't try to fix things.

Delight in your kids' quirks and talents. Encourage them to follow their passions, not the passions of the crowd. Avoid indulging their material wants, which will be plenty. Instead, focus their energies on enlivening experiences like reading, playing instruments, or participating in sports. Let them try many new things so they can discover their own path in life, built by their chosen passions. This also involves permitting your child to have input into the big decisions in their lives, such as the schools they attend or the subjects they study. Allow that.

Expectations are fine, even ambitious ones, but work with your child to set them and, above all, make sure they're realistic. If they hit their targets, don't go overboard with raucous applause; just hug them, congratulate them, and praise their efforts (*not* the grade). And if they should fall short? Hug them still, praise their effort, and put things like scores and grades into their proper context, reminding them, all the time, that a test or piece of coursework is just one measure of learning among hundreds of other possible measures. It's not a blotch on their intelligence, it hasn't ruined their life chances, it doesn't determine how highly a teacher thinks of them, or whether their parents are proud. There's enough pressure to be perfect out there, so do everything you possibly can to put setbacks into perspective and create a home environment in which your kids feel comfortable to open up about how they feel when they encounter them.

And finally, parent by example. Show your kids through your own failures that failure is humanizing, not humiliating. Talk openly with them. Let them talk openly with you. Teach them that negative emotions are normal. Be there, always, to support them. Care about the planet and the ecosystem that your child will inherit. Be kind to your surroundings and those close to you. Respect the authority of teachers. If they've had to dish out some consequence for whatever good reason, have their back. Thank them for their commitment to your child's development whenever you see them.

Your children idolize you. Show them why it's important to grow up embracing the joy of their imperfect humanity. Face your own struggles in the way you want them to face theirs: with courage, conviction, and compassion. Do all these things and you'll teach your child that perfection is not necessary to live an active and fulfilling life.

Last week, I rewatched *Operation Varsity Blues*, Netflix's serialization of Rick Singer's college admissions racket. In true Hollywood style, it's a polished, dramatized piece of cinematography that's dripping with jeopardy and suspense. Moody sequences of Singer sitting in his dim-lit home, glaring intently at a computer screen, phone to ear, scheming, are mixed with scenes of affluent clients on the other end of the line who're always somewhere exotic, standing on a veranda, overlooking acres of luscious landscape, and listening intently as Singer explains the intricate details of how their child's going to pose as a mercurial water polo prospect.

It's a fantastic screenplay. And yet, somehow, you can't help but feel it's all a bit straightforward. The director firmly fixes the viewer's gaze on what took place, but facts are just about all we learn. It was an elaborate scam. Singer and his wealthy clients behaved reprehensibly. They were tried, some went to jail. The end.

The convicted families were indeed complicit in a monstrous fraud. And they deserved their fate for effectively stealing elite college spots from less privileged kids. But what *Operation Varsity Blues* fails to tell is the more uncomfortable story about why Singer's racket needed to exist at all. To tell that, the filmmakers would've needed to pan back and ask searching questions about our economy and the society that economy has created.

Of course, this failure to ask the more searching questions is not unique to problems of parenting. The very same stumbling block applies to social media, as we saw in chapter 8. In search of comfortable answers, there's a tendency in modern culture to view a whole host of societal ills—predatory advertising, addictive social media platforms, pressures in school and college, pushy parents, and so on—as a set of unconnected, interesting happenstances, which appear like magic, in a puff of smoke, unbidden among us.

But that can't be true, can it? If you dig deep enough, you'll find that everything is interconnected.

This isn't intuitive, since we're taught to think of the world in terms of individual parts, rather than complex wholes. Indeed, that's how we're taught to think of ourselves—as *individuals.* So naturally, we overlook the intricate relationships that are operating between things. Parents push kids to always do better, work more, and shoot for perfectionistic standards not because they've spontaneously combusted into hovering worrywarts. They push because they're the economy's psychological agents. Just like Kevin and Ian consume as their economy requires them to consume, or social media companies write their algorithms as their economy requires them to write their algorithms, parents parent in the way their economy requires them to parent.

Sure, *Operation Varsity Blues* wouldn't have been the same all-action docudrama had that been the plotline. But nonetheless, it would've got us much closer to the root of the problem.

Karen Horney was perhaps the first to pick away at our impulse to blame neuroses like perfectionism on the people afflicted. Instead, she wanted us to interrogate the societal and cultural conditions into which those neuroses flourished. She was right about that; we just haven't caught up with her. Helicopter parenting isn't a natural, hardwired form of child-rearing—it's the emblematic parenting style of an economy fixated on growth and spellbound by money and merit. It's a cultural phenomenon, in other words. And just like advertising, social media, and overwhelming pressures to excel in school and college, it, too, is contributing to those skyrocketing levels of socially prescribed perfectionism.

And we're not done quite yet. Because there's one last realm of modern culture that's jacking up the volume on our obsession with perfection. A realm most of us—young and old, rich or poor—encounter almost every day: work. So let's talk about our high-octane, modern-day jobs, and the unrelenting culture of hustle that's fast infecting our entire psyche.

CHAPTER ELEVEN

Hustle Is a Six-Letter Word
Or How Insecurity in the Modern Workplace Creates a Reliance on Perfectionism Just to Get By

"At the root of this is the American obsession with self-reliance, which makes it more acceptable to applaud an individual for working himself to death than to argue that an individual working himself to death is evidence of a flawed economic system."

Jia Tolentino[1]

When I lived in Bath, there was a café I loved to go to. Located on the ground floor of a converted Georgian mansion, it was a cozy space tucked away in a shortcut just a stone's throw from the city's famous Royal Crescent. You walked down a set of stone stairs into a bunting-lined basement filled with colorful art and reclaimed items of furniture. Admittedly, it wasn't the most polished of places, and it barely turned a profit, but it was Emma's haven—her kingdom.

Emma leased a vacant unit to open the café in late 2018. A year earlier, she'd left her role as an advertising director in London, where she'd lived and worked for almost a decade. It was the logical thing to do; she was tired, needed a new challenge, and London's house prices were shooting up. Emma would often receive lucrative offers to return to the rat race, but she resisted. She no longer wanted the pressure, late nights, and panicked requests from demanding clients. To Emma, her café was more than money in her bank account; it was her refuge and restoration.

That particular change of pace seems unusual nowadays. If someone suddenly decides to take their foot off the gas and place themselves firmly in the slow lane, we tend to view that decision with passive suspicion. Especially in metropolitan bubbles like London or New York, where the trendy answer to "How's it going?" is always "So busy," simply standing still can be a sign of decay. Because if you're not moving forward in these places, if you're failing to make something of yourself, then you're not going to climb the slippery career ladder. And let's be honest: Who doesn't want to make *something* of themselves?

I got to know Emma when I first moved to Bath. On my daily coffee run one morning I cracked a joke about the city's hapless tourists, and she laughed raucously. Months passed. The café became a frequent haunt. When it was quiet, Emma would ask me how life was going, and I, in turn, did the same. We struck up a friendship and slowly began learning bits and pieces about each other, which is how I got to know about her past life. I recently reached out to see how she was doing and asked whether she wouldn't mind sharing some of those experiences for this book.

Emma's work history is fascinating. Back in her early twenties, young and full of energy, she was eager to graduate and get started in life, head to the big city, and carve out an exciting career. She told me, "When I graduated, I was so excited. I had a first-class degree in English from Warwick, and I soon found myself in demand for stuff like marketing blurbs, social media covers, and branding content.

"Freelance," Emma told me, "was the obvious starting point."

But the sparkle soon wore off. Although freelancing promised freedom, it actually delivered stress and isolation. Emma frequently found herself submerged in a trough of unstimulating tasks, like creating biographies for consultants or writing inane corporate story lines. "I felt ineffectual and unrecognized," she reflected, "and London can be a lonely place." People had no obligation to respond to her pitches, let alone give her feedback. Agreements, she complained, were mostly a waste of time. "You sail one way or the other in response to the changing whims of those who pay." And if you can't meet their impossible demands? "You'll just get a shitty rating and critical review."

It was a dispiriting existence. Before long, Emma was cramming all her experience into a résumé and applying for more stable jobs. After many rejections, she persevered, and was rewarded with a starting role at a small but hip PR firm in London's West End. "That move was really an escape from the insecurity of gigging," she told me. "It was time—I needed more control over my life."

Even so, there was still an element of risk attached. The pay for entry-level marketing roles is notoriously low, and the contracts are almost always precarious. "Although I was formally employed for two years," Emma recalled, "my boss was very clear from the get-go that I could be released at any time."

But the risk paid dividends. Emma spent the next couple of years expanding her role inside the company and building a glowing reputation with several high-profile clients. Not without sacrifice, of course. "I was working relentlessly," she told me. "I stayed late most nights, routinely came in on weekends, and always made myself visible at important parties and events." It got to the point, she recalled, when doing anything nonwork felt a bit like goofing off. "There were times, I'm ashamed to say, when I'd go away with family or friends and wasn't totally there. I was just thinking, 'I should be working' the whole time."

Going above and beyond like this looks like a personal choice. And I suppose, on one level, it's a free country—you're either willing to overextend yourself or you're not. But we know it's not quite that simple. Sure, you can say no to those little pieces of unpaid labor, and you can keep saying no, but that'll be noted after a while. Staying in your lane, refusing to yield when leaned on, failing to go the extra yard—these are traits that are frowned upon in the modern workplace. "Nobody ever changed the world on forty hours a week," American businessman Elon Musk once tweeted. You need to be doing "about eighty [hours] sustained, peaking at one hundred at times."[2]

For several more years, Emma kept up her routine of overwork. She hopped between several more jobs, briefly returned to freelancing, before finally landing a senior managerial role in an international advertising firm. By then, she'd achieved a lot in the industry—far more than she'd ever imagined. But her patience was wearing thin and, worse, she'd grown increasingly pessimistic.

"I started out wearing my job on my sleeve, treating it like a lifestyle, giving it a kind of spiritual dimension and believing it was my calling." But Emma's job didn't love her back. And soon, her industry's more superficial features began to gnaw at her. "Aspirational, even though it's such a meaningless phrase, that's all companies really care about these days. Not make it funny, complex, or thoughtful, but just sprinkle a bit of glitter and make it aspirational.

"But here's the thing: How do you keep on doing that? How do you keep on churning out twinkling campaigns convincing people to chase some mythical ideal without at some point growing deeply cynical?" She explained that "even though I had this vague sense that I was getting ahead, I never truly felt I was making any progress." Like most industries in the new economy, advertising is notorious for having nebulous measures of success. The criteria are "ambiguous," Emma told me, and often invented after the fact. "All that unknown is scary, especially when you're on a time-limited contract, have expenses, and need to know if you'll be in a job next year."

Emma journeyed to London convinced that she'd find her place in the world, but she left it exhausted, dazed, and more uncertain than ever. She told me that what most wore her down was that chronic feeling of insecurity. "I never felt I had a firm enough footing in advertising to weather the relentless pressures to perform, which kept coming and coming." In the end, she said, "I wasn't sure of my convictions or whether I even believed in what I was doing. Younger people were coming up who were hungrier and more willing to make the necessary sacrifices. I couldn't keep pushing myself like them, I began resenting the daily grind and, if I'm being honest, I was completely exhausted, burned out."

The café was Emma's getaway. In sleepy Bath, serving cakes and cappuccinos to local moms and weary professors from the nearby university, she finally had a vocation. One that gave her something back, provided some semblance of security, and offered a crystal clear sense of purpose.

A supply-side economy exhausts as many human and natural resources as possible so as to make as much money as possible in the shortest possible time. Living under this set of rules for several decades now, it's certainly true that we've amassed a staggering level of affluence—far more than even people a few decades ago could have possibly imagined. But it's also true that, just like Emma found, we can't enjoy it. We're not even allowed to appreciate it. For appreciation would block precisely the type of overwork this economy needs to keep itself growing. Should we slow down, rest more, and strive less, the consequences of that rest would be to put other workers on the sidelines.

All of which means our economic system, in a rather circular way, needs to keep us working just to keep us working. How does it do that? The answer, of course, is insecurity.

Being an adult in the modern workforce means being insecure. No matter how much you earn, or more to the point, how hard you work, it's never going to be enough—the job is never really done. It just moves on, shape-shifts, or is replaced with something new. Rarely will we experience lasting satisfaction—much less security—from the fruits of our labor. We'll get paid, we'll work, and we'll grind and get paid some more as everything seems to go on forever, grinding after more and more money just to hang on to the standard of living that we've already got.

Emma's experiences with that insecurity aren't unique, nor are her emotional responses to them. When we talk about work these days, we often talk about how much work we're doing, or how dreadfully burned-out we all are. Which is true. The added extras, main hustles, side hustles, and time spent simply catching up on what we couldn't do in the working day make a mockery of payroll data suggesting we're dutifully working our forty hours a week.[3] Self-reported working habits reveal the truth: the average working week is closer to forty-eight hours, and a whopping 18 percent of workers are clocking well in excess of sixty hours a week.[4]

But there's something else going on behind those staggering numbers. In the past, the basic rhythms and routines of work were straightforward, even if the work itself was exhausting and at times backbreaking. That's changed. Those patterns of doing work are being completely dispensed with, while the work itself has become no less laborious. Emma's story is a testament to the psychological toll of that switchover in the context of a new economy where the rules of work are being radically rewritten.

As organizations limber up and adapt to an environment of quick-fire growth, old-fashioned securities like a stable place to live and a routine time to work are disintegrating. In their place is a completely different set of priorities. Whereas our parents worked for firms that rewarded dedication, the honing of specialist skills, and loyalty to the organization, the modern firm rewards agile and flexible risk-takers who can cope with instability and change, and who are willing to jostle among themselves for time-limited, episodic contracts.

I say willing, but it's not as though we've got a choice. The scrapping of old-era labor protections has enabled firms to hire and fire at will, and make casual forms of employment more or less de facto. Between 2005 and 2015, almost all new jobs added to the American economy were casual in some way, with the biggest growth in independent contractors, freelancers, and contract company workers.[5] "Don't get too comfortable" is one interpretation of this new, fluid labor market. "You're disposable" is another.

Hired on a short-term basis and with no securities, a new generation is emerging for whom a career might as well be a foreign concept. They view themselves not as personnel climbing up an organizational ladder, but as rentable assets to be exchanged on the employment trading floor for a maximum price. Under this set of rules, working identities, rather like our identities as consumers, must be plastic and constantly rebranded. Hustling (what else?) is the common-sense logic underpinning this way of viewing ourselves. And it's a logic that cuts through educational competition and Instagram-based grifting just as much as it does gigging for Uber or consulting for McKinsey.

"The old model of work where you could expect to hold a steady job with good benefits for an entire career is long gone," US presidential candidate Hillary Clinton told an audience in North Carolina. And she's absolutely right. The kind of unassuming dedication to a skill or trade she's talking about, the kind people like my grandfather made an honest livelihood out of, seems decidedly archaic. "People in their twenties and thirties," Clinton continued, "have come of age in an economy that's totally different."[6]

Inside this different economy, the important thing isn't how deeply you can master something, but how quickly you can get it done and move on to something else. It's work, sure, but work for work's sake—

what anthropologist David Graeber calls make-work[7]—which is a constant, humming, almost empty state of hurried busyness in place of patient perseverance and mastery. You've got to "rise and grind," according to a recent Nike campaign; "hustle harder" in the words of rapper 50 Cent; and use each of your "24 hours in the day" like fast-fashion mogul Molly-Mae Hague. We learn from this culture that it doesn't matter what you're doing, so long as you never stop. Because if you're slacking, slowing down or, worse, taking a moment to simply think about what all the relentless grinding is even for, then you're going to be left behind.

Work-life balance invariably gets messy under these kinds of pressures. And it becomes increasingly difficult to divorce your job from everything else. As Emma's story shows, it's hard to enjoy or gratuitously waste free time if you're constantly worrying about how that time is harming your bottom line. According to a 2016 study of work habits, many workers say they regularly forgo trips and holidays because they want to show "complete dedication" to their employers, are fearful of being viewed as "replaceable," and would "feel guilty" about taking time off.[8]

Guilt about not working enough escapes no one. And if anything, it intensifies the higher up the ladder you go. For the first time in living memory, the wealthiest members of society make raucous virtue of the amount of time they work. Not because they want to—although we all know one of *those* guys—but because earning an income sufficient to maintain their social position requires eye-watering hours in a very narrow set of elite professions like law, finance, and medicine. Junior lawyers at some firms in London, for example, are averaging fourteen-hour workdays.[9] And on Wall Street, bankers have what's called a "banker nine-to-five," which starts at 9:00 a.m. on one day and goes to 5:00 a.m. the next.[10]

As working demands rise, so, too, do expectations. Get a satisfactory rating in your annual review, for instance, and you'll instantly discover that this is in no way satisfactory. Nowadays, its even become trendy for some companies to sing about their unrelenting standards. Our "bar is very high" Britain's most valuable fintech company, Revolut, warned prospective employees on it's website. If staff fall short of "perfection," the company goes on, they'll be assessed "accurately, not kindly," even though "it might hurt."[11]

Certainly, fintech companies like Revolut are far more open than most would be about the perfectionistic demands they place on their staff. But that doesn't mean such demands aren't equally widespread in other workplaces, including universities. As many of my colleagues will attest, you need to be consistently hitting student ratings well in excess of four out of five for promotion. Around four gets you through to the next year. Three gets you swiftly whisked away to undertake further training. Less than three, and you're going to need a Nobel Prize just to survive probation.

I mention academics because they used to be somewhat insulated from these ludicrous pressures. But not any longer. As universities adapt for survival inside a supply-side economy, they've begun to restructure themselves in the image of private corporations. Such restructuring has hit young academics especially hard. They're the ones who must contort themselves most elastically for a new administration, and they're also the ones who must forever justify their precarious positions by demonstrating productivity, or "output," as the Research Excellence Framework calls it.

Competition is ferocious. Where once one or two published articles would suffice to secure an academic position, today you'll be lucky if you're short-listed with less than four. And don't forget the "optional" extras: seminar attendance, evening lectures, conferences, networking functions, teaching, and other forms of unpaid admin. You could sit them out. But should you do so, you'll discover via a string of rejection letters that those activities were essential to lifting yourself above hundreds of other job applicants.

In fact, academic positions are so scarce that even if you do all those added extras, you still can't afford to be rooted in one place. You've got to be footloose and move where opportunities arise. Which brings me to another hidden injury of insecure work: flux. The question for the budding professional these days isn't so much "How much do you want it?," but rather "How much putting your life on hold—not settling down, not laying roots, not finding a community, not having a long-term relationship, not having kids—are you prepared to do for it?" On the rocky road to becoming a moderately successful professor, I myself have put most of my life on hold. Since 2013, for example, I've had seven jobs, in seven cities, across three continents, moving about once every two years. And although that sounds extreme, it's not remotely unusual for academics.

It's not remotely unusual for most other industries, either. The average adult, as a rule, can expect to job-hop around twelve times during their working lives and spend much of it in that most dispiriting of places: the gig economy.[12] That's daunting, and I haven't even mentioned the rocketing cost of rent, house prices, debt, general living expenses, and how it feels to grind day in, day out, inside an unequal economy that dishes out the consequences of effort so lopsidedly. In this hustle culture, those who're hustling, and giving everything they've possibly got—including their health and happiness—are rarely those who're benefiting. Eight million young workers in the UK—a quarter of the workforce—have never worked in an economy where average real wages were consistently rising.[13] They have, though, worked in one where corporate profits soared.[14]

A supply-side economy is indeed an impressive vehicle of growth. But what's less explicit is where all that growth goes—to the companies and their shareholders—and the price that everyone else pays for it—stagnant wages, declining living standards, and bucketloads of insecurity. Think about it this way: the modern firm, which needs to grow or go under, will ideally want, if it can possibly get away with it, the productivity of employees without incurring the costs of responsibilities like social security, health insurance, and a constant, dependable schedule. So instead of employing workers like they used to, they now contract with workers, and the workers themselves assume the costs of those responsibilities, with no attendant increase in pay, and all under the auspices of a farce that says they're members of an exciting new hustler class.

My concern here is not so much with the injustice of these hidden transfers of security—from the worker to the firm—but their psychological consequences and why perfectionism is foremost among them.

Insecurity can feel like liberation at first. And from the outside, it certainly looks like a dream gig. You're in the driver's seat, you can work where and whenever you want, and untethered from the demands of an overbearing boss—you can be the author of your own destiny. That was precisely Emma's excitement as she embarked on her initial career: taking risks, learning new skills, and pushing boundaries along the way. But after a honeymoon period came a brute realization: insecurity is not a one-time thing. Day in, day out, she found herself starting over with renewed apprehension that she might not be doing enough. And as she lifted herself into the corporate world, which expected plenty of output, with few assurances, the daily pressures just kept on coming.

Insecurity, by definition, means we lack the affirmations required to reassure us that we're doing okay, that we're making a difference, that we're not going to be let go next week, next month, or next year. Without those affirmations, life can feel pretty unsteady. We constantly fear being discarded, become hypervigilant for validation and positive feedback, and grow wary of revealing too much of ourselves. Shame is a regular occurrence, especially if we slip up ("How could you be so stupid?"). And a tremendous amount of guilt is stirred when not working, making it difficult to enjoy life outside the daily grind.

To guard against these emotions, we'll invariably take on more and more. By being the ideal worker in the eyes of those around us, we'll ease the pent-up emotional pressures produced from working under the vise of insecurity. But only momentarily. Because sooner or later, something will come up—an updated target, an unforeseen roadblock, a global pandemic—to set the tempo even faster. And rather like moving through levels of Tetris, once you've gotten up to that new pace, up goes the tempo once again.

And so on, and so on.

We simply can't rest when our working identities (not to mention economic survival) depend on this breathless chase. Fully 80 percent of adults in the US describe themselves as "hardworking"—just 3 percent say they're lazy.[15] And that's fine; we *are* hardworking. But the question is—who's benefiting? Is it us or is it the firms who contract us? Because no matter how hard we work, insecurity means there can never be enough assurance. Our accomplishments matter far less in this economy than the relentless grind toward them. Arguably, our accomplishments don't matter at all.

We've internalized, in other words, the common sense of an economic system that values people only insofar as they work themselves ragged—and then some.

The more we sacrifice ourselves at the altar of our jobs, the more perfectionism will become cemented as an essential component of our working lives. And we're already seeing that in the vernacular of young people. Of all the slogans in meme culture, "Fake it till you make it" is perhaps the perfect crystallization of perfectionism's ubiquity in the modern workplace. Translated, it means "I'm deeply unsure of myself and extremely apprehensive about my ability to do this job, but I'm going to *act* like I'm absolutely smashing it anyway." Insecurity traps us inside anxious fears of working hard enough, playing an unwinnable game of pretend: always striving relentlessly for more success, but never believing we've made enough progress.

Insecure work etches this perfectionism into us; not by choice, but necessity. We truly believe that we don't have the smarts, skills, or sheer physical energy needed to cope, let alone succeed. Such immobilizing anxiety occupied Emma for many years, until she decided to pack it in and do something different. For her, it was the right decision. But for many others, with fewer resources, and even fewer alternatives, the only viable option is to keep on grinding alongside everyone else and hope for the best.

Every year, millions of young people like Emma enter the workforce. Their perfectionism is already at a high watermark and along comes job insecurity to take it even higher. Although I can't prove this—we simply don't have the data—it certainly seems like it. Forty percent of eighteen- to twenty-nine-year-olds are frequently or nearly always concerned about their work-life balance and levels of stress at work.[16] Office workers typically rate their working lives just six out of ten.[17] And more than half of working people say they feel exhausted and completely burned-out.[18]

The coronavirus pandemic has exacerbated these long-standing trends. According to the American Psychological Association's Work and Well-being Survey, American workers saw heightened rates of burnout in 2020 and 2021. Eight in ten reported work-related stress, a third reported lack of interest and effort at work, another third reported cognitive weariness and emotional exhaustion, and almost half reported physical fatigue—a figure that's almost 40 percent higher than 2019.[19] And it's not just America. A 2022 survey of nearly fifteen thousand employees across thirteen countries found that one in four of them were reporting burnout symptoms.[20]

So burned-out are workers that an online movement has surfaced to promote what's called "quiet quitting."[21] The phrase is generating millions of shares on social media, and it's all in celebration of *not* going above and beyond for our jobs. This movement suggests that attitudes are shifting in response to the stress and tension in the modern workplace. We seem to be figuring out that hustling and grinding and hustling some more are needlessly punishing ways to work, especially if they come with insecurity, no surety of reward, and at the expense of our health and happiness.

Of course, intolerable levels of insecurity are not the only reason for this downed-tools protest. But they're likely to be a pretty sizable one. In a recent US survey, just one-fifth of workers felt their job was secure.[22] In fact, so insecure are jobs these days that an astonishing 30 percent of salaried employees say that freelancing—the most insecure of insecure work—would actually offer them more security. Which goes some way to explaining why 38 million Americans left their jobs in 2021 alone.[23] Thirty percent of them, just like Emma, started their own businesses and a great majority of the rest went freelance. At current rates of switching, most US workers will be self-employed by 2027.[24]

Will we find more security working for ourselves? The answer to that question doesn't really matter, since security is an alien concept anyway to a new generation whose working histories contain a long list of job swaps from one temporary gig to the next. When insecurity is an inevitable part of your working life—when it's all you know—taking complete ownership of your circumstances makes perfect sense. If there's anything to learn from the "great resignation" or "quiet quitting," it's that people are concluding there's simply no alternative to insecure work. So either grind it out for yourself or refuse to grind it out at all.

If that's the case, then maybe it really is time to start navigating the workplace in a way that doesn't require perfectionism. Forging that path won't be easy in this economy, and you'll need to trust yourself.

Trust that you can slow down, trust that you can be happy when things are good enough, trust that you can go home to your family, visit your friends, and spend time doing the things you love outside of the office without worrying or feeling guilty about what's being lost.

At first, that's a surprising discovery for the perfectionist. But the more you encounter it, the more familiar good enough becomes, the more you'll be able to accept when it's time to let things go. Research shows that employees who give themselves work-life balance are far more productive than those who're burned out.[25] With every piece of affirmative feedback in your decision to slow down, your confidence will grow, and you'll become inclined to allow yourself the space to rest, unfazed by insecurity and that little voice telling you to do more.

If you're a manager, be aware that rising numbers of young people entering your organization will be perfectionistic. They'll expect that you're looking for perfection. Let them know from day one that that's not the case. Try to create a culture of psychological safety in which employees can feel comfortable enough to fail without fear of recrimination or judgment. Encourage healthy risk-taking, allow people to speak their minds, and promote and reward creativity. Make sure your colleagues know that no question is a stupid question and let them stick their necks out without fear of having them cut off.

But also, don't expect perfectionistic employees to take to their new environment straightaway. Perfectionists tend to be risk-averse, after all. Be patient. Give them time and support. As they become more comfortable, their strengths will begin to show. Make the most of those strengths; perfectionistic people think deeply, are attentive to detail, and can solve complex problems given an atmosphere that allows them to do so. If they happen to screw up or struggle with things like procrastination, intervene with compassion. Let them know that good enough is good enough. Keep letting them know.

Because getting things done is way better than getting things perfect.

*   *   *.

I popped in to see Emma recently. Her café still has its very own eccentric charm, but it was striking how quiet it was. This was a business emerging from the wreckage of a global pandemic into a cost-of-living crisis, and it showed. "Foot traffic is way down," Emma told me. "Tourists aren't coming in the same numbers, people seem to be doing more work from home, and the locals are cutting back." The café wasn't massively profitable before the pandemic—Emma didn't open it for that. But now it barely breaks even. "I'm dipping into my savings to pay myself, and I don't know how long I'm prepared to do that."

"Will you go back to advertising?" I asked.

"Maybe," she replied. "But I feel like I'm dead wood now. I'm not even sure I'd get back in."

She would, and I think deep down Emma knows that. Even so, that this hugely successful woman doubts herself is telling.

Emma opened her café hoping for liberation from the daily grind. But even here, there's no escape from the indifference of circumstances far from her control. Work these days, no matter what you do, is so insecure, built on such shaky ground that we're vulnerable to every single setback, roadblock, conflict, ailment, and economic shock—no matter how big or small. And the pandemic was undoubtedly catastrophic for those starting out in the modern economy.

In telling Emma's story, and the broader story of work's plummeting security, my aim is not to dwell on how shitty work has become, or even to bemoan how tough this generation has it. Instead, I want to emphasize, one last time, how things connect. Nobody waved a magic wand and said work must be insecure, casual, time-limited, and completely free of employer obligations. Our economy did that, following the prime directive, which is to generate as much growth as possible in the shortest possible time.

And when you really think about the lingering and unshakable insecurity we all feel, you'll notice that everything is indeed connected. The reason we're so insecure at work is the same reason we're pushed to breaking point by schools, colleges, and helicopter parents, or made to feel so inadequate by predatory advertisers: we live in an economy that needs to grow far more than we need to feel content. Perfectionism is just the collateral damage. The price we must pay for our economy's morbid dependence on the insecurity of each and every one of us.

So with that in mind, what on earth can we do?

PART FOUR

HOW CAN WE EMBRACE IMPERFECTION IN THE REPUBLIC OF GOOD ENOUGH?

CHAPTER TWELVE

Accept Yourself

Or the Power of Good Enough in Our Less Than Perfect Lives

*"What I am is good enough if
I would only be it openly."*
Carl Rogers[1]

Paul Hewitt may be a clinician, but his hardest challenge with struggling perfectionists is not their treatment—it's getting them to accept that they need it. "Perhaps the worst thing about perfectionism," he told me recently, "is the unwillingness of perfectionists to see that their perfectionism is at the root of their problems." Almost every perfectionist, he said, "is extraordinarily adept at hiding their pain behind a mask of high functioning, maximization, and competency."

A recovering perfectionist, I find that Paul's words ring painfully true. When you're entangled in the thicket of never enough, when you're convinced that the only way to matter is to be perfect, you don't think perfectionism is a problem. On the contrary. You think perfectionism is the one thing holding you up in the world, while everything and all around you is going up in flames.

Society doesn't recognize perfectionism as much of a problem, either. Straining on tiptoe, lifting ourselves above other people, grasping incessantly at bigger and better things—these are the behaviors society says it rewards and they're the blueprint for the way most people live. Any problems that these behaviors generate are therefore hidden behind a weight of conventional wisdom that says perfectionism is the way to get ahead, a badge of honor, our favorite flaw.

But perfectionism isn't a badge of honor, and it's not holding you up in the world. At root, as this book has tried to explain, perfectionism is the response to deficit thinking so extreme that we live our entire lives in the shadow of shame. Shame about what we don't have, how we don't appear, and what we haven't done. That's not an emblem of success. That's a loathing of the very things that make us so enliveningly human: our flaws.

Just knowing that, I hope, is a solace of sorts, a call to action, an impetus to acknowledge the problem and take the first steps in a different direction. We'll talk about those steps in a moment. But before that, I want to reflect briefly on what we've learned about where perfectionism comes from. Because here, too, there's an opportunity for solace through nothing more than the asset of awareness.

In our individualistic culture, it's hard to envisage perfectionism as anything other than a *personal* trait. However, my work rose to prominence on the back of a curious finding. Perfectionism, I discovered, is rising for everyone. And socially prescribed perfectionism—the belief that our environment demands perfection—is rising most rapidly. Those two facts point not to something going wrong within us, but rather to something going wrong within our society. That something, I've tried to argue, is the pressure to overwork and overconsume in a culture fixated on more, bigger and better—forever.

Every trait emerging from those fixations—perfectionism foremost among them—has been drilled so deeply into our interiors that we view their presence in our characters as normal, natural, even desirable. Afflicted by a Stockholm syndrome of the soul, we've burrowed into this economic habitat and conspired with those who've built it to accept the inevitability of our discontent. That syndrome is probably the most astounding—most chilling—psychological relic of the supply-side revolution. Because what's going on right now isn't normal and natural. There were alternative paths; there still *are* alternative paths. And we'll talk about some of them in the next chapter.

For now, though, let's just reflect on the idea that after genes and early life experiences are subtracted out, perfectionism is brought to bear on us not by our own agency, but by pressures out there in wider culture. I realize that's a somewhat nihilistic outlook, for it suggests that perfectionism isn't within our individual gift to remedy. Even so, I'd argue that it's a decidedly more hopeful one than the alternative, which essentially says that perfectionism is our problem and *our problem alone* to solve.

Many would no doubt object. They'd say that pinning the blame on "the system" could be read as an almost total erasure of hope that we can change ourselves from the inside out. But it's only false hope that I wish to erase. In this culture, it's not sufficient to say that with a bit of positive thinking we can overcome immobilizing perceptions of not being enough. These are more than just *perceptions*; they're logical and rational feelings equal in intensity to the relentless conditioning that's generating them. We only experience more distress, not less, when at the end of all the life hacks, mindfulness and self-care, we discover an economy that feeds off our insecurity, still there, right where we left it.

Finding that your best efforts to escape perfectionism are made harder by your personal inability to snap out of it can seem incredibly distressing. I get that. Yet finding that your best efforts to escape it are made harder because your economy needs you to internalize the core belief that you're not enough is something else entirely. And although it seems counterintuitive to say so, that something else, I sincerely believe, is reassurance rather than distress.

Why do I say that?

Because, in sizing up the forces working against you, you realize that needing to be perfect isn't in any way, shape, or form your fault. You *are* enough. The culture you live inside, the one that consumes and surrounds you, just doesn't give you the permission to breathe in your incomprehensible existence and truly accept it.

If you can get your head around that, if you can value and love yourself for the breathtaking human being that you are, if you can know that everything you feel that you *should* be is but a set of ideas conditioned by your culture, ideas that are there purely to grow your economy, and that your ability to fully transform yourself within those structural constraints is limited, at least for now, then you'll be able to take the very worst that this world can throw at you. That's what *real* hope looks like. Hope that's honest. Hope that confronts the world as it actually is. Hope that's not going to mislead you with false promises of individual transformation without first awakening you to the fact that it's not you who needs transforming.

We can break the cycle of perfectionism. But first, we must arm ourselves with the knowledge that enables us to recognize, and then accept, that there are limits to the things we can control. Often, and without warning, our dreams get shattered, and things can pan out in ways we hadn't planned. The trick is not to sink into a pit of regret and self-loathing as our economy wants us to (did someone say retail therapy?), but rather, to try and live contentedly inside that unairbrushed reality, knowing that, whatever happens, time still marches onward, and we go on existing.

I dedicated much of this book to demystifying the root causes of our obsession with perfection for that very reason. Knowledge, as they say, is power. And if we let it, knowledge can also be the source of extraordinary healing. All of which brings me to something I've been practicing a lot in my own rehabilitation: acceptance. Acceptance that the simple act of moving, breathing, and existing means we matter—that we're enough. And acceptance that through no fault of our own, our culture will continually try to inject us with insecurity, and that's okay, we can sit next to that reality, not needing to react in the way we're supposed to, not needing to constantly improve things, not needing to be perfect.

Acceptance isn't giving up, nor does it mean simply accepting the injustices that surround us. You can want things to change and agitate for that change and still meet the world where it is. That's our challenge. So let's take a closer look at the act of acceptance, starting with that most primary of cultural fixations: growth.

★   ★   ★

I should confess that before I wrote this book I was quite attracted to the idea of psychological growth. The growth mindset, it seemed to me, was a powerful corrective strategy to the rigid behaviors and irrational beliefs that characterize perfectionism. After all, growth is about all those controllable goodies—process, challenge, learning, development, and so on. This mindset, in which we're always carrying our setbacks forward, or failing better, so to speak, provides the foundation for a fuller and more intrinsically satisfying life.

But then I wrote the book. And the more I thought about growth, the more I felt that this mindset was not all it seems. For one thing, I don't really want my mind to be set on anything, even if it is supposedly healthy. The rigidity of that imperative is just as inhibiting as the things it's supposed to be correcting. But more important than that, pitting striving for growth against striving for perfection misses the point. Just like the growth-is-everything economy it came from, a growth-is-everything mindset can only allow us to grow. And that means when we stumble, hit a setback, run into a roadblock, or simply screw up—we need to turn those very ordinary experiences of failure into something else, anything else, that signifies growth.

"You can't let your failures define you," Barack Obama famously said in his 2009 address to America's schoolchildren, "you have to let your failures teach you."[2]

Which sounds like sage advice. But look closer, and the essential message advocates something decidedly unhuman. Because the implication is that our failures and shortcomings can't be allowed to simply wash through us as a joyous reminder of what it means to be a fallible human being. Quite the contrary. The lesson we learn from "fail better" rhetoric like Obama's is that we must always be hypervigilant of failure, concocting a way, whenever we encounter it, to rehabilitate it on the redemptive arc of growth so that no trace of it is left as a lingering reminder.

Every last "fail better" cliché attempts to sprinkle fairy dust on failure—to sterilize it, pop a bow tie on it, and send it out into the world with a shiny lapel labeled "growth." In not one of these "feel good" bromides is there the permission to leave our fragile humanity alone and simply let setbacks, failures, disappointments, vulnerabilities, and shortcomings seep into our lives, where they can be as important a form of sustenance as eating or drinking. Why do we have to *grow* and *excel* all the time? Why does failure *require* constant rehabilitation? Why can't we just let it be exactly what it *is*—a normal and natural part of our mortal existence?

To put it bluntly, the growth mindset purports to celebrate failure when in actual fact it does completely the opposite.

Growth followed by more growth followed by even more growth and overlaid with perfectionism—this is the essential psychology of growth-is-everything economics. But you and I aren't a business model to be continually redrawn for maximum profit, nor are we a machine cog to be endlessly fine-tuned for maximum performance. We're exhaustible human beings. We age and decay. Our resources to grow are not limitless.

Yet even if we did possess superhuman powers of endurance, we'd be wise to remind ourselves that often there's little we can learn in failure. We knew exactly what to do; we just got ourselves muddled up, had a rough night's sleep, or came up against someone more qualified or privileged. That's life. Shit happens. And when shit happens, growth-is-everything psychology seriously backfires because rather than compassionate self-reflection, it traps us in a cage of unrelenting self-betterment, pushing ourselves ever harder in pursuit of "growth"—whatever that looks like— ultimately to be imprisoned by the need to be perfect.

Although that's the cage most of us are trapped in right now, it's not the only one we could unwittingly end up in. Taken at face value, my blaming of the system's fixation on growth for our obsession with perfection could easily trap us in the polar opposite cage of victimhood. Our imprisonment in that case would proceed from anger, bitterness, and resentment, which, no matter how well justified, will only create misery for those trapped there.

So that's why, in moving ourselves away from perfectionism and toward acceptance, we mustn't let ourselves leap from one cage straight into the other. Yes, the supply-side economy is largely to blame for our insecurities, and yes, there's good reason to feel aggrieved that the rich and powerful have contrived to place us inside a society that crumbles under the first signs of widespread contentment. But "the system" is not within our personal control to straighten out—that's a political question, answered with collective action.

What *is* within our control is how we respond to that knowledge. Because if we could just find a way to push past the formidable weight of cultural conditioning, we'd learn that it's perfectly possible to embrace our imperfect minds and bodies without needing to constantly grow, update, or improve them. And learn as well that those minds and bodies can go in many different directions, at many different speeds. Yes, sometimes we'll indeed charge forward toward growth. But other times we'll creep there more slowly, scarcely recognizing that we're growing at all. And still other times, we might have to change direction completely, or shrink into ourselves, or simply let the passing passage of time age and decay us.

If we only allow ourselves the psychological space to grow, we deny ourselves the acceptance of those other realities. Allowing the acts of slowing down, regression, and failure into our lives, letting them sit alongside us in amicable if sometimes uncomfortable conversation, helps us to think clearly about what being human *really* means. And what's more, it also helps us to think clearly about why growing, and constantly searching for more, bigger, and better is not the answer to our problems that we think it is.

So how can we set ourselves in the direction of acceptance? The more I've thought about that question, the more I've come to realize that there's so much to unpack. "Good enough" seems a good enough place to start. However here, too, it's not straightforward. One thing to say to ourselves, "I'm good enough"; quite another to sincerely believe it in a culture committed to telling you otherwise. Acceptance, therefore, cannot just be acceptance of ourselves. As we've learned throughout this book, it must also be acceptance that the culture we live inside will make that acceptance the hardest possible thing to do.

Start with looking that truth in the eye and build from there.

Karen Horney, who put culture at the front of her therapeutic alliances, never sanitized the truth. She always called a spade a spade. She didn't hide from her patients the immense challenges involved in taking off perfectionism's armor plate in a culture that requires it. "Our limitations are for the greater part," she said, "culturally and socially conditioned."[3] She knew there'd be conflict between intrinsic needs for belonging, self-esteem and contentment, and the upstream swimming required to have those needs fulfilled. And she recognized that there'll be times when we must go with culture's current to get by.

This is acceptance, but it's acceptance rooted in a crystal-clear consciousness of ourselves, our limitations, and how the things we can't control out there in the wider world impact on our innermost tensions. In what can be a "menacing world," Horney said, accepting oneself will be a "difficult journey" that "may never be fully realized," but that's eminently worthy of our "wholehearted commitment" all the same.[4] If you're prepared to embark on that journey, if you're ready to take off the mask of perfection, let go of your idealized image, and open up to others, then you'll experience, as Horney herself did, more and more of the joy of being somewhere near at one with your actual self—the essence of who you really are under the perfect facade.

Then, without even realizing it, without even consciously trying, you'll find less and less need for perfectionism.

The key to beginning that journey, says Horney, is to recognize that "adaptation to psychic normal" is what has generated the problem of perfectionism in the first place.[5] And by adaptation to psychic normal, she means what I've rather provocatively called our "Stockholm syndrome of the soul." We must gain the perspective that it's acculturation doing us the harm, and then we must do the hard work of unlearning the impulses of our culture, and learning to enjoy what Horney called "psychic health" instead.[6]

Psychic health is Horney's term for accepting all of yourself and all of your feelings. Her own struggles with adaptation to a patriarchal culture in the 1930s and '40s taught her that the first steps toward such acceptance will be extremely tough, and they'll be taken with absolutely no guarantee of success. But Horney also reassured us that, in time and with practice, things will start to *feel* different.

Trust the process and know that accepting yourself will be unfamiliar territory. You'll sometimes despair, and you'll often feel that you can't possibly embrace all of yourself, since all of yourself is simply too much unmasking. And mark my words, like most things in life, that unmasking will be far harder if you're from an underprivileged or minority background. Which means patience is going to be a virtue, especially for those who must bend themselves most out of shape to conform to society's "ideal." The way to think about it, I suppose, is that no one picks up a guitar for the first time and starts riffing "Hotel California." By the same logic, that almost instinctual urge to manage impressions can't simply be unlearned overnight.

However, underneath the impression management is a set of more basic anxieties that we can start to work with: fear of judgment, fear of rejection, fear of failure.

Confronting these anxieties head-on is perhaps the most important next step. Doing so will be extremely hard, but commit to it. A good way to do this is to make a list of what perfect looks like to you. Then browse the list and pick something that'll challenge your basic anxieties in uncomfortable ways. Perhaps strike up a conversation with a friendly face at work; don't filter that selfie; take a social media hiatus; be kind to yourself whenever you fail; ask questions, even if you think they're stupid ones; speak up in situations you ordinarily feel uncomfortable; send off that job application; talk to your boss about the raise or promotion you deserve; say no to that unpaid piece of work; give up a status possession; do the things you love but aren't world champion at.

Then observe what happens. How did it turn out? How do you feel?

Go through the anxiety that these first small steps will generate. Sit with it and reflect on that feeling. Don't react, repress it or recycle it into something else. Just let it wash through you; just let it be. You'll discover that your trepidation tells you something significant. The approval that you're so desperately in need of, not to mention terrified of losing, is simply a prop for your perfect self. Let that realization soak in and ask, "Is that impossible version of me really worth living in fear for?"

Keep confronting that fear, and as you get more comfortable showing yourself, allow more and more of the outside in. Let the forces far from you, and far from your sphere of influence, wash over you, and resist the urge to constantly try and fight against the tides of fate, fortune, and time—as if somehow everything and all around you can be perfected. What's going to happen is going to happen. Friends and acquaintances are going to say and do things that hurt. Bosses and politicians are going to make difficult, life-altering decisions. Natural disasters, extreme weather events, and deadly pandemics are going to be part and parcel of a "new normal."

Not one of these certainties can be predicted, never mind controlled. They just spring up on us, often when we least expect them. Yet despite the indifference of fortune and fate, our instinct is to cling on to what clinical psychologist David Smail calls "magical volunteerism"—or the fallacy that we can decide the trajectory of our lives with our own efforts and nothing but our own efforts.[7] So as well as working on accepting yourself, it's vital you also work on accepting the inevitability of the things you cannot change. Which means confronting your fears of judgment, rejection, and failure head-on, putting yourself out there, accepting pain, distress, and hard times as intractable parts of life, and in doing so, not letting them turn into unnecessary suffering and self-loathing.

Psychologist Tara Brach calls this acceptance, "radical acceptance."[8] Radical because it describes the acceptance of life as it is, for what it is, rather than constantly worrying about why life isn't better or how we should be doing more. Of course, life circumstances—*and the consequences of those circumstances*—mean that such acceptance will be far harder for some to practice than it is for others. But that doesn't make it any less essential. In many ways, having a hard go of life makes radical acceptance *all the more* essential.

And I also want to be clear about something else: radical acceptance isn't giving up and accepting your lot in life. You can be radically accepting of what's happening to you, and still work hard, forge your own path, and on that path, achieve great things. It's just that in striving, as in life, we must, as far as possible, let the *flow* of our experiences carry us—the process, learning, development, enjoyment, self-discovery, and so on—not the outcomes, benchmarks, awards, statuses, league positions, or any of the many other measures and metrics that we can aspire to ride high on, sure, but can't directly control.[9]

Think about that kind of striving like piloting a sailboat over the waves. When you strive for great things knowing that not everything is within your gift to control, you'll have a general idea of where you're going and you'll be able to set yourself on a course to get there. But unlike those who believe in magical volunteerism, you'll do so with full knowledge that conditions will dictate how difficult the journey is going to be and how long it'll take to get there.

On the voyage, you'll move jaggedly up and down as you meet the wind, waves, crests, and breaks that life will invariably throw at you. Sometimes you'll be assisted by a friendly tailwind, and that's great— ride that thing for all it's worth! Other times you'll need to work with all your might just to keep yourself moving forward, which is fine, up to a point. And still other times circumstances will dictate that you must float to wherever the tide is taking you, at least for a little while.

Keep practicing the acceptance of those realities, endure it, because it's worth every second of discomfort—especially when conditions are against you. It won't be straightforward. In the most challenging times, when you're filled with doubt and despair, you'll succumb often and sometimes painfully to the impression management of social media, the ruthless pull of advertising, or the pressure to compete in school or at work. And you'll paint that perfect facade right back on.

You might feel dispirited, but remember: *the struggle is the point.* It's the *road* to acceptance we're aiming to travel; it's not about resting comfortably at the destination. Each setback is a fresh reminder of the seriousness of going against the grain of your individualistic, have-everything culture. So be kind to yourself, always, know that this is incredibly hard, and also know that, irrespective of whether you think you're getting anywhere, the mere act of working on acceptance—of getting comfortable in your own skin and with your own circumstances—is one of the bravest things you can possibly do.

Keep going. Do not yield. Every time you get up and put yourself back in the firing line, your confidence grows a little bit more, acceptance comes a tiny bit closer into view, and you'll experience more and more of the spontaneous joy that pours out when you make authentic decisions, and take full responsibility for them, in ever greater regularity. Trust me, there is nothing that makes you more uncomfortable than trying to be somebody else—somebody perfect. And there is nothing that gives you more joy than to think, feel, and say what is yours.

The aim of therapy, according to Karen Horney, is to achieve exactly that kind of joy. The kind that shows the patient has been returned to themselves and feels "a genuine integration and a sound sense of wholeness, oneness [because] not only are the body and mind, deed and thought or feeling, consonant and harmonious, but they function without serious inner conflict."[10] As one of Horney's most perfectionistic patients puts it in a letter:

> *Until now, I have known nothing, understood nothing, and therefore could love nothing for the simple, unbelievable reason that I wasn't here! For over forty years of my life, I have been exiled from myself without even suspecting it. Merely to understand this, now, is tremendous. It is not only the end of all that dying, it is to begin life.*[11]

Like that patient, we can gain perspective on the life that perfectionism is draining from our lives. And then, with a great deal of patient perseverance, we can set ourselves on a course to accept ourselves, or "begin life," as Horney's patient rather powerfully puts it. "I am how I look, what I have, or what I've accomplished" becomes "I am what I am and what I am is good enough." That's when you know you're finally free from the perfection trap.

Paul Hewitt has devoted his working life to helping perfectionists because perfectionism poses an extremely tricky challenge. As he's observed time and time again, patients rarely intuit perfectionism as being at the root of their problems. Some even struggle to recognize that they even have it. Which means to defeat perfectionism we sufferers must first be brought to the understanding that our perfectionism isn't doing what we think it's doing. It's not holding us up on a pedestal of competency and hyperfunctioning; it's insecurity and shame masquerading as those things.

My hope is that this book has helped convince you of that. And armed with a new knowledge about this most curious of traits, you'll find yourself resolving to tread a different path. Choosing that new path will entail making several changes to the way you interact with and view the world, quite a few of which I've described throughout this book. But the most significant changes are to be found in this chapter. They include, first, identifying perfectionism as a *problem to be reckoned with and worked on*; second, recognizing that we suffer this affliction because our economy and culture *requires and celebrates it*; and third, inside that reality, making a wholehearted commitment to *acceptance of who we are and where we're at in life*, knowing that such acceptance may never be fully realized, but that the joy one experiences in glimpsing it with ever more regularity will be more than worth the challenge to get there.

And finally, I should be clear, since it's important: we can be ambitious, and we can commit ourselves to doing great things. There's absolutely no problem with striving. What I'm saying is simply that the focus should be on striving in the same way Karen Horney describes it, and my grandfather did it. Which is for the very *flow* of the experience itself and for what that experience leaves in the world, not worrying about the outcomes or other people's approval, not constantly fretting about what can be learned, how we might "fail better," or whether we "made it" or didn't "make it" at all. "We are what we are," we must always remind ourselves, "and what we are is good enough."

That's what we can personally do to escape the perfection trap. Now, how about society?

CHAPTER THIRTEEN

Postscript for a Post-Perfectionism Society
Or Life in the Republic of Good Enough

"Not everything that is faced can be changed;
but nothing can be changed until it is faced."
James Baldwin[1]

The last chapter, in many ways, was the hardest to write. I'm not a clinician, so naturally I feel uncomfortable dishing out advice. However, I wanted to give readers struggling with perfectionism hope, and some things to bear in mind as they grapple with their predicament. If we exercise enough patient perseverance, then we can arm ourselves with acceptance—both of ourselves and our circumstances. Then, slowly, unevenly, and with a great deal of unpeeling, we can begin to discover more and more of the spontaneous joy that just seems to engulf you when you realize you love another human being; or that floods you in those flashes of connection with the natural world; or indeed that you see in children everywhere, of just being alive, with all of themselves and all of their feelings.

Such joy is what happens when we encounter contentment, or to be more exact, *enoughness*. That it even exists, that we have access to it, is the good news.

The bad news is that you and I aren't supposed to access it. In putting the onus on *us* to wake up to this reality, and change *ourselves* accordingly, there's a danger, once again, of making personal accountability the centerpiece of salvation. We can, and should, do all the things that help to release the pressure—be brave, be vulnerable, show up, try and let things go, practice self-compassion, sit with setbacks, decide on a path to living inside ourselves, and embrace the journey of self-acceptance. Yet doing those things won't change the fact that we're constantly squeezed in our economy, which inundates us with perfectionistic fantasies—keeping us on tiptoe, reaching always for more. Rather than accept that our ability to conquer those pressures is extremely limited, we're turned in the direction of perfectionism, and we blame ourselves for not being able to conquer them.

I've tried to show you that you can push back against that pressure and do something in yourself to bring about greater contentment and self-acceptance. And *something*, of course, is better than nothing.

But we can't stop there. We're citizens living in a shared society, one that we must agree to manage collectively if we're going to make any noticeable inroads on our shared tensions. Perfectionistic people may be ideal workers and consumers in the eyes of our politicians, economists, and social planners. But their ever-increasing presence tells us that something is deeply wrong if the only things we care about are work and consumption. The absence of intrinsic needs like camaraderie, mattering, belonging, unconditional love, mercy, compassion, and honesty, and the presence of alienated feelings like discontentment, insecurity, depression, anxiety, and unhappiness, are the fault of a malfunctioning society. And a malfunctioning society is a decidedly political matter.

★　　★　　★

In this book, I've tried to argue that perfectionism is a cultural phenomenon. Our obsession with perfection, and the knock-on toll perfectionism takes on our mental health and relationships, is part of a deficit treadmill on which we're all forced to run, ever more frantically and with ever more tension, devoting more and more of ourselves to perfecting the things we're led to believe are imperfect. What we don't need right now, at this critical juncture in time, is to keep on running. What we need is a way off the treadmill.

We'll make few meaningful inroads into perfectionism until we accept that fact. Until we've decided that we'd rather care for the health of ourselves, our communities, and our planet than have a few more toys and gadgets. Until we move toward people rather than against them, conserve rather than waste, and refuse to profit from activities that cause harm to other humans or the natural world. Until, in other words, we realize that more growth is desirable, yes, but not essential, especially if it comes at the expense of our health and happiness.

If we could just imagine such a society, if we could suppose that people will indeed be enthusiastic about living in that world, then we could envisage change being at least a possibility. And possibility is the blueprint for hope. It means that things don't have to be this way. It means that things could be different.

To paint a vision of what this future would look like, this chapter is a thought experiment of sorts. I want to draw out the logic of a citizenry whose priorities have radically shifted, and who've given their wholehearted consent to living in a world that has learned how to thrive within human and planetary limits. If that were to be the case, what kinds of things would we change and what policies would we implement? Mine are not exhaustive propositions, nor are they intended to be in any way prescriptive. I simply ask you to consider them with an open mind and imagine what would happen if one, several, or all were to materialize. Would we be better off? Would we be happier? Would perfectionism still be our favorite flaw?

THE PURSUIT OF GROWTH AT ALL COSTS is harmful and unsustainable—could we become more agnostic toward it?

Economic growth—immortalized in units of the gross domestic product—is the almighty secular god. We worship at its altar and place it on a gilded pedestal high above all other considerations. Whatever the economy needs in order to grow, no matter the human or environmental costs, it'll invariably get. During the coronavirus pandemic, for example, I read in the newspaper that the British government did a cost-benefit analysis on containment measures. Some economists from high in their Whitehall perches worked out that the economic "benefits" of *not* locking down the British economy would be justified if the annual death rate could be kept below fifty thousand. Just to be clear: that's fifty thousand "acceptable" deaths for the sake of economic growth.[2]

Evaluating public health crises from the standpoint of growth is rather symbolic of the times. And it's not just public health; every last monetizable piece of society is being sliced up and sold off in exchange for an extra basis point of GDP. If an alien were to descend from space, they'd be forgiven for thinking that human beings exist merely for the sake of their economy. We speak of the economy as if it were a living, breathing organism. As if it, rather than us, were the sentient agent in need of constant nourishment.

"What's good for the economy?" we ask. "What's bad for the economy?"

Of course, pursuing economic growth isn't inherently problematic. In fact, when societies are in their early, agrarian phase of development, getting growth going is fundamental because it's the only way we know how to end destitution, suffering, and avoidable death. More than 1 billion people worldwide have been lifted out of extreme poverty in the last twenty-five years, and broad-based economic growth is an important reason why that's happened.[3]

Indeed, the extraordinary affluence enjoyed by developed nations these days is in large part due to the proceeds of growth. Its story is one of remarkable success.

But eventually, with enough growth, the dilemma of scarcity is resolved and the general level of abundance passes the point at which growth's relationship with improved living standards begins to weaken. That's exactly where we've been for some time in the West. The problem we've got is not scarcity, it's actually maintaining that scarcity so the economy continues to grow despite reaching a level of abundance that—reasonably shared—would provide a good enough standard of living for everyone. How that's done is quite straightforward: you simply manufacture scarcity into existence. And throughout this book we've talked about many of the ways scarcity, or the feeling of not having or being enough, is manufactured.

Which begs the question: Now we've solved the dilemma of scarcity, can we afford to be a little more agnostic about growth, and switch to an economy that's powered by something more optimistic than shortage, deficit, and lack?

That question, in many ways, might soon be moot. Because adopting that kind of economy might not be a choice; it might be a necessity. First, because structural trends such as aging populations, lagging rates of innovation, eye-watering ratios of debt, and rising costs of energy on top of the long-run effects of climate change and COVID-19 mean the global economy is *already* slowing down.[4] And second, because each basis point of economic expansion requires an equivalent expansion in energy consumption to power it—accelerating the already alarming effects of climate change (and making the transition to renewables far harder than it already is).[5,6]

So I suppose the real question is, Will we come to our senses in time?

In a paper titled "Data Check on the World Models That Forecast Global Collapse," Dutch economist and sustainability researcher Gaya Herrington reported an analysis showing exactly the difficulty we're headed for if we don't change soon. Modeling the impact of several growth scenarios on things like the global food supply, natural resource capacity, and ecological sustainability, she discovered that we face an ecological "collapse pattern" in every single one, which can only be slowed to a "moderate decline" under extremely optimistic assumptions of technological innovation.[7] "Humanity is on a path," Herrington concludes, "to having limits to growth imposed on itself rather than consciously choosing its own."[8]

A similar pattern is also a possibility for the financial system. "The world economy is a mess," writes British economist Ann Pettifor, because of unsustainable levels of sovereign, corporate, and household debt. So unsustainable are debt levels that we've effectively backed ourselves into a corner. "Going cold turkey would finish off a dysfunctional financial system," Pettifor says, "that's now hopelessly addicted to emergency infusions."[9]

And there's something else that should make us question our pursuit of growth at all costs. On a individual level, there's only so much insecurity we can tolerate. If we can never feel enough, if we must always strive and work and consume and strive and work some more, in perpetuity, forever, and if we aren't allowed at some point to slow down and taste something like contentment, or enoughness, then eventually we'll also succumb to our own collapse pattern. Epidemics of stress, anxiety, burnout, and socially prescribed perfectionism are perhaps leading indicators of what happens when we're continually squeezed like that.

"The only solution," according to Pettifor, "is surgery on the system itself."

What Pettifor means by surgery is an economic reset. British economist Kate Raworth has been thinking about that reset and about how economic rules might be written in a new economy where growth *isn't* everything. This growth-agnostic economy—an economy she calls the "doughnut economy"—is a road map for reorientation.[10] Raworth's doughnut is a ring of sustainability that places a floor and ceiling on how much growth an economy needs. With too little, it won't provide for the basic requirements of its citizens; with too much, it'll shoot past ecologically viable boundaries to inflict significant damage on people and the environment.

In Raworth's analysis, we've already shot past most of those boundaries. And indeed, calls for doughnut economies come mostly from those concerned with the impact of unsustainable expansion on pollution, global warming, ocean acidification, rising sea levels, melting glaciers, drought, food security, and biodiversity loss. Raworth's solution is to set an environmental boundary and to let economic growth oscillate within the doughnut of sustainability. There, she says, GDP will bob and dip "in response to the constantly evolving economy." The key is not simply to tolerate oscillating growth, but to actively target it as a policy goal.

Go ahead and say that's a load of impractical kumbaya—you won't be the first. I'd simply reply that we should at least listen to the likes of Herrington, Pettifor, and Raworth. Because what these women are saying is that the continued pursuit of growth as our one and only policy goal is a poisoned chalice, which leads us down a challenging path to a destination where we'll have to manage—in ever greater regularity—fragilities in the natural world, the financial system, and human beings.

Raworth's doughnut economy shows us that we don't have to set ourselves down that path. In developed nations, we could aim for a more steady-state, growth-agnostic economy as a matter of course. Not only will that give us our best chance of slowing climate change sufficiently for green technologies to catch up, but it'll also help us to rehabilitate ourselves from the many and varied injuries of lives lived constantly under the sword of scarcity. It'll show us that sometimes enough really is plenty; that we can have the things we need without always feeling like we must have more of the things we don't. It'll give us the permission to appreciate time away from the rat race in our homes and communities. And it'll focus our minds on what's really important in life: sustainability, quality relationships, and happiness.

GDP IS A MEAN MEASURE of growth—so could we calculate progress with other metrics as well?

Democratic nations will always need metrics and benchmarks by which to measure their progress. In the wealthier ones, economic growth is ill-suited to this challenge for the reasons we've just discussed. Which begs the question: What measure of progress should we use instead? The answer, I believe, is human and social progress.

Because if instead of prioritizing goods and services, we prioritize human and social progress, then we can ask what the trade-offs are each time a new policy is proposed. What are the human and social progress trade-offs if employees are stripped of their right to take parental leave or paid vacations? What are the trade-offs if healthcare is outsourced to the private sector? What are the trade-offs if a public library is sold to a property developer? Is the boost to the GDP worth it? Or will these policies make people's lives more insecure and less fulfilling?

British economist Richard Layard thinks human and social progress should be the focal criteria for public policy.[11] His research shows that economic growth is poorly correlated with well-being across a population and therefore governments should prioritize other outcomes—human outcomes— like mental health, happiness, and healthy life expectancy. Layard's work has been hugely influential and has provided the springboard for global initiatives aiming to measure prosperity in a way that puts people above profits.

The UN's Human Development Index is perhaps the most notable. Each year, it ranks countries' societal progress according to three dimensions of human development: living a long and healthy life, being educated, and having a decent standard of living. Other international metrics, like the Happy Planet Index, the World Happiness Report, and the Social Progress Index do similar things, albeit on smaller scales.

Why are these metrics important? Well, they show just how hollow economic growth has been in the past few decades. Since 2010, for example, the United States' per capita GDP has grown by $8,000, yet there's been zero growth in the country's human development score.[12] To put it in perspective: that's $10 trillion worth of aggregate expansion doing absolutely nothing to improve core indicators of human and social progress.

It's growth, yes, but it's wasted growth if it doesn't benefit people.

For this reason, human development metrics are beginning to influence governments. New Zealand has become the first high-income nation to incorporate measures of happiness and well-being into policy considerations. Bhutan has an index called Gross National Happiness, which they use to determine whether policies should be implemented. Maryland and Vermont have a Genuine Progress Indicator, which takes GDP and subtracts out the negative impacts of growth. Canada has developed the Canadian Index of Wellbeing. And there are others in the pipeline.

No developed nation puts human prosperity ahead of economic growth. Yet. But these are encouraging steps in the right direction.

WORK WILL UNDERGO SIGNIFICANT CHANGE with the acceleration of automation—so could we embrace that change to replace insecurity with meaning and purpose?

A century ago, British economist John Maynard Keynes began to think about what possibilities lay in store for the grandchildren of his generation. His 1930 essay, "Economic Possibilities for Our Grandchildren," contains several predictions.[13] One was that technology would rid the world of what he called man's "economic problem," the toil of work, because robots would do the heavy lifting for us.

He was right. With the advent of technologies like robots and artificial intelligence (AI), researchers estimate that automation will replace about half of all jobs in the next decade.[14]

In the same essay, Keynes made another, more famous forecast. Given the economy would become so productive, he said, future generations would barely need to work at all. "Three-hour shifts or a fifteen-hour week," according to Keynes, would be quite enough to satisfy the basic needs for purpose and routine.

On that prediction, though, he couldn't have been more wrong. Technology hasn't meant we can get stuff done quicker and knock off early. What's actually happened is that our political class decided it was far more important for five men to be richer than God.

Rather than enjoyed, we've filled the time saved by advances in technology with yet more work. Dishwashers freed up time to work more. Washing machines freed up time to work more. Hell, even central heating meant we didn't have to collect and chop firewood so we could . . . work more. And now, ominously, AI is emerging to free up huge amounts of work that's being used to, yep, you guessed it, have us work more. That's the hamster wheel of growth in action.

Until, of course, AI isn't used for that reason. In the not-too-distant future, white-collar workers are going to find that AI can do most of their jobs for them. We won't be working more then, because we won't be working at all.

We need, of course, to work. It gives us dignity, purpose, and self-respect, not to mention that society would collapse in rather short order if everyone downed tools. But Keynes wrote "Economic Possibilities for Our Grandchildren" as a record of hope for future generations, letting them know that, one day, work won't need to be arduous, backbreaking, and necessary for survival. He envisaged a society in which the productivity gains of automation were broadly shared. And as a result, people could enjoy a shorter working life, immersed in the vocation of their jobs, doing them to fuel their passions and dreams rather than for mere survival.

The obvious retort is that some people love to work and want to do more of it. Why stop them? I'm not saying we should. Nor was Keynes.

If work is what gives you meaning and purpose, go for it. Fill your boots.

What I'm saying is that the tail shouldn't wag the dog. Those with the penchant for overwork, and who are privileged enough to have the capacity to do so, shouldn't be allowed to warp working norms to such an extent that they pollute the entire workplace. Human progress, if it means anything, is about freeing ourselves from that kind of hyper-competitive, breathless, relentless striving.

So, if our agreement about the "correct" number of working hours can move from sixty to forty, then surely it can keep moving from forty to Keynes's recommended fifteen.

Those who want to work more absolutely can. The point is that advancement in automation and AI means we don't have to. Or at least we don't have to in *theory*. The reality of shorter workweeks will depend on where we decide the proceeds of automation should go: to ordinary people, in the form of more time in our homes and communities, or to shareholders, in the form of stock valuations and dividends.

In essence, who benefits from automation is—and always has been—a question of priorities. Keynes's mistake was to naively assume we'd use automation to enhance the lives of people.

Then there's the rather tenuous assumption that more work equals more productivity. Global initiatives like the four-day week and a concerted transition toward more flexible working arrangements are showing that it's not quite that simple.[15] The number of companies embracing such initiatives is on the rise, and they're finding that their employees are happier, less stressed, healthier, and more productive having embraced them.[16]

A recent review of thirty-three companies experimenting with a four-day week, for example, found that employee burnout was reduced by a third, and fatigue and sleep problems by almost 10 percent, compared to a five-day week.[17] Work-life balance and life satisfaction also improved, as did company revenues. Indeed, when it comes to revenues, perhaps the highest-profile company to experiment with a four-day week—Microsoft Japan—saw a staggering 40 percent increase in productivity when its employees took an extra day off.[18]

So just imagine, for a moment, another world. One where we use technology not to enhance shareholder value, but, as Keynes prophesied, to free us from the drudgery of unnecessary work. Imagine how much more of our working lives would be spent on taking calculated risks, pushing boundaries, creating, and innovating, and how much more time we'd spend trying new things, building new relationships, and appreciating newfound leisure.

I don't pretend that the transition to that world will be easily accomplished. But I do believe it'll be essential, especially if we're serious about breaking free from perfectionism and the many other physical and psychological stresses that come from insecure overwork. What will also be essential for any of this to materialize is a dramatic reduction in inequality. Because none of it—placing well-being ahead of goods and services, working fewer hours, enjoying more leisure—will be possible unless gaps between rich and poor are brought under some sort of control.

INEQUALITY IS THE GREAT SOCIETAL SICKNESS—so could we possibly rebalance the scales?

"Tax us now." That was the plea from a group of millionaires who joined protests at the 2022 gathering of financial and political elites in Davos, Switzerland.[19] The top 1 percent in America, these millionaires pointed out, have more wealth than the bottom 92 percent combined, and the fifty wealthiest Americans, their posters read, own more wealth than the entire bottom half of American society. Although the United States is a clear outlier, the divergence of rich and poor is a distinguishing feature of most economies in the modern world. "How can this be right," the millionaire protesters asked, "when cost-of-living crises are playing out in multiple nations?"

It can't be right, but it is the inevitable consequence of supply-side economics. Several decades of pandering to capital—tax cuts for the rich, deregulation, deunionization, and so on—have culminated in a lopsided economy where the gains of economic expansion are stockpiled among the elite. Since 2020, two-thirds of all the new wealth we've collectively produced has been captured by the richest 1 percent.[20]

And it's not just income and assets. The elite live longer, healthier lives. They have more spacious homes; access to private healthcare; two, perhaps three vacations a year; and, most crucially, possess disproportional power over their own lives and the lives of others.

Problem is: it's not just rapidly growing economies that create these inequities. According to French economist Thomas Piketty, inequalities get out of hand in economies with low or no growth, too. More so, in fact, because his research shows that gaps between the rich and poor increase in the long run when the rate of returns to wealth—rents from real estate, dividends from stocks, et cetera—outstrip the rate of economic growth.[21] Assuming he's correct about that, and there's plenty of evidence to suggest he is, then slowing rates of economic growth will actually create more inequality and social unrest than we already have.

Unless, of course, strong preventative measures are taken to bring about a more even distribution of income, wealth, and power.

In his new book, *Capital and Ideology*, Piketty proposes some such measures.[22] A global wealth tax with a rate that goes as high as 90 percent for those worth a billion dollars is the most eye-catching. But there are others. He suggests progressive inheritance and income taxes at top marginal rates in excess of 80 percent, just like they were between 1950 and 1970. With the money raised, Piketty suggests we fund an endowment of capital, given to everyone at age twenty-five, which should boost investment and entrepreneurial activity.

For Piketty, progressive taxes are not just about redistributing resources and power. They're also about conservation. "It is increasingly clear that the resolution of the climate challenge will not be possible without a strong movement in the direction of the compression of social inequalities at all levels," he writes in *Le Monde*.[23] Because, he says, "at world level, the richest 10% are responsible for almost half the emissions and the top 1% alone emit more carbon than the poorest half of the planet." Taxing billionaires out of existence would create a "drastic reduction in purchasing power of the richest [and] would therefore in itself have a substantial impact on the reduction of emissions at a global level."

Progressive taxation was what those millionaires in Davos wanted. But creating a more equitable distribution of income and wealth isn't just about progressive taxation; other preventative measures must also be considered. In a 2020 paper for the *Review of Political Economy*, political economists Tilman Hartley, Jeroen van den Bergh, and Giorgos Kallis proposed several such measures.[24] These include promoting worker co-operatives, which distribute corporate profits more evenly; imposing interest-rate caps and rent controls; strengthening labor protections that boost the security of working people; basic income; land and carbon taxes; and higher investment in public goods such as housing, healthcare, and education.

All work to bring down inequality. And reducing inequality will invariably take pressure off our political classes' current crusade of growing the economic pie to meet human needs. A crusade that looks increasingly untenable against a backdrop of zero-sum accounting. In the last three years alone, the world's five richest men have more than doubled their already vast fortunes, while the world's poorest 60 percent—almost 5 billion people—have gotten even poorer.[25]

There isn't scarcity, just inequality.

Which is why it's time we focused on how the economic pie is sliced instead. If we could do that, it's perfectly possible to reduce poverty, pollution, and food and shelter insecurity, and increase life expectancy, well-being, and social progress without relying on GDP to magically meet those objectives.

To this end, I want to focus on one policy: basic income. Because basic income won't just reduce inequality, although it will do that in good measure. It'll also reduce a great deal of the perfectionism that comes from living inside an economy that gets a great deal of its growth from the vice of scarcity.

BASIC INCOME GIVES PEOPLE REAL FREEDOM to flourish— so could we implement it in place of welfare?

A minimum assumption of any decent society is that people have an unconditional right to exist. People shouldn't need to justify or earn their existence, and they certainly shouldn't have to prove themselves in order to eat or sleep somewhere warm. Instead, people should be free to express themselves however they wish, take as many risks in self-exploration as they want, and if they should fail, have the right not to starve or find themselves destitute.

These ideals are at the core of basic income—a centralized economic program that guarantees income to everyone. Under the policy, all people receive no less than is minimally required to sustain themselves, but also no more. This fundamental right seems odd viewed through the lens of today's culture. Yet the idea is far from a new one: basic income is ordained in Christian theology and practiced all over the world in many Indigenous communities.

Basic income expands personal freedom. It means that no person is economically dependent upon another. Entrepreneurs can take whatever risks they like without fear of losing the clothes off their backs. Creatives are free to create whatever they want, provided they're willing to live on necessities. All who work get paid on top of a basic income, which only becomes helpful should they need it. With the sheer size and bulkiness of our present welfare state, it's hard to imagine that a basic income would cost much more than we already spend. Perhaps less, if we consider the knock-on savings for healthcare, mental health services, and policing.

Just like getting a bit more agnostic about growth, basic income might not be a choice; it may very well become a necessity. As we've just seen, major technological advances like AI are taking jobs away from people at a rapid clip, and that trend will only accelerate into the future. Unconditional support will invariably be needed to backstop demand and stabilize the economy as it undergoes these unprecedented disruptions.

But there are wider benefits than economic stabilization. If everyone is unconditionally trusted with the same resources as everyone else, widespread insecurity falls, and so does inequality. By providing a universal starting point in life, one that's above the poverty line, basic income provides a secure foundation—alleviating the chronic stress, and perfectionism, associated with scarcity.

Indeed, this is perhaps the most important benefit of basic income: it flips our purpose in life on its head. Rather than existing in the quicksand of deficit, basic income harnesses our intrinsic motivation and provides the firm footing needed to explore, innovate, and contribute to society in personally meaningful and socially useful ways. In the basic income world, income fuels work, not the other way around, and that enables us to live our lives free from the suffocating guilt and shame of not doing or having enough.

Where trialed, the scheme has shown promising results. German policy advisor Claudia Haarmann, for example, found that when basic income was piloted in Namibia, it increased the rate of work by 10 percent, and school attendance by 90 percent. It also reduced child malnutrition by 30 percent and overall crime by 42 percent.[26]

Canadian economist Evelyn Forget had similar findings in her famous Manitoba Basic Annual Income Experiment.[27] The guaranteed income scheme she ran dramatically improved the mental health of Manitoban families, increased the time young people spent at school, and reduced hospital admissions by almost 10 percent.

The impact of basic income on mental health is indeed enormous. One study, over twelve years and including 100 million people in Brazil, found that unconditional cash transfers reduced suicide risk by 61 percent.[28] These transfers have even been tested against psychotherapy and found to be far more effective at improving mental health than any individual intervention.[29]

Time and time again, these findings are replicated. A recent review of almost forty studies, for example, finds that expansions in social security correlate with improved mental health outcomes, while reductions correlate with poorer outcomes.[30] For these reasons, several public and professional health associations have officially endorsed basic income, including the Canadian Medical Association, the Canadian Public Health Association, and the Chronic Disease Prevention Alliance.

Most arguments for basic income hinge on the easing of poverty. And in that respect, its promise is indeed substantial. But I see benefits well beyond the policy's redistributive potential. Money worries are an inescapable feature of modern life for everybody. Having enough to make a good impression, or even make ends meet, are things that preoccupy our daily thoughts—not to mention our nightmares. Basic income releases us from that jeopardy. There'll still be competitive and professional hierarchies, which are necessary. We just won't need to justify ourselves continually, we'll feel far less fear, and we'll be inclined to appreciate people for who they are, not for what they have or what they're worth.

In other words, we won't need to be perfect just to get by.

If you're reading this book, I imagine that you're probably where I was a few years ago: struggling with a burning desire to be perfect and wondering why on earth you feel like this. So I hope this book's been the same journey for you as it's been for me. I hope it's given you permission to appreciate your precious, fallible humanity. And I hope it's given you a different way of thinking about our obsession with perfection not as some inner drive or compulsion that we can't tame, but as a relational trait and cultural phenomenon arising from difficulty resisting, in the words of Erich Fromm, "public pressure to be a wolf with the wolves."[31]

We've come of age inside an all-consuming culture of flawlessness and exceptionalism, which doesn't give us a moment's respite from the relentless messaging about what we lack. Inside that culture, there's a collective, almost unconscious, scramble for perfection. And although that sounds very "big picture," it does give us a straightforward way out. For if we can somehow alter the values that society holds, and implement the changes I've discussed in this chapter, then without doing anything in ourselves, without even thinking about it, breaking free of perfectionism will lose most of its difficulty.

Why? Because perfectionism cannot thrive under conditions of safety, security, and plenty.

Of course, that's easy to say, not so easy to do. But is there hope? Of course there's hope! Young people aren't following the "natural" conservative path on economics, climate policy, or social issues taken by their parents. They want something different.[32]

I see and hear evidence for this in the corridors of university campuses, at presentations and events, in sessions of conferences and in the bars and cafés that surround them. It's remarkable really. How they just won't be ground down. How they continue to reject what they've been told their entire lives to understand is "just the way things are." How they just keep arguing, mostly out of view, for reforms as radical in their outlook as those that kick-started the supply-side revolution all those decades ago.

These men and women are nearly two decades younger than I am. But they already seem to know what took me almost my entire adult life to figure out: *it's society that needs mending, not us.*

As long as we can hold on to that fact, we're not lost. We can help young people to secure their futures. We can fight with them and on their behalf. We can work together, plan together. We can vote together.

But we must act fast together because the shadows are lengthening and the powers in charge show no signs of changing course. Left to their own devices, they'll surely waste our remaining human and natural resources, keeping a teetering system upright just about long enough to extract the last few trillions for themselves, rather than creating something truly sustainable for everyone.

Such a movement can only come from the ground, not the dusty pages of this book. So get out there, organize, agitate, and tell the powerful with your voices and your votes that you demand change. Things might seem difficult now. But the time is upon us, the winds are slowly changing, and we do, have what's left of democracy.

If we can use it, then piece by piece, we can build something resembling a Republic of Good Enough—one that respects human and planetary limits.

All of which is why, on a crystal clear day, if I creak my neck out really far, if I squint as hard as I possibly can into the distance, I can just about make out what looks like a path. And on that path, I can see a long queue of smart, thoughtful, compassionate, generous, and thoroughly decent human beings just like you, walking toward the light of hope. Hope that we can live in a place where we don't have to feel insecure or less than. Where abundance is enjoyed, by everyone. Where we don't need to be perfect just to get by.

For your presence on this earth, and for reading this book, I am eternally grateful.

I hope it's helped you to better understand your perfectionism. I hope it's helped you to situate it in the bigger picture and discover where most of it originates. Genes and early life experiences do matter, and they matter rather a lot. But beyond them, the overbearing weight of modern culture has smothered us with impossible pressures to be perfect. Pressures that are inescapable. Pressures that are unrelenting. Pressures that are always there to remind us, heaven forbid we should ever forget, that we're not enough. Knowledge reveals the true source of all that errant pressure—our growth-at-all-costs economy—and with it the political movements and policies that provide an escape.

Reader: we *are* enough. Every last one of us. The lonely night porter at the Hind Hotel and the worn-out engineer at the hydro plant, the hard-up cleaner scrubbing muck from bathroom floors and the frazzled banker cutting million-dollar swaps. Beneath our brittle exteriors, we're the same bone, flesh, and blood. If we could just accept that common humanity, if we could know that no one is perfect or could ever be made perfect, then we'd discover that yearning, wanting, craving, and constantly trying to update, fix, and improve things are fleeting and meaningless conditions, and that their ubiquity in this culture disconnects us from the astonishing, animating spirit of our imperfections and their coursing, vitalizing energies, which are real and alive and within us and accessible if only we could be allowed to access them.

You have the right to love and live contentedly inside your beautiful, imperfect self, on your beautiful, imperfect planet. Fight for it.

ACKNOWLEDGMENTS

This book very nearly didn't get written. Many a month spent procrastinating, reworking the structure, adding a comma, removing a comma, swapping the opening word and then swapping it back again put this book well over two years past its deadline. Having skillfully smoothed over the fallout from all that indecision—having fielded countless panicked "It's not ready yet!" messages and emails—my agent, Chris Wellbelove, has probably learned his lesson: don't, for Christ's sake, talk a perfectionist into writing a book on perfectionism.

Thanks, Chris, for seeing the project way before I did and sticking with it through to the end.

Thanks, too, belong to my long-suffering editors, Helen Conford of Cornerstone Press and Rick Horgan of Scribner. It took a while, but we got there. Your guidance (not to mention patience) has made this book an immeasurably better read. On the editing front, I would also like to thank Hazel Adkins, Emily Herring, Rob, Isabel, Katya, Vanessa, and Olivia for reading and commenting with care and sensitivity.

It's also the case that this book would not exist without the guidance of my doctorate supervisor and close friend Andrew Hill. Thank you for supporting me and continuing to work with me closely as I've tried to understand perfectionism better. I'd also like to make a special mention of my first supervisor, Howard Hall, who was an instrumental figure in my academic development and to whom I owe a debt of gratitude for taking a long-shot punt on me in the first place.

On my professional journey, there have also been many doctorate students, faculty, and support staff who've made a significant imprint on my development and thinking. These people include, in no particular order: Sandra Jovchelovitch, Chris Hunt, Gareth Jowett, Sarah Mallinson-Howard, Paul Appleton, Marianne Etherson, Daniel Madigan, Andrew Parker, Mustafa Sarkar, Rachel Arnold, Paul Dolan, Bradley Franks, Sana Nordin-Bates, Martin Smith, Liam Delaney, Catherine Sabiston, Mike McKenna, Martin Jones, Mark Beauchamp, Champa Heidbrink, Nikos Ntoumanis, Anthony Payne, Sean Cumming, Michael Butson, Joan Duda, Michael Muthukrishna, Miriam Tresh, Patrick Gaudreau, Anika Petrella, Chris Niemiec, Richard Ryan, Maria Kavussanu, Robert Vallerand, Nicolas Lemyre, Jennifer Sheehy-Skeffington, Jens Madsen, and Alex Gillespie.

Thanks are also due to the focal characters of this book—Paul Hewitt and Gordon Flett—who gave their time to talk with me and share their wisdom about perfectionism in a way no other could. I would also like to thank Martyn Standage for being a constant source of support and banter (and favorite 4W coffee drinker). And to Fred Basso for listening to me muse about philosophy I only half understand, for reading my drafts, and for exchanging after-lecture debate about economics and psychology in the pubs outside LSE.

A big thank you, too, to Liam, Stuart, and Peter for their friendship.

And finally, above all, I am grateful to my family. Your unwavering support, guidance, and love (and shed, where I wrote large chunks of this book) have been and continue to be an immense source of solace and have improved this book, and me, beyond words. Although I seem to move all over the place, you're the one constant in my all-too-hectic life. I love you all very much.

NOTES

Chapter One: Our Favorite Flaw
Or Modern Society's Obsession with Perfection

1. Gino, F. (2015). "The Right Way to Brag about Yourself." *Harvard Business Review.* Available online: https://hbr.org/2015/05/the-right-way-to-brag-about-yourself.

2. Pacht, A. R. (1984). "Reflections on Perfection." *American Psychologist* 39(4): 386.

3. Horney, K. (1937). *The Neurotic Personality of Our Time.* New York: W. W. Norton.

Chapter Two: Tell Me I'm Enough
Or Why Perfectionism Is So Much More Than High Standards

1. Sullivan, H. S. (1953). *The Interpersonal Theory of Psychiatry.* New York: W. W. Norton.

2. American Psychiatric Association (2013). *Diagnostic and Statistical Manual of Mental Disorders* (5th ed.). Arlington, VA: American Psychiatric Association.

3. Hewitt, P. L., & Flett, G. L. (1991). "Perfectionism in the Self and Social Contexts: Conceptualization, Assessment, and Association with

Psychopathology." *Journal of Personality and Social Psychology* 60(3): 456.

4. McRae, D. (2008). "I'm Striving for Something I'll Never Achieve—I'm a Mess." *The Guardian*. Available online: https://www.theguardian.com /sport/2008/oct/28/victoriapendleton-cycling.

5. Dinh, J. (2011). "Demi Lovato Tells Teens That 'Love Is Louder' Than Pressure." MTV. Available online: https://www.mtv.com/news/46d7mo/demi -lovato-love-is-louder.

6. Isaacson, W. (2011). *Steve Jobs*. New York: Simon & Schuster.

7. Greenfield, R. (2011). "The Crazy Perfectionism That Drove Steve Jobs." *The Atlantic*. Available online: https://www.theatlantic.com/technology /archive/2011/11/crazy-perfectionism-drove-steve-jobs/335842/.

8. Gladwell, M. (2011). "The Tweaker: The Real Genius of Steve Jobs." *The New Yorker*. Available online: https://www.newyorker.com/magazine /2011/11/14/the-tweaker.

9. Tate, R. (2011). "What Everyone Is Too Polite to Say about Steve Jobs." *Gawker*. Available online: https://www.gawker.com/5847344/what-every one-is-too-polite-to-say-about-steve-jobs.

10. This is an informal, adapted version of Paul and Gord's Multidimensional Perfectionism Scale. Unlike the rigorously validated instrument itself, these items have not been scientifically corroborated and are merely intended to be illustrative.

Chapter Three: What Doesn't Kill You
Or Why Perfectionism Does So Much Damage to Our Mental Health

1. Woolf, V. (1979). *The Diary of Virginia Woolf, Volume One: 1915–1919.* Boston: Mariner.

2. Hewitt, P. L., Flett, G. L., & Mikail, S. F. (2017). *Perfectionism: A Relational Approach to Conceptualization, Assessment, and Treatment.* New York: Guilford.

3. Limburg, K., Watson, H. J., Hagger, M. S., & Egan, S. J. (2017). "The Relationship between Perfectionism and Psychopathology: A Meta-Analysis." *Journal of Clinical Psychology* 73(10): 1301–26.

4. Smith, M. M., Sherry, S. B., Chen, S., Saklofske, D. H., Mushquash, C., Flett, G. L., & Hewitt, P. L. (2018). "The Perniciousness of Perfectionism: A Meta-Analytic Review of the Perfectionism–Suicide Relationship." *Journal of Personality* 86(3): 522–42.

5. Smith, M. M., Sherry, S. B., Rnic, K., Saklofske, D. H., Enns, M., & Gralnick, T. (2016). "Are Perfectionism Dimensions Vulnerability Factors for Depressive Symptoms after Controlling for Neuroticism? A Meta-Analysis of 10 Longitudinal Studies." *European Journal of Personality* 30: 201–12.

6. Hewitt, P. L., & Flett, G. L. (1991). "Perfectionism in the Self and Social Contexts: Conceptualization, Assessment, and Association with Psychopathology." *Journal of Personality and Social Psychology* 60: 456–70.

7. Hill, R. W., Zrull, M. C., & Turlington, S. (1997). "Perfectionism and Interpersonal Problems." *Journal of Personality Assessment* 69: 81–103.

8. Hill, R. W., McIntire, K., & Bacharach, V. R. (1997). "Perfectionism and the Big Five Factors." *Journal of Social Behavior & Personality* 12: 257–70.

9. Nealis, L. J., Sherry, S. B., Lee-Baggley, D. L., Stewart, S. H., & Macneil, M. A. (2016). "Revitalizing Narcissistic Perfectionism: Evidence of the Reliability and the Validity of an Emerging Construct." *Journal of Psychopathology and Behavioral Assessment* 38: 493–504.

10. Habke, A. M., Hewitt, P. L., & Flett, G. L. (1999). "Perfectionism and Sexual Satisfaction in Intimate Relationships." *Journal of Psychopathology and Behavioral Assessment* 21: 307–22.

11. Haring, M., Hewitt, P. L., & Flett, G. L. (2003). "Perfectionism, Coping, and Quality of Intimate Relationships." *Journal of Marriage and Family* 65: 143–58.

12. Flett, G. L., Hewitt, P. L., Nepon, T., Sherry, S. B., & Smith, M. (2022). "The Destructiveness and Public Health Significance of Socially Prescribed Perfectionism: A Review, Analysis, and Conceptual Extension." *Clinical Psychology Review* 93: 102130.

13. Smith, M. M., Sherry, S. B., Chen, S., Saklofske, D. H., Mushquash, C., Flett, G. L., & Hewitt, P. L. (2018). "The Perniciousness of Perfectionism: A Meta-Analytic Review of the Perfectionism–Suicide Relationship." *Journal of Personality* 86(3): 522–42.

14. Sutton, J. (2021). "Even the Bleakest Moments Are Not Permanent." *The Psychologist*. Available online: https://www.bps.org.uk/psychologist/even-bleakest-moments-are-not-permanent.

15. Hill, A. P. (2021). "Perfectionistic Tipping Points: Re-Probing Interactive Effects of Perfectionism." *Sport, Exercise, and Performance Psychology* 10(2): 177.

16. Curran, T., Hill, A. P. (2018). "A Test of Perfectionistic Vulnerability Following Competitive Failure among College Athletes." *Journal of Sport and Exercise Psychology* 40(5): 269–79.

17. Sturman, E. D., Flett, G. L., Hewitt, P. L., & Rudolph, S. G. (2009). "Dimensions of Perfectionism and Self-Worth Contingencies in Depression." *Journal of Rational-Emotive & Cognitive-Behavior Therapy* 27: 213–31.

18. Dang, S. S., Quesnel, D. A., Hewitt, P. L., Flett, G. L., & Deng, X. (2020). "Perfectionistic Traits and Self-Presentation Are Associated with Negative Attitudes and Concerns about Seeking Professional Psychological Help." *Clinical Psychology & Psychotherapy* 27(5): 621–29.

Chapter Four: I Started Something I Couldn't Finish
Or the Curious Relationship between Perfectionism and Performance

1. Burns, D. D. (2008). *Feeling Good: The New Mood Therapy*. New York: HarperCollins.

2. Hamachek, D. E. (1978). "Psychodynamics of Normal and Neurotic Perfectionism." *Psychology* 15: 27–33.

3. Greenspon, T. S. (2000). "'Healthy Perfectionism' Is an Oxymoron!: Reflections on the Psychology of Perfectionism and the Sociology of Science." *Journal of Secondary Gifted Education* 11(4): 197–208.

4. Pacht, A. R. (1984). "Reflections on Perfection." *American Psychologist* 39(4): 386.

5. Stoeber, J., Haskew, A. E., & Scott, C. (2015). "Perfectionism and Exam Performance: The Mediating Effect of Task-Approach Goals." *Personality and Individual Differences* 74: 171–76.

6. Stoeber, J., Chesterman, D., & Tarn, T. A. (2010). "Perfectionism and Task Performance: Time on Task Mediates the Perfectionistic Strivings–Performance Relationship." *Personality and Individual Differences* 48(4): 458–62.

7. Harari, D., Swider, B. W., Steed, L. B., & Breidenthal, A. P. (2018). "Is Perfect Good? A Meta-Analysis of Perfectionism in the Workplace." *Journal of Applied Psychology* 103(10): 1121.

8. Ogurlu, U. (2020). "Are Gifted Students Perfectionistic? A Meta-Analysis." *Journal for the Education of the Gifted* 43(3): 227–51.

9. Madigan, D. J. (2019). "A Meta-Analysis of Perfectionism and Academic Achievement." *Educational Psychology Review* 31(4): 967–89.

10. Harari, D., et al. (2018). "Is Perfect Good? A Meta-Analysis of Perfectionism in the Workplace."

11. Adapted from: Gaudreau, P. (2019). "On the Distinction between Personal Standards Perfectionism and Excellencism: A Theory Elaboration and Research Agenda." *Perspectives on Psychological Science* 14(2): 197–215.

12. Hill, A. P., & Curran, T. (2016). "Multidimensional Perfectionism and Burnout: A Meta-Analysis." *Personality and Social Psychology Review* 20(3): 269–88.

13. Gaudreau, P., Schellenberg, B. J., Gareau, A., Kljajic, K., & Manoni-Millar, S. (2022). "Because Excellencism Is More Than Good Enough: On the Need to Distinguish the Pursuit of Excellence from the Pursuit of Perfection." *Journal of Personality and Social Psychology* 122(6): 1117–45.

14. Gaudreau, P., et al. (2022). Ibid.

15. At the very end, we let participants know their "failure" was just sham feedback for the purposes of the experiment. Expletives followed.

16. Curran, T., & Hill, A. P. (2018). "A Test of Perfectionistic Vulnerability Following Competitive Failure among College Athletes." *Journal of Sport and Exercise Psychology* 40(5): 269–79.

17. Hill, A. P., Hall, H. K., Duda, J. L., & Appleton, P. R. (2011). "The Cognitive, Affective and Behavioural Responses of Self-Oriented Perfectionists Following Successive Failure on a Muscular Endurance Task." *International Journal of Sport and Exercise Psychology* 9(2): 189–207.

18. Sirois, F. M., Molnar, D. S., & Hirsch, J. K. (2017). "A Meta-Analytic and Conceptual Update on the Associations between Procrastination and Multidimensional Perfectionism." *European Journal of Personality* 31(2): 137–59.

19. Hewitt, P. L., Flett, G. L., & Mikail, S. F. (2017). *Perfectionism: A Relational Approach to Conceptualization, Assessment, and Treatment.* New York: Guilford.

Chapter Five: The Hidden Epidemic
Or the Astonishing Rise of Perfectionism in Modern Society

1. Flett, G. L., & Hewitt, P. L. (2020). "The Perfectionism Pandemic Meets COVID-19: Understanding the Stress, Distress and Problems in Living for Perfectionists during the Global Health Crisis." *Journal of Concurrent Disorders* 2(1): 80–105.

2. Georgiev, D. (2022). "How Much Time Do People Spend on Social Media?" Review 42. Available online: https://review42.com/resources/how-much-time-do-people-spend-on-social-media/.

3. Flannery, M. E. (2018). "The Epidemic of Anxiety among Today's Students." NEA News. Available online: https://www.nea.org/advocating-for-change/new-from-nea/epidemic-anxiety-among-todays-students.

4. Association of Child Psychotherapists (2018). "Silent Catastrophe: Responding to the Danger Signs of Children and Young People's Mental Health Services in Trouble." Available online: https://childpsychotherapy.org.uk/sites/default/files/documents/ACP%20SILENT%20CATASTROPHE%20REPORT_0.pdf.

5. Royal College of Psychiatrists (2021). "Country in the Grip of a Mental Health Crisis with Children Worst Affected, New Analysis Finds." Available online: https://www.rcpsych.ac.uk/news-and-features/latest-news/detail/2021/04/08/country-in-the-grip-of-a-mental-health-crisis-with-children-worst-affected-new-analysis-finds.

6. Survey reported in Flett, G. L., & Hewitt, P. L. (2022). *Perfectionism in Childhood and Adolescence: A Developmental Analysis.* Washington, DC: American Psychological Association.

7. Girlguiding (2016). "Girls' Attitudes Study." Available online: https://www.girlguiding.org.uk/globalassets/docs-and-resources/research-and-campaigns/girls-attitudes-survey-2016.pdf.

8. Flett, G. L., & Hewitt, P. L. (2022). *Perfectionism in Childhood and Adolescence.*

9. Flett, G. L. & Hewitt, P. L. (2022). Ibid.

10. Curran, T., & Hill, A. P. (2019). "Perfectionism Is Increasing Over Time: A Meta-Analysis of Birth Cohort Differences from 1989 to 2016." *Psychological Bulletin* 145(4): 410.

11. Smith, M. M., Sherry, S. B., Vidovic, V., Saklofske, D. H., Stoeber, J., & Benoit, A. (2019). "Perfectionism and the Five-Factor Model of Per-

sonality: A Meta-Analytic Review." *Personality and Social Psychology Review* 23(4): 367–90.

12. Haidt, J., & Twenge, J. (2021). *Adolescent Mood Disorders Since 2010: A Collaborative Review.* Unpublished manuscript, New York University.

13. The interested reader can find an overview of all other perfectionism theories in Joachim Stoeber's excellent book *The Psychology of Perfectionism* (2017). London: Routledge.

Chapter Six: Some Perfectionists Are Bigger Than Others
Or the Intricate Nature and Nurture of Perfectionism's Development

1. Mead, M. (1939). *From the South Seas.* New York: Morrow.

2. Plomin, R. (2018). *Blueprint: How DNA Makes Us Who We Are.* Cambridge, MA: MIT Press.

3. Iranzo-Tatay, C., Gimeno-Clemente, N., Barberá-Fons, M., Rodriguez-Campayo, M. Á., Rojo-Bofill, L., Livianos-Aldana, L., & Rojo-Moreno, L. (2015). "Genetic and Environmental Contributions to Perfectionism and Its Common Factors." *Psychiatry Research* 230(3): 932–39.

4. Quoted in: Seelye, K. Q. (2019). "Judith Rich Harris, 80, Dies; Author Played Down the Role of Parents." *New York Times.* Available online: https://www.nytimes.com/2019/01/01/obituaries/judith-rich-harris-dies .html.

5. Harris, J. R. (1998). *The Nurture Assumption: Why Children Turn Out the Way They Do.* New York: Simon & Schuster.

6. Harris, J. R. (1995). "Where Is the Child's Environment? A Group Socialization Theory of Development." *Psychological Review* 102(3): 458.

7. Harris, J. R. (1998). *The Nurture Assumption.*

8. I should emphasize this point since it's extremely important. Early life trauma has a profound effect on perfectionism. Indeed, in case reports and across

hundreds of clinical studies, perfectionism is a well-documented coping mechanism against mistreatment. I'm not a clinical psychologist so I cannot talk with any authority on these matters. Nor, frankly, should I attempt to. This book sheds light on perfectionism as a cultural phenomenon, which is to say perfectionism as it afflicts everyone in the aggregate. Readers interested in early trauma and perfectionism might consult the excellent books: *Overcoming Perfectionism* by Ann W. Smith (1990), and *Perfectionism: A Relational Approach* by Paul Hewitt, Gordon Flett, and Samuel Mikail (2017).

9. Paris, B. J. (1996). *Karen Horney: A Psychoanalyst's Search for Self-Understanding*. New Haven, CT: Yale University Press.

10. Paris, B. J. (1996). Ibid.

11. Horney, K. (1937). *The Neurotic Personality of Our Time*. New York: W. W. Norton.

12. Horney, K. (1937). Ibid.

13. Horney, K. (1937). Ibid.

14. Horney, K. (1950). *Neurosis and Human Growth*. New York: W. W. Norton.

15. Horney, K. (1975). *The Therapeutic Process: Essays and lectures*. New Haven, CT: Yale University Press.

16. Kaufman, S. B. (2020). "Finding Inner Harmony: The Underappreciated Legacy of Karen Horney." *Scientific American*. Available online: https://blogs.scientificamerican.com/beautiful-minds/finding-inner-harmony-the-underappreciated-legacy-of-karen-horney/.

Chapter Seven: What I Don't Have
Or How Perfectionism Grows in the Soil of Our (Manufactured) Discontent

1. Adorno, T. W. (1974). *Minima Moralia*. London: Verso.

2. US Census Data (2022). "U.S. Retail Sales (2012 to 2022)." Oberlo. Available online: https://www.oberlo.ca/statistics/us-retail-sales.

3. eMarketer (2022). "Total Retail Sales Worldwide (2020 to 2025)." Oberlo. Available online: https://www.oberlo.ca/statistics/total-retail-sales.

4. Fischer, S. (2021). "Ad Industry Growing at Record Pace." *Axios Media Trends*. Available online: https://www.axios.com/2021/12/07/advertising-industry-revenue.

5. In Jacobsen, M. F., & Mazur, L. A. (1995). *Marketing Madness: A Survival Guide for a Consumer Society.* New York: Routledge.

6. "You can't have a strong National Health Service," we keep being told, "without a strong economy."

7. Morgan, T. (2013). *Life after Growth.* Petersfield, UK: Harriman House.

8. I realize this sounds like a completely batshit way to organize an economy that would prefer to avoid complete collapse, but it is, I assure you, the very serious logic of our debt-propelled, forever-growth consensus.

9. Roper-Starch Organization (1979). *Roper Reports 79-1.* Roper Center, University of Connecticut, Storrs.

10. Roper-Starch Organization (1995). *Roper Reports 95-1.* Roper Center, University of Connecticut, Storrs.

11. Pew Research Center (2007). "How Young People View Their Lives, Futures and Politics: A Portrait of 'Generation Next.'" Retrieved from http://people-press.org/report/300/a-portrait-of-generation-next.

12. Easterlin, R. A. (1974). "Does Economic Growth Improve the Human Lot? Some Empirical Evidence." In *Nations and Households in Economic Growth*, ed. David, P. & Melvin, W. (89–125). Palo Alto: Stanford University Press.

13. Myers, D. G. (2000). "The Funds, Friends, and Faith of Happy People." *American Psychologist* 55: 56–67.

14. Kahneman, D., & Deaton, A. (2010). "High Income Improves Evaluation of Life but Not Emotional Well-Being." *Proceedings of the National Academy of Sciences of the USA* 107: 16489–93. I've adjusted their $75,000 plateau point for inflation.

15. Phillips, A. (2010). *On Balance.* London: Picador.

16. Brown, B. (2012). *Daring Greatly: How the Courage to Be Vulnerable Transforms the Way We Live, Love, Parent, and Lead.* New York: Penguin.

17. Germer, C. K., & Neff, K. D. (2013). "Self-Compassion in Clinical Practice." *Journal of Clinical Psychology* 69(8): 856–67.

18. Kernis, M. H. (2000). "Substitute Needs and the Distinction between Fragile and Secure High Self-Esteem." *Psychological Inquiry* 11(4):, 298–300.

19. Neff, K. D. (2022). "Self-Compassion: Theory, Method, Research, and Intervention." *Annual Review of Psychology*, 74.

20. MacBeth, A., & Gumley, A. (2012). "Exploring Compassion: A Meta-Analysis of the Association between Self-Compassion and Psychopathology." *Clinical Psychology Review* 32(6): 545–52.

21. Albertson, E. R., Neff, K. D., & Dill-Shackleford, K. E. (2015). "Self-Compassion and Body Dissatisfaction in Women: A Randomized Controlled Trial of a Brief Meditation Intervention." *Mindfulness* 6(3): 444–54.

Chapter Eight: What She Posted
Or Why Social Media Companies Thrive on Pressures to Be Perfect

1. This quote was part of a verbal testimony from Adam Mosseri, head of Instagram, before a Senate committee on Protecting Kids Online in December 2021. The testimony is available to view at: https://www.commerce.senate.gov/2021/12/protecting-kids-online-instagram-and-reforms-for-young-users.

2. Statista (2022). "Meta: Annual Revenue and Net Income 2007–2021." Available online: https://www.statista.com/statistics/277229/facebooks-annual-revenue-and-net-income/.

3. Statista (2022). "Meta: Monthly Active Product Family Users 2022." Available online: https://www.statista.com/statistics/947869/facebook-product-mau/.

4. Wells, G., Horwitz, J., & Seetharaman, D. (2021). "Facebook Knows Instagram Is Toxic for Teen Girls, Company Documents Show." *Wall Street Journal.* Available online: https://www.wsj.com/articles/facebook-knows-instagram-is-toxic-for-teen-girls-company-documents-show-11631620739.

5. Wells, G., Horwitz, J., & Seetharaman, D. (2021). Ibid.

6. Wells, G., Horwitz, J., & Seetharaman, D. (2021). Ibid.

7. Wells, G., Horwitz, J., & Seetharaman, D. (2021). Ibid.

8. Twenge, J. M., Haidt, J., Lozano, J., & Cummins, K. M. (2022). "Specification Curve Analysis Shows That Social Media Use Is Linked to Poor Mental Health, Especially among Girls." *Acta Psychologica* 224: 103512.

9. Freitas, D. (2017*). The Happiness Effect: How Social Media Is Driving a Generation to Appear Perfect at Any Cost.* Oxford: Oxford University Press.

10. Etherson, M. E., Curran, T., Smith, M. M., Sherry, S. B., & Hill, A. P. (2022). "Perfectionism as a Vulnerability Following Appearance-Focused Social Comparison: A Multi-Wave Study with Female Adolescents." *Personality and Individual Differences* 186: 111355.

11. Twenge, J. (2017). "Have Smartphones Destroyed a Generation?" *The Atlantic.* Available online: https://www.theatlantic.com/magazine/archive/2017/09/has-the-smartphone-destroyed-a-generation/534198/.

12. Salinas, S. (2018). "Sheryl Sandberg Delivered a Passionate, Defiant Defense of Facebook's Business." CNBC. Available online: https://www.cnbc.com/2018/04/26/facebooks-sheryl-sandbergs-brilliant-defense-of-the-ad-business.html.

13. Statista Research Department (2022). "Global Facebook Advertising Revenue 2017–2026." Available online: https://www.statista.com/statistic/544001/facebooks-advertising-revenue-worldwide-usa/.

14. Davidson, D. (2017). "Facebook Targets 'Insecure' Young People." *The Australian*. Available online: https://theaustralian.com.au/business/media/digital/facebook-targets-insecure-young-people-to-sell-ads.

15. Levin, S. (2017). "Facebook Told Advertisers It Can Identify Teens Feeling 'Insecure' and 'Worthless.'" *The Guardian*. Available online: https://www.theguardian.com/technology/2017/may/01/facebook-advertising-data-insecure-teens.

16. Fairplay for Kids (2021). "How Facebook Still Targets Surveillance Ads to Teens." Available online: https://fairplayforkids.org/wp-content/uploads/2021/11/fbsurveillancereport.pdf.

17. Fairplay for Kids (2021). "Open Letter to Mark Zuckerberg." Available online: https://fairplayforkids.org/wp-content/uploads/2021/11/fbsurveillanceletter.pdf.

18. Sung, M. (2021). "On TikTok, Mental Health Creators Are Confused for Therapists. That's a Serious Problem." Mashable. Available online: https://mashable.com/article/tiktok-mental-health-therapist-psychology.

19. Wells, G., Horwitz, J., & Seetharaman, D. (2021). "Facebook Knows Instagram Is Toxic for Teen Girls, Company Documents Show."

20. Brailovskaia, J., Delveaux, J., John, J., Wicker, V., Noveski, A., Kim, S., & Margraf, J. (2022). "Finding the 'Sweet Spot' of Smartphone Use: Reduction or Abstinence to Increase Well-Being and Healthy Lifestyle?! An Experimental Intervention Study." *Journal of Experimental Psychology: Applied*. Advance online publication. https://doi.org/10.1037/xap0000430.

21. Heller, A. S., Shi, T. C., Ezie, C. E., Reneau, T. R., Baez, L. M., Gibbons, C. J., & Hartley, C. A. (2020). "Association Between Real-World Experiential Diversity and Positive Affect Relates to Hippocampal–Striatal Functional Connectivity." *Nature Neuroscience:* 23(7): 800–804.

22. Wier, K. (2020). "Nurtured by Nature." *Monitor on Psychology* 51: 50.

23. O'Neill, E. (2015). "Why I Really Am Quitting Social Media." YouTube.

Video online: https://www.youtube.com/watch?v=gmAbwTQvWX8&t=579s.

24. Flett, G. L., & Hewitt, P. L. (2022). *Perfectionism in Childhood and Adolescence*. Washington, DC: American Psychological Association.

25. Min, S. (2019). "86% of Young Americans Want to Become a Social Media Influencer." CBS News. Available online: https://www.cbsnews.com/news/social-media-influencers-86-of-young-americans-want-to-become-one/.

Chapter Nine: You Just Haven't Earned It Yet
Or How Meritocracy Has Set a Standard of Perfection in School and College

1. Sandel, M. J. (2020). *The Tyranny of Merit*. London: Allen Lane.

2. Burns, J., & Campbell, A. (2017). "Social Mobility: The Worst Places to Grow Up Poor." BBC News. Available online: https://www.bbc.co.uk/news/education-42112436.

3. White House (2013). "Remarks by the President on Investing in America's Future." Office for the Press Secretary: Speeches and Remarks. Available online: https://obamawhitehouse.archives.gov/the-press-office/2013/10/25/remarks-president-investing-americas-future.

4. Markovitis, D. (2019). "How Life Became an Endless, Terrible Competition." *The Atlantic*. Available online: https://www.theatlantic.com/magazine/archive/2019/09/meritocracys-miserable-winners/594760/.

5. Markovitis, D. (2019). Ibid.

6. Semuels, A. (2016). "Poor at 20, Poor for Life." *The Atlantic*. Available online: https://www.theatlantic.com/business/archive/2016/07/social-mobility-america/491240/.

7. Desilver, D. (2018). "For Most U.S. Workers, Real Wages Have Barely Budged in Decades." Pew Research Center. Available online: https://www

.pewresearch.org/fact-tank/2018/08/07/for-most-us-workers-real-wages -have-barely-budged-for-decades/.

8. De Botton, A. (2005). *Status Anxiety.* London: Vintage.

9. Jacobs, D. (2015). *Extreme Wealth Is Not Merited.* Oxfam Discussion Papers. Available online: https://www-cdn.oxfam.org/s3fs-public/file_attachments/dp -extreme-wealth-is-not-merited-241115-en.pdf.

10. Geisz, M. B., & Nakashian, M. (2018). "Adolescent Wellness: Current Perspectives and Future Opportunities in Research, Policy, and Practice." Robert Wood Johnson Foundation. Available online: https://www.rwjf.org/en /library/research/2018/06/inspiring-and-powering-the-future--a-new-view -of-adolescence.html.

11. Resmovits, J. (2015). "Your Kids Take 112 Tests between Pre-K and High School." *Los Angeles Times.* Available online: https://www.latimes.com /local/education/standardized-testing/la-me-edu-how-much-standardized -testing-report-obama-20151023-story.html.

12. Hausknecht-Brown, J., Dunlap, N., Leira, M., Gee, K., & Carlon, A. (2020). "Grades, Friends, Competition: They Stress Our High Schoolers More Than You Might Think." *Des Moines Register.* Available online: https:// www.desmoinesregister.com/story/news/2020/04/20/sources-of-high -school-stress-iowa-how-to-help-grades-social-fitting-in/5165605002/.

13. Anderson, J. (2011). "At Elite Schools, Easing Up a Bit on Homework." *New York Times.* Available online: https://www.nytimes.com/2011/10/24/ education/24homework.html.

14. Top Tier Admissions (2022). "Admission Statistics for the Class of 2024." Available online: https://toptieradmissions.com/counseling/college/2024-ivy -league-admissions-statistics/.

15. Wallace, J. (2019). "Students in High-Achieving Schools Are Now Named an 'At-Risk' Group, Study Says." *Washington Post.* Available online: https:// www.washingtonpost.com/lifestyle/2019/09/26/students-high-achieving -schools-are-now-named-an-at-risk-group/.

16. Luthar, S. S., Kumar, N. L., & Zillmer, N. (2020). "High-Achieving Schools Connote Risks for Adolescents: Problems Documented, Processes Implicated, and Directions for Interventions." *American Psychologist* 75(7): 983–95.

17. Markovitis, D. (2019). *The Meritocracy Trap*. New York: Penguin Press.

18. Flett, G. L., & Hewitt, P. L. (2022). *Perfectionism in Childhood and Adolescence*. Washington, DC: American Psychological Association.

19. Vaillancourt, T., & Haltigan, J. D. (2018). "Joint Trajectories of Depression and Perfectionism across Adolescence and Childhood Risk Factors." *Development and Psychopathology* 30(2): 461–77.

20. Sandel, M. J. (2020). *The Tyranny of Merit*. New York: Macmillan.

21. Rimer, S. (2003). "Social Expectations Pressuring Women at Duke, Study Finds." *New York Times*. Available online: https://www.nytimes.com/2003/09/24/nyregion/social-expectations-pressuring-women-at-duke-study-finds.html.

22. Wilgoren, J. (2000). "More Than Ever, First-Year Students Feeling the Stress of College." *New York Times*. Available online: https://www.nytimes.com/2000/01/24/us/more-than-ever-first-year-students-feeling-the-stress-of-college.html.

23. Schwartz, K. (2017). "Anxiety Is Taking a Toll on Teens, Their Families and Schools." KQED. Available online: https://www.kqed.org/mindshift/49454/anxiety-is-taking-a-toll-on-teens-their-families-and-schools.

24. Mental Health Foundation (2018). "Stressed Nation: 74% of UK 'Overwhelmed or Unable to Cope' at Some Point in the Past Year." Available online: https://www.mentalhealth.org.uk/about-us/news/stressed-nation-74-uk-overwhelmed-or-unable-cope-some-point-past-year.

25. Adams, R. (2022). "Thousands of Students Drop Out of University as Pandemic Takes Its Toll." *The Guardian*. Available online: https://www.theguardian.com/education/2022/mar/17/thousands-of-students-drop-out-of-university-as-pandemic-takes-its-toll.

26. Schleicher, A. (2018). "PISA 2018: Insights and Interpretations." OECD. Available online: https://www.oecd.org/pisa/PISA%202018%20 Insights%20and%20Interpretations%20FINAL%20PDF.pdf.

27. Clark, K. (2022). "D.C. Schools Should Step Up amid a Perfect Storm of Mental Health Challenges." *Washington Post.* Available online: https:// www.washingtonpost.com/opinions/2022/02/18/dc-schools-should-step -up-amid-perfect-storm-mental-health-challenges/.

28. Goodman, C. K., & Moolten, S. (2022). "'The Perfect Storm': Worries Mount That Florida's Colleges Face a Mental Health Crisis Like No Other." *South Florida Sun Sentinel.* Available online: https://www.sun-sentinel .com/health/fl-ne-college-mental-health-crisis-20220818-cq27gflhuzgtp cks5q3aacqjdu-story.html.

29. Kacmanovic, J. (2022). "Why Tween Girls Especially Are Struggling So Much." *Washington Post.* Available online: https://www.washingtonpost .com/health/2022/08/08/tween-girls-mental-health/.

30. Allstate Corporation (2016). "Americans Say Hard Work and Resiliency Are the Most Important Factors." Available online: https://www.prnewswire.com/news -releases/americans-say-hard-work-and-resiliency-are-the-most-important-factors -in-success-ahead-of-the-economy-and-government-policies-300210377.html.

31. Even though these families make up about 25 percent of the UK population.

32. Friedman, S., & Laurison, D. (2020). *The Class Ceiling: Why It Pays to Be Privileged.* Bristol University Press.

33. To name a few: low-paid and casual forms of employment, student debts, rising costs of living (most notably energy, healthcare, and rents), zero percent interest rates returning below-inflation yields on anything you do manage to save, and houses within an hour of the office with price tags that are affordable only to oligarchs, money launderers, and children of the very wealthiest.

34. Deloitte (2022). "The Deloitte Global 2022 Gen Z & Millennial Survey." Available online: https://www2.deloitte.com/content/dam/Deloitte/global /Documents/deloitte-2022-genz-millennial-survey.pdf.

Chapter Ten: Perfectionism Begins at Home
Or How Pressure to Raise Exceptional Kids Affects How We Parent

1. Fromm, E. (1944). "Individual and Social Origins of Neurosis." *American Sociological Review* 9(4): 380–84.

2. Doepke, M., & Zilibotti, F. (2019). *Love, Money, and Parenting: How Economics Explains the Way We Raise Our Kids*. Princeton, NJ: Princeton University Press.

3. Doepke, M., & Zilibotti, F. (2019). Ibid.

4. Ramey, G., & Ramey, V. A. (2010). "The Rug Rat Race." *Brookings Papers on Economic Activity* 41(1): 129–99.

5. Challenge Success (2021). "Kids Under Pressure: A Look at Student Well-Being and Engagement during the Pandemic." Available online: https://challengesuccess.org/resources/kids-under-pressure-a-look-at-student-well-being-and-engagement-during-the-pandemic/

6. Doepke, M., & Zilibotti, F. (2019). *Love, money, and parenting*.

7. Curran, T., & Hill, A. P. (2022). "Young People's Perceptions of Their Parents' Expectations and Criticism Are Increasing Over Time: Implications for Perfectionism." *Psychological Bulletin* 148(1–2): 107–28.

8. Fleming, D. J., Dorsch, T. E., & Dayley, J. C. (2022). The Mediating Effect of Parental Warmth on the Association of Parent Pressure and Athlete Perfectionism in Adolescent Soccer." *International Journal of Sport and Exercise Psychology*, 1–17.

9. Curran, T., Hill, A. P., Madigan, D. J., & Stornæs, A. V. (2020). "A Test of Social Learning and Parent Socialization Perspectives on the Development of Perfectionism." *Personality and Individual Differences* 160: 109925.

10. Ko, A. H. C. (2019). *Parenting, Attachment, and Perfectionism: A Test of the Perfectionism Social Disconnection Model in Children and Adolescents*. Doctoral dissertation, University of British Columbia.

Chapter Eleven: Hustle Is a Six-Letter Word
Or How Insecurity in the Modern Workplace
Creates a Reliance on Perfectionism Just to Get By

1. Tolentino, J. (2017). "The Gig Economy Celebrates Working Yourself to Death." *The New Yorker*. Available online: https://www.newyorker.com/culture/jia-tolentino/the-gig-economy-celebrates-working-yourself-to-death.

2. Umoh, R. (2018). "Elon Musk Pulls 80- to 90-Hour Work Weeks—Here's How That Impacts the Body and the Mind." CNBC. Available online: https://www.cnbc.com/2018/12/03/elon-musk-works-80-hour-weeks--heres-how-that-impacts--your-health.html?&qsearchterm=Elon%20musk%20pulls%2080%20to%2090%20hour%20weeks.

3. Giattino, C., Ortiz-Ospina, E., & Roser, M. (2020). "Working Hours." Our World in Data. Retrieved from: https://ourworldindata.org/working-hours.

4. McGregor, J. (2014). "The Average Work Week Is Now 47 Hours." *Washington Post*. Available online: https://www.washingtonpost.com/news/on-leadership/wp/2014/09/02/the-average-work-week-is-now-47-hours/.

5. Kopf, D. (2016). "Almost All the US Jobs Created Since 2005 Are Temporary." *Quartz*. Available online: https://qz.com/851066/almost-all-the-10-million-jobs-created-since-2005-are-temporary/.

6. Quote in: Gimein, M. (2016). "The Fallacy of Job Insecurity." *The New Yorker*. Available online: https://www.newyorker.com/business/currency/the-fallacy-of-job-insecurity.

7. Graeber, D. (2013). On the Phenomenon of Bullshit Jobs. *Strike! Magazine*. Available online: http://gesd.free.fr/graeber13.pdf.

8. Carmichael, S. G. (2016). "Millennials Are Actually Workaholics, According to Research." *Harvard Business Review*. Available online: https://hbr.org/2016/08/millennials-are-actually-workaholics-according-to-research.

9. Ames, J. (2022). "US Law Firms Exact Pound of Flesh from Juniors with 14-Hour Days." London *Times*. Available online: https://www.thetimes.co.uk/article/us-law-firms-exact-pound-of-flesh-from-juniors-with-14-hour-days-f5tfz0s07.

10. Markovitis, D. (2019). *The Meritocracy Trap*. London: Penguin.

11. Makortoff, K. (2023). "Fintech Firm Revolut Calls In Psychologists After Criticism of Its Corporate Culture." *The Guardian*. Available online: https://www.theguardian.com/business/2023/jan/16/fintech-revolut-psychologists-criticism-corporate-culture-uk-banking-licence.

12. US Bureau of Labor Statistics (2021). "Number of Jobs, Labor Market Experience, Marital Status, and Health." Available online: https://www.bls.gov/news.release/pdf/nlsoy.pdf.

13. Office for National Statistics (2022). "Average Weekly Earnings in Great Britain: March 2022." ONS Statistical Bulletin. Available online: https://www.ons.gov.uk/employmentandlabourmarket/peopleinwork/employmentandemployeetypes/bulletins/averageweeklyearningsingreatbritain/march2022/pdf.

14. Office for National Statistics (2022). "Average Weekly Earnings in Great Britain: March 2022." ONS Source Dataset: GDP First Quarterly Estimate Time Series (PN2). Available online: https://www.ons.gov.uk/economy/grossdomesticproductgdp/timeseries/cgbz/pn2.

15. Malesic, J. (2022). "Your Work Is Not Your God: Welcome to the Age of the Burnout Epidemic." *The Guardian*. Available online: https://www.theguardian.com/lifeandstyle/2022/jan/06/burnout-epidemic-work-lives-meaning.

16. GFK Custom Research North America (2011). "A Disengaged Generation: Young Workers Disengaged by Pressures of Work Worldwide." PR Newswire. Available online: https://www.prnewswire.com/news-releases/a-disengaged-generation-young-workers-disengaged-by-pressures-of-work-worldwide-122581838.html.

17. De Neve, J-E., & Ward, G. (2017). "Does Work Make You Happy? Evidence from the World Happiness Report." *Harvard Business Review*. Available online: https://hbr.org/2017/03/does-work-make-you-happy-evidence-from-the-world-happiness-report.

18. Threlkeld, K. (2021). "Employee Burnout Report: COVID-19's Impact and 3 Strategies to Curb It." Indeed. Available online: https://www.indeed.com/leadershiphub/preventing-employee-burnout-report.

19. Abramson, A. (2022). "Burnout and Stress Are Everywhere." *Monitor on Psychology* 53: 72.

20. Brassey, J., Coe, J., Dewhurst, M., Enomoto, K., Giarola, R., Herberg, B., & Jeffery, B. (2022). "Addressing Employee Burnout." McKinsey Health Institute. Available online: https://www.mckinsey.com/mhi/our-insights/addressing-employee-burnout-are-you-solving-the-right-problem.

21. Ellis, L., & Yang, A. (2022). "If Your Co-Workers Are 'Quiet Quitting,' Here's What That Means." *Wall Street Journal*. Available online: https://www.wsj.com/articles/if-your-gen-z-co-workers-are-quiet-quitting-heres-what-that-means-11660260608.

22. DiRenzo, Z. (2022). "Even in a Hot Labor Market, Workers Are Worried about Job Security." CNBC. Available online: https://www.cnbc.com/2022/05/21/even-in-a-hot-labor-market-workers-are-worried-about-job-security.html.

23. Kaplan, J., & Kiersz, A. (2021). "2021 Was the Year of the Quit: For 7 Months, Millions of Workers Have Been Leaving." *Business Insider*. Available online: https://www.businessinsider.com/how-many-why-workers-quit-jobs-this-year-great-resignation-2021-12.

24. Pofeldt, E. (2017). "Are We Ready for a Workforce That Is 50% Freelance?" *Forbes*. Available online: https://www.forbes.com/sites/elainepofeldt/2017/10/17/are-we-ready-for-a-workforce-that-is-50-freelance/.

25. Beauregard, T. A., & Henry, L. C. (2009). "Making the Link between

Work-Life Balance Practices and Organizational Performance." *Human Resource Management Review* 19(1): 9–22.

Chapter Twelve: Accept Yourself
Or the Power of Good Enough in Our Less Than Perfect Lives

1. Rogers, C. R. (1995). *On Becoming a Person.* Boston: Mariner Books.

2. White House. (2009). "Remarks by the President in a National Address to America's Schoolchildren." Office for the Press Secretary: Speeches and Remarks. Available online: https://obamawhitehouse.archives.gov/the-press-office/remarks-president-a-national-address-americas-schoolchildren.

3. Horney, K. (1935). "Women's Fear of Action." Talk delivered to the National Federation of Professional and Business Women's Clubs. In Paris, B. J. (1996). *Karen Horney: A Psychoanalyst's Search for Self-Understanding.* New Haven, CT: Yale University Press.

4. Horney, K. (1950). *Neurosis and Human Growth.* New York: W. W. Norton.

5. Horney, K. (1950). Ibid.

6. Horney, K. (1950). Ibid.

7. Smail, D. (2005). *Power, Interest and Psychology: Elements of a Social Materialist Understanding of Distress.* Ross-on-Wye, UK: PCCS Books.

8. Brach, T. (2000). *Radical Acceptance.* New York: Bantam.

9. Rogers, C. R. (1995). *On Becoming a Person.*

10. Horney, K. (1950). *Neurosis and Human Growth.*

11. Horney, K. (1949). "Finding the Real Self: Foreword to a Letter." *American Journal of Psychoanalysis* 9: 3–7.

Chapter Thirteen: Postscript for a Post-Perfectionism Society
Or Life in the Republic of Good Enough

1. Baldwin, J. A. (1962). "As Much Truth as One Can Bear." *The New York*

Times. Available online: https://www.nytimes.com/1962/01/14/archives/as-much-truth-as-one-can-bear-to-speak-out-about-the-world-as-it-is.html.

2. Parsley, D. (2021). "Boris Johnson 'Privately Accepts' up to 50,000 Annual Covid Deaths as an Acceptable Level." *The Independent*. Available online: https://inews.co.uk/news/boris-johnson-privately-accepts-up-to-50000-annual-covid-deaths-as-an-acceptable-level-1170069.

3. The World Bank (2018). "Decline of Global Extreme Poverty Continues but Has Slowed: World Bank." Available online: https://www.worldbank.org/en/news/press-release/2018/09/19/decline-of-global-extreme-poverty-continues-but-has-slowed-world-bank.

4. The World Bank (2024). *Subdued Growth, Multiple Challenges*. Available online: https://thedocs.worldbank.org/en/doc/661f109500bf58fa36a4a46eeace6786-0050012024/original/GEP-Jan-2024.pdf

5. Garrett, T. J., Grasselli, M., & Keen, S. (2020). "Past World Economic Production Constrains Current Energy Demands: Persistent Scaling with Implications for Economic Growth and Climate Change Mitigation." *PLOS One* 15(8): e0237672.

6. Paulson, S. (2022). "Economic Growth Will Continue to Provoke Climate Change." *The Economist*. Available online: https://impact.economist.com/sustainability/circular-economies/economic-growth-will-continue-to-provoke-climate-change.

7. What Herrington is saying here is that there's no assured "green" solution that will allow us to follow current trajectories of exponential growth without at some point falling into a "collapse pattern." This is a view shared by energy economist Tim Morgan. "The major growth stimulus of the industrial era—low-cost energy from oil, natural gas, and coal—is winding down," he writes in his essay "The Dynamics of Global Repricing." "Transition to renewables is imperative," he continues, "but there's no guarantee that an economy based on wind-turbines, solar panels and batteries can be as large

as the fossil-based economy of today—the probabilities are that it will be smaller." Technology will no doubt be one answer to the "growth problem," and an important one at that. But it's not the silver bullet many think it is. As well as innovating our way to a sustainable future, we'll also, at some point, need to reckon with the fact that a steady-state economy will be needed to avoid that collapse pattern. And rather than seeing that as an existential crisis, we could choose to see it as an opportunity to reassess our priorities and rebalance the economy instead.

8. Herrington, G. (2021). "Data Check on the World Model That Forecast Global Collapse." Club of Rome. Available online: https://www.clubof rome.org/blog-post/herrington-world-model/.

9. Pettifor, A. (2021). "Quantitative Easing: How the World Got Hooked on Magicked-Up Money." *Prospect.* Available online: https://www.prospect-magazine.co.uk/magazine/quantitative-easing-qe-magicked-up-money-finance-economy-central-banks.

10. Raworth, K. (2017). *Doughnut Economics: Seven Ways to Think Like a 21st Century Economist.* Chelsea, VT: Chelsea Green.

11. Layard, R. (2020). *Can We Be Happier? Evidence and Ethics.* London: Pelican.

12. Tønnessen, M. (2023). "Wasted GDP in the USA." *Humanities and Social Sciences Communications* 10, 681.

13. Keynes, J. M. (1930). "Economic Possibilities for Our Grandchildren." In *Essays in Persuasion*, 358–73. New York: W. W. Norton.

14. McKinsey & Company. (2023). "The Economic Potential of Generative AI: The Next Productivity Frontier."

15. Veal, A. J. (2022). "The 4-Day Work-Week: The New Leisure Society?" *Leisure Studies* 42(2): 172–87.

16. Henley Business School (2019). *Four Better or Four Worse? A White Paper from Henley Business School.* Available online: https://assets.henley.ac.uk/v3/ fileUploads/Journalists-Regatta-2019-White-Paper-FINAL.pdf.

17. Schor, J. B., Fan, W., Kelly, O., Bezdenezhnykh, T., & Bridson-Hubbard, N. (2022). "The 4 Day Week: Assessing Global Trials of Reduced Work Time with No Reduction in Pay." www.4dayweek.com.

18. Davis, W. (2022). "A Big 32-Hour Workweek Test Is Underway. Supporters Think It Could Help Productivity." NPR. Available online: https://www.npr.org/2022/06/07/1103591879/a-big-32-hour-workweek-test-is-underway-supporters-think-it-could-help-productiv.

19. Neate, R. (2022). "Millionaires Join Davos Protests, Demanding 'Tax Us Now.'" *The Guardian*. Available online: https://www.theguardian.com/business/2022/may/22/millionaires-join-davos-protests-demanding-tax-us-now-taxation-wealthy-cost-of-living-crisis.

20. Christensen, M. B., Hallum, C., Maitland, A., Parrinello, Q., & Putaturo, C. (2023). "Survival of the Richest: How We Must Tax the Super-Rich Now to Fight Inequality," Oxfam. DOI. 10.21201/2023.621477.

21. Piketty, T. (2013). *Capital in the Twenty-First Century.* Cambridge, MA: Harvard University Press.

22. Piketty, T. (2020). *Capital and Ideology.* Cambridge, MA: Harvard University Press.

23. Piketty, T. (2019). "The Illusion of Centrist Ecology." *Le Monde.* Available online: https://www.lemonde.fr/blog/piketty/2019/06/11/the-illusion-of-centrist-ecology/.

24. Hartley, T., van den Bergh, J., & Kallis, G. (2020). "Policies for Equality under Low or No Growth: A Model Inspired by Piketty." *Review of Political Economy* 32(2): 243–58.

25. Christensen, M. B., Hallum, C., Maitland, A., Parrinello, Q., & Putaturo, C. (2023). "Survival of the Richest."

26. Haarmann, C., Haarmann, D., & Nattrass, N. (2019). "The Namibian Basic Income Grant Pilot." In *The Palgrave International Handbook of Basic Income* (357–72). London: Palgrave Macmillan.

27. Simpson, W., Mason, G., & Godwin, R. (2017). "The Manitoba Basic Annual Income Experiment: Lessons Learned 40 Years Later." *Canadian Public Policy* 43(1): 85–104.

28. Machado, D., Williamson, E., Pescarini, J., Rodrigues, L., Alves, F. J., Araújo, L., & Barreto, M. L. (2021). "The Impact of a National Cash Transfer Programme on Reducing Suicide: A Study Using the 100 Million Brazilian Cohort." Available at SSRN: https://ssrn.com/abstract=3766234.

29. Haushofer, J., Mudida, R., & Shapiro, J. P. (2020). "The Comparative Impact of Cash Transfers and a Psychotherapy Program on Psychological and Economic Well-Being" (No. w28106). National Bureau of Economic Research.

30. Simpson, J., Albani, V., Bell, Z., Bambra, C., & Brown, H. (2021). "Effects of Social Security Policy Reforms on Mental Health and Inequalities: A Systematic Review of Observational Studies in High-Income Countries." *Social Science & Medicine* 272: 113717.

31. Fromm, E. (1976). *To Have or To Be?* New York: Harper & Row.

32. Burn-Murdoch, J. (2022). "Millennials Are Shattering the Oldest Rule in Politics." *The Financial Times.* Available online: https://www.ft.com/content/c361e372-769e-45cd-a063-f5c0a7767cf4.

INDEX